An OPUS book

The Two Irelands
1912–1939

David Fitzpatrick is Associate Professor of
Modern History at Trinity College Dublin

The Two Irelands

1912–1939

David Fitzpatrick

Oxford   New York

OXFORD UNIVERSITY PRESS

Oxford University Press, Great Clarendon Street, Oxford OX2 6DP

Oxford New York
Athens Auckland Bangkok Bogota Bombay
Buenos Aires Calcutta Cape Town Dar es Salaam
Delhi Florence Hong Hong Istanbul Karachi
Kuala Lumpur Madras Madrid Melbourne
Mexico City Nairobi Paris Singapore
Taipei Tokyo Toronto Warsaw
and associated companies in
Berlin Ibadan

Oxford is a trade mark of Oxford University Press

First published as an Oxford University Press paperback 1998

British Library Cataloguing in Publication Data
Data available

Library of Congress Cataloging in Publication Data
Fitzpatrick, David.
The two Irelands, 1912–1939 / David Fitzpatrick.
Includes bibliographical references and index.
1. Ireland—Politics and government—1910–1921. 2. Ireland—Politics and
government—1922–1949. 3. Ulster (Northern Ireland and Ireland)—Politics and
government. 4. Irish question. I. Title.
DA960.F575 1998 941.5082—dc21 97–23908
ISBN 0-19-289240-1

3 5 7 9 10 8 6 4 2

Typeset by Best-set Typesetter Ltd., Hong Kong
Printed in Great Britain by
Mackays of Chatham plc
Chatham, Kent

For D.M.F.
my first and most critical reader
with love and gratitude

Preface

The partition of Ireland created two states embodying rival ideologies and representing two hostile peoples. Roman Catholic nationalists acquired effective control over twenty-six counties in the Irish Free State, while Protestant Unionists secured the six counties of Northern Ireland. By dividing Ireland according to the religion and politics of the local majority in each region, Lloyd George's government hoped to avert further sectarian conflict within Ireland and to absolve the United Kingdom from future responsibility for the 'restoration of order'. This book concerns the revolution which prompted partition, and the legacies of that revolution for the two Irish states. Part I analyses not one but two revolutionary movements, each characterized by massive popular mobilization tending to subvert British control over Ireland. The Ulster Unionist struggle against Home Rule after 1912, though largely bloodless, was initially far more menacing than its nationalist adversary. It also provided a valuable model for the republican revolutionaries who won widespread public support after the 1916 Rising. Essential to the success of both revolutionary movements was the subordination of individual choice to communal solidarity, expressed and regulated through fraternal networks such as the Orange Institution and the Irish Republican Brotherhood.

The ideas and methods of the revolutionary period constituted a formidable and inhibiting legacy for the two new states, discussed in Part II. Each new government was immediately threatened by civil war, leading to the ruthless suppression of disaffected republicans in the south and alienated Catholic nationalists in Northern Ireland. The subsequent maintenance of local power by the dominant majority in each state was not softened by respect for the freedom of individuals or dissident minorities. In the Irish Free State, de Valera's republicans succeeded in winning electoral power in 1932, within eight years of their leader's release from internment, only to suppress their opponents from both flanks with matching severity. The small Protestant minority, though mostly free from physical persecution after 1922, suffered increasingly from the legal incorporation of Catholic moral precepts. In Northern Ireland, the familiar techniques of coercion and discrimination often assumed sectarian form, despite a half-hearted initial attempt to achieve a *modus vivendi* with the substantial Catholic population excluded from the southern state by partition. While governments in each state asserted their power with considerable effect, their subjects did not in general secure the civil liberties promised by the two revolutionary movements. Furthermore, the political alignments cemented in the two civil wars continued to dominate political debate, restricting the opportunity for social and economic reform. Freedom had been subordinated to the pursuit and defence of power.

This book explores the parallels, as well as the rivalries, between nationalism and Unionism. Many writers have noted that the antipathy between 'the two Irelands' was all the more bitter because of their cultural, social, and political similarities. Yet no previous interpretation of twentieth-century Ireland has attempted to define and elaborate these parallels by giving equal attention to the two political movements and the two states. This design presented a daunting challenge to a writer such as myself, for whom Ulster Unionism and Northern Ireland were until quite recently unfamiliar territory. Instead of attempting a comprehensive synthesis of northern and southern history, I have selected certain themes and examples for parallel study in both terrains. My sources, although diverse and often drawn from archives in Dublin, Belfast, or London, constitute only a fraction of the vast and fast expanding available documentation for recent Irish history. Even so, I hope that this attempt to integrate interpretation of the two Irelands will provide an unexpected and perhaps provocative slant on each individual history. Though the mutual recognition of shared histories cannot in itself reconcile Ireland's divided peoples, it is surely desirable for historians to probe that common legacy. Any such attempt is likely to touch many raw nerves. I can only hope that if offence is given by this book, it will have been given even-handedly.

In piecing together this interpretation of two complex and interlocking histories, I have drawn remorselessly on the published research of other scholars, not all of whom could be named in the notes or the guide to Further Reading. I am also grateful to the many librarians and archivists who have catered to my sometimes insistent demands over the last quarter-century, and the custodians who have enabled me to cite or quote archival materials in the National Archives, the National Library, the Public Record Office of Northern Ireland, the House of Orange, and other institutions listed in the notes. My interest in twentieth-century Ireland has been maintained and revived through supervision of theses by innovative scholars such as Peter Hart, Tom Crean, Patrick Murray, and Fearghal McGarry. I am no less indebted to the many undergraduate historians whom I have taught in Trinity College Dublin since 1979, and especially to the members of the Trinity History Workshop who have published two fine volumes of essays on Ireland between 1914 and 1923. My colleagues have again tolerated my nocturnal raids on the departmental printer, and allowed me leave of absence at an opportune moment. Georgina, Brian, and Meg Fitzpatrick have as always suffered long, an experience shared by my unflappable editor, George Miller. Jane Leonard interrupted her pursuit of commemoration in modern Ireland to criticize the entire text, which silently incorporates many of her comments and erudite suggestions. Much of this book was concocted in turret and cottage, or on bicycle-back, deep in Co. Down, where I meditated on the two Irelands without ready access to notes or books. Perhaps a trace of its secretive drumlined landscape may be detected between the lines that follow.

Contents

Conventions

Since Irish political and religious terminology is peculiarly loaded and contested between rival factions, it is desirable to indicate and define the key labels chosen for use in this book. The term *loyalism* (signifying the profession of loyalty to the British monarch) is usually preferred to *Unionism*, except in the case of organized political activity; *unionism* refers to organized Labour. The word *nationalism* embraces *republicanism*, *constitutionalism*, and other programmes for Irish self-determination. The *IRA* is used as a formal term for the *(Irish) Volunteers* in 1920–1 and interchangeably with the *Irregulars* in 1922–3, thereafter referring to the military instrument of anti-treaty republicanism. *Catholics* are Roman Catholics; *Protestants* are adherents of all churches recognizing the Reformation. English renderings of Irish terms are given in parentheses.

Where place names were changed after 1921, the earlier form is normally used: thus, *King's Co.* (not *Offaly*); *Connaught* (not *Connacht*). *Derry* is used for the city, *Londonderry* for the county. *Ulster* refers to the province of nine counties; *Ireland* to all thirty-two counties. The terms *southern* or *northern*, when applied to governments or administrations, refer to the (Irish) Free State (Éire from 1937, the Republic of Ireland from 1949); or to Northern Ireland (also called the *province*, or the *six counties*). *Britain* excludes Ireland, yet the *British* government and army signify those of the United Kingdom.

Reforms are normally dated according to their implementation rather than enactment: thus the Union is assigned to 1801 (not 1800). Most large numbers are rounded to two significant figures, so avoiding spurious precision. Rates of participation in organizations are approximate, being derived from census returns in 1911 or 1926. In such calculations, 'adults' are assumed to have comprised three-fifths of the population (as for persons aged 20 or more in Ireland, 1911).

The brief biographical asides specify religion or birthplace when these are unexpected (as in the case of Catholic loyalists, Protestant nationalists, or southern-born Ulster Unionists). Future titles and honorifics do not appear in the text, but the highest honour is given along with the surname in the index. This also provides dates of birth and death, where ascertained. Citations are mainly confined to the sources of quotations and statistics, unless obviously extracted from readily accessible material such as censal or electoral returns; but the major sources of fact and interpretation are specified in the guide to Further Reading.

Abbreviations

CID	Criminal Investigation Department
CIGS	Chief of the Imperial General Staff
GAA	Gaelic Athletic Association
GDP	Gross Domestic Product
GHQ	General Head Quarters
IRA	Irish Republican Army (Óglaigh na hÉireann)
IRB	Irish Republican Brotherhood
ITGWU	Irish Transport and General Workers' Union
LOL	Loyal Orange Lodge
MP	Member of Parliament
NA	National Archives (Dublin)
NCO	Non-Commissioned Officer
NLI	National Library of Ireland (Dublin)
OC	Officer Commanding
PRO	Public Record Office (London)
PRONI	Public Record Office of Northern Ireland (Belfast)
RIC	Royal Irish Constabulary
RM	Resident Magistrate
RUC	Royal Ulster Constabulary
TCD	Trinity College Dublin (University of Dublin)
TD	Teachta Dála (Deputy of Dáil Éireann)
TUC	Trades Union Congress
UCD	University College Dublin
USC	Ulster Special Constabulary
UULA	Ulster Unionist Labour Association
UVF	Ulster Volunteer Force
UWUC	Ulster Women's Unionist Council

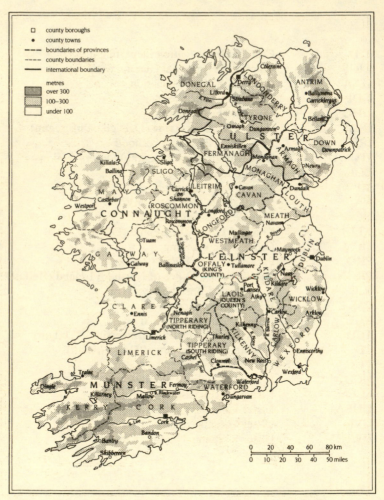

Map 1. Modern Ireland: towns, counties, and provinces

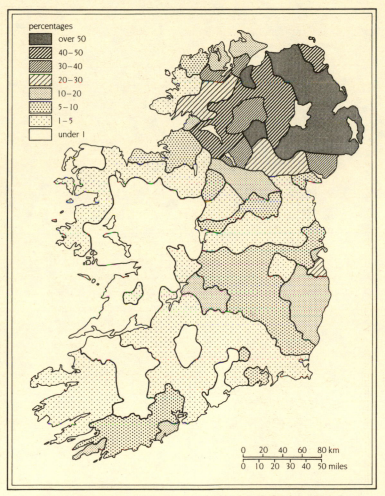

percentages

- over 50
- 40 – 50
- 30 – 40
- 20 – 30
- 10 – 20
- 5 – 10
- 1 – 5
- under 1

0   20   40   60   80 km
0 10 20 30 40 50 miles

Map 2. Percentage of Protestants in each rural district, 1936–7

PART I

What Revolution?

Ireland, 1912–1922

Introduction

Between 1912 and 1922, Ireland experienced revolution in several senses. Its constitutional status, as defined in British statutes, was transformed by the dual 'settlement' of 1921–2. All but six of Ireland's thirty-two counties were withdrawn from the United Kingdom as constituted in 1801, becoming a dominion-like 'Irish Free State' within the British empire. Six of the nine counties of Ulster became a 'province' within the United Kingdom, unique in possessing an autonomous parliament and a form of 'Home Rule'. These constitutional revolutions enabled local élites to take over political control from the British government and its Irish-based agents. In Northern Ireland, political control was monopolized by Unionists (otherwise 'loyalists'), hitherto implacable opponents of all forms of Home Rule and of all governments threatening devolution. Power in the Free State passed to the more moderate section of those who had battled with Britain in pursuit of a republic, simultaneously marginalizing intransigent republicans, unrepentant Home Rulers, and loyalists (whether lapsed or incorrigible).

The constitutional revolution masked a more far-reaching though informal religious settlement, whereby the major churches and their doctrines exercised far greater political influence than was any longer possible in the increasingly secular and liberal British system. The victors in each state self-consciously embodied the religion as well as the political ideology of the majority. Northern Ireland, where Protestants outnumbered Catholics by two to one in 1926, was unmistakably a 'Protestant state' from the outset. In the Irish Free State, where Protestants, Jews, freethinkers, and other oddities comprised less than a thirteenth of the population, the new rulers blatantly identified Catholic with national values. After partition, the outlook for northern Catholics and southern Protestants seemed bleak indeed.

The means by which the two revolutionary élites secured local power ranged from violence and the threat of violence to collective protest, propaganda, parliamentary and diplomatic struggle, and negotiation. The Ulster Unionists relied primarily on parliamentary agitation backed by the menace of armed resistance; the republicans shunned parliament but used propaganda even more effectively than armed force. Thus the creation of the two Irish states, though not achieved by purely revolutionary methods, entailed a revolutionary shift in power-holding. These changes carried the promise, admittedly not fully realized, of concomitant social and cultural transformations. The alterations in Irish political organization were sufficiently lasting and profound to merit the term 'revolution'.

The first part of this book examines the character of Ireland's major revolutionary movements, the bitter conflict between them, and their underlying similarities. Chapter 1 ('Whose Revolution?') concerns the organization and influence of the major protagonists in Irish politics around 1912. Chapter 2 ('Why?') examines the ideologies of those involved, and the recurrent tension between doctrines of liberation and the pursuit of power. Chapter 3 ('How?') narrates the slide towards revolution and partition between 1912 and 1922, emphasizing the importance of external interventions in changing the course of Irish politics. In the absence of uncontrollable factors such as the outbreak and termination of the Great War, the eruption of the Easter Rising, and the vagaries of British party politics, the antagonism between Irish nationalists and loyalists might have generated different forms of conflict and different constitutional outcomes. Ireland's revolution was the product of crisis, not only in Ireland, but in Britain and beyond.

The origins of that revolution can be explored only cursorily in a book devoted to the twentieth century. The antipathies between Ireland and England, and those between Catholics and

Protestants, fed upon centuries of bitter conflict and self-replicating rhetoric which cannot be chronicled here. It would be ludicrous, however, to discuss the interaction of nationalism and loyalism without first examining Ireland's status within the United Kingdom, the focus for every major political struggle over the last two centuries. The 'Union' effected in 1801 was partial and, from many perspectives, fictitious. Ireland had not been smoothly transferred from the colonial subjection of the eighteenth century (ending with a brief phase of spurious independence after the British 'renunciation act' of 1783) to full integration with Britain. The religious union proved transitory as well as artificial, the 'United Church of England and Ireland' being dissolved by Irish disestablishment in 1869–71. This undermined the much resented supremacy of a church that served scarcely an eighth of the Irish population, by allowing formal parity to Roman Catholics (three-quarters) and Presbyterians (one in ten).

Political assimilation was also incomplete. It is true that Irish constituencies supplied over a seventh of the House of Commons, whereas Ireland provided less than a tenth of the United Kingdom's population by 1911. Yet Ireland was still governed in the style of a colony, with a lord lieutenant or 'viceroy' whose chief secretary headed a cluster of 'Irish' boards and departments centred in Dublin Castle. 'The Castle' worked uneasily with a smaller network of Whitehall departments with Irish branches. Unlike Scotland, also shackled to England by an imperfect union, Ireland had no autonomous code or body of law. It was nevertheless subjected to a range of 'coercion acts' and suspensions of normal process with Indian but few English counterparts; whereas measures of social reform were only sporadically extended to Ireland. By contrast with England's local and largely gunless police forces, the armed Royal Irish Constabulary provided a model of centralized paramilitary policing that was widely imitated in both the dominions and the colonies. It was supported by numerous military detachments, which were far more likely than in England to be called out 'in aid of the civil power'.

The economic union was more nearly complete, following the amalgamation of the exchequers (1817), the belated introduction of free trade between Britain and Ireland (1824), the assimilation of the currencies (1826), and the equalization of excise duties, customs duties, and most taxes (1853). However, the local authorities responsible for administering many services, and for collecting 'rates' from occupiers of land and buildings, remained under far stricter central control than in England. According to most calculations, Ireland was 'undertaxed' by 1912, in the sense that the cost of providing 'Irish services' exceeded the return to the exchequer of Irish-raised taxes and duties. That reversal of the nineteenth-century imbalance was mainly attributable to introduction of the old-age pension (1909), for which a mysteriously large proportion of the Irish population claimed to be qualified. Since, however, these 'Irish services' also included the upkeep of armed police, the viceregal establishment, and a host of other English impositions, the boon to Ireland was not universally acknowledged. Both in form and in practice, the government of Ireland was a bizarre blend of 'metropolitan' and 'colonial' elements. Ireland could therefore be pictured either as a partner in Britain's empire or as her colony, interpretations that fostered conflicting revolutionary programmes. While loyalists mustered to defend their metropolitan privileges, republicans inveighed against their colonial oppressors.

One index of Ireland's assimilation into the United Kingdom was the extent of Irish and Catholic involvement in the civil, military, and colonial services. Though patronage remained important, competitive examinations had provided the standard entry to the Irish civil service since 1871. This reform further enfeebled the so-called 'Ascendancy', an ill-defined yet deeply resented élite drawn from the landed gentry and the professions, exclusive of nonconformists as well as Catholics, and closely identified with Trinity College, gentlemen's clubs, and freemasonry. Irish Catholics and Protestants alike took advantage of competitive recruitment to the Indian and other colonial services, though mandarin resistance had stemmed the flow by the turn of the century. At home, relatively few Catholics managed to secure army and police commissions or senior administrative posts. Despite vigorous 'affirmative action' on the part of Augustine Birrell as chief secretary after 1909, Protestants continued to predominate in the judiciary and the magistracy. By contrast, Catholics were over-represented among police constables, and no less likely to enlist in the pre-war British army than Irish Protestants, Englishmen, or Scots. Catholics comprised only a third of the unpaid justices of the peace in 1908; but the introduction of a fairly broad franchise for local authorities in 1899 had broken the Ascendancy's residual power in local government. The partial transfer of public administration from the Ascendancy to upwardly mobile Catholics reinforced the belief that the Union was at last becoming a reality, for better or worse. Gaelic revivalists as well as English optimists detected evidence of cultural assimilation or 'Anglicization', which they deplored or commended according to taste. Catholic intrusion into public offices also caused resentment and fear among Irish Protestants as they saw their privileges slipping away, a reaction comparable to the indignation of the Hindu 'collaborator' class as Muslims infiltrated the colonial élite during the last decades of British rule in India. Thus, while a growing minority of Catholic Irishmen had an interest in maintaining the institutions which supported them, this process only intensified disaffection with the prevailing government of Ireland on the part of cultural nationalists and loyalists alike.

In addition to religion, both class and sex remained sources of severe inequity in popular access to the benefits of Union. Despite the Reform (or 'mud cabin') act of 1884, which enfranchised male householders of all valuations as well as many 'lodgers', only about half of Irish adult males were parliamentary electors in 1910 (compared with two-thirds in both England and Scotland). This anomaly was not corrected until 1918, when the electorate throughout the United Kingdom was extended to embrace virtually all non-migratory adult males and also women over thirty. Before the war, however, women occupiers had by degrees gained the right to vote and compete in local elections, and a few had been elected as poor law guardians. Working men were slower in Ireland than in Britain to achieve political office, partly because the proletariat was disproportionately small in a country still predominantly rural. Even in towns, the small scale of Irish firms and heavy unemployment had impeded Labour's development as an industrial and political force. Far more numerous and politically active were the third-of-a-million tenant farmers, who had not only become prominent in local government, but were also well advanced in buying their properties from landlords using long-term government loans. Yet tenant grievances remained intense, since landlords outside the impoverished 'congested districts' could not normally be compelled to sell and the process of negotiation was often prolonged and acrimonious. Moreover, leaseholds and town properties were unaffected by the land purchase legislation. Discrimination against women, workers, and tenants generated lingering disaffection and contributed to the revolutionary spirit, though there was no intrinsic reason for these grievances to be linked with the political campaigns of either nationalists or loyalists. The constitutional future of Ireland, deeply disunited and insecurely unified with England, remained disturbingly unpredictable in 1912.

Whose Revolution?

Irish Politics in 1912

Unionists

Oddly, the most active threat to the Union in 1912 came from Unionists, in particular from Ulster Unionists. Since almost all pre-war Unionists demanded the retention of all four Irish provinces within the United Kingdom, the term 'Ulster Unionists' signified those Unionists who resided in Ulster (home to three-quarters of all Irish Protestants). Their main forum was the Ulster Unionist Council, formed in 1905 as an adjunct to the Irish Unionist Alliance (1891). The Council linked local activists with the caucus of about twenty Irish Unionists in the House of Commons (all normally from Ulster with the exception of the two members for Dublin University) and their numerous colleagues in the House of Lords. Though a tight-knit and highly effective unit, the Ulster Unionists acted not as a distinct party but as a lobby within Conservatism. Their leader until his death in 1906 was Colonel Edward Saunderson of Castle Saunderson in Cavan, for most of his career a prominent Orangeman. His successors were an Englishman (Walter Long), and then, between 1910 and 1921, a Dubliner (Sir Edward Carson). Though somewhat mitigating the Ulsterness of the organization, the enrolment of a former chief secretary for Ireland and a celebrated advocate helped Ulster Unionists to extend their political influence among British Conservatives. This was further encouraged by the retention of twenty-eight Irish representative peers in the House of Lords, which also included many magnates with Irish estates but British titles such as the mighty 5th marquess of Lansdowne. The voice of Irish and particularly Ulster

Unionism was thus more audible and authoritative than might have been expected from so small a constituency.

Although Unionism in Ulster was supported by a network of clubs and local associations similar to those in Britain, its popular appeal was distinctively fraternal. Dominant in the Ulster Unionist Council, and in the selection of parliamentary candidates, were the representatives of the Loyal Orange Institution (1795). Through most of the nineteenth century, the Grand Lodge in Dublin had exercised a potent if reticent influence upon the various public organizations promoting Protestant and loyalist causes. Tightly organized by counties and districts, an array of about 1,500 'private' or local lodges provided the cosy, sociable, and secure setting for easy talk among Protestants of all classes. There farmers, labourers, or weavers could share their indignation against nationalist and Catholic disloyalty, and also elect delegates to higher lodges incorporating landlords, businessmen, and grandees. All classes mingled in the annual 'walk' on 12 July, commemorating the victory of William of Orange at the Boyne (1690), which typically involved a public procession with banners and bands, sometimes followed by an Orange ball. An élite of experienced and dutiful Orangemen were initiated into the still more shadowy Imperial Grand Black Chapter (1797), which was likewise closely modelled on the arcane hierarchies of freemasonry. Orangemen and 'Blackmen', though no longer oath-bound to secrecy, were forbidden to discuss their meetings outside the lodge. Breaches of the Institution's 'laws and ordinances', ranging from non-payment of dues to voting for unsuitable electoral candidates, and from 'conduct unbecoming to an Orangeman' to marrying a Roman Catholic, were punished by suspension or expulsion and publication of the offender's name and lodge. Nearly 5,500 members were expelled between 1851 and 1975, out of a membership ranging between about 50,000 and 100,000. Indiscipline peaked in the Edwardian decade, when over 800 Orangemen were ejected.[1] These figures attest to an energetic but far from unchallenged system of management.

In Tyrone, probably the most densely organized county, over a third of adult male Protestants were Orangemen in 1912. In Belfast, where the solidarity of Protestants was fragile and dissident organizations flourished, the corresponding proportion was only about a sixth. Belfast had been particularly affected by the creation in 1903 of the Independent Orange Order, a product of proletarian and evangelical resentment against the patrician hierarchy of the regular Grand Lodge. Though men and the ethos of manliness predominated, the Orange Institution developed auxiliary networks of lodges for women, just as the Ulster Women's Unionist Council (1911) provided assertive support for its male counterpart. Orangeism, though formally committed to the pursuit of individual liberty and religious toleration, acted as a powerful sectarian influence which made loyalism increasingly unappetizing for Irish Catholics. It was the political and fraternal manifestation of a wider-ranging polarization between Catholic and Protestant peoples, evident in the close correlation between the proportion of Protestants in the Irish population (26 per cent in 1911) and of Unionist votes in contested elections (28 per cent in December 1910). That balance was replicated in Ulster, where Unionists secured 52 per cent of the vote while Protestants comprised 56 per cent of the population. Centuries of social segregation, reinforced by episodes of bitter sectarian conflict, had rendered political and religious affiliations almost interchangeable.

Unionist precepts, though strikingly invariant in content and rhetoric over the quarter-century up to 1912, required an external menace to translate them into popular mobilization. Since the existing Union was held to be the immaculate and immutable specification of the Anglo-Irish link, the motive force behind Unionism was its defence against the disloyal Irishry and reforming governments. As indicated in the next chapter, Ulster loyalism was vested in an idealized vision of the 'British constitution', the empire and the monarchy. Any party, government, or even monarch caught tampering with the Union thereby surrendered all entitlement to loyalty, being instead excoriated

for sedition compounded (in the case of erring governments) by
treachery. Conservative administrations were not immune:
indeed, the formation of the Ulster Unionist Council was
prompted by chief secretary Wyndham's flirtation with devolution in 1904–5. But the main impetus for loyalist mobilization
was the reiterated attempt by Liberal governments, under Gladstone and later Asquith, to introduce 'Home Rule' through the
creation of a subsidiary parliament controlling domestic services
for the entire island of Ireland.

The Government of Ireland bills of 1886 and 1893 (defeated
respectively in the Commons and the Lords) had each provoked
frenzied parliamentary and propagandist campaigns, as well as
clandestine drilling under the supervision of the Orange Institution. As in the revolutionary years of 1798, 1848, and 1867,
Orangemen constituted themselves as the armed guardians of
Protestant Ascendancy. The demand for Home Rule, despite its
modest scope and subordination to the imperial parliament, was
considered no less threatening to the Union than earlier agi-
tations for repeal or for the republic. Few loyalists followed the
path of Robert Lindsay Crawford, an Antrim-born Dubliner
who became imperial grand master of the Independent Orange
Order, in seeking accommodation with devolutionists and Home
Rulers.[2] The rhetorical verities of Ulster loyalism seemed
eternal, yet the focus and pace of its activity were mutable and
largely dictated by the reformist programmes of Liberal governments. The introduction of a further Government of Ireland
bill in April 1912 was to precipitate Unionist resistance of such
ferocity that a revolutionary uprising seemed probable.

Nationalists

Though depicted in loyalist rhetoric as revolutionary conspirators and subverters of the Union, monarchy, and empire, most
Irish nationalists in 1912 viewed themselves as 'constitutionalists'. This signified their desire to alter Ireland's constitutional
status through 'constitutional' or legal means, using the agencies
of propaganda and parliamentary lobbying, instead of 'physical

force' or rebellion. The constitutional strategy was patiently and shrewdly pursued by the Irish Parliamentary Party, reunited in 1900 out of several warring factions under the chairmanship of John Redmond from Wexford, an urbane Catholic graduate of Dublin University. Redmond resuscitated Parnell's alliances with the Liberal Party and subsequently the Roman Catholic hierarchy, despite clerical antagonism to Liberal policies such as state support for secular education. The hierarchy found in the Irish Party a valuable advocate for most Catholic causes, and looked forward to moulding the morality of the emerging nation-state. The Liberal commitment to Home Rule, almost inaudible after Campbell-Bannerman's sweeping victory of 1906, rang loud and clear upon Asquith's failure to secure a majority of seats in either election of 1910. With the government's survival in his discretion, Redmond prepared confidently to take power in an Irish parliament created in accordance with the new Government of Ireland bill. The Parliament act of the previous year had restricted the House of Lords to postponing rather than rejecting legislation, so protecting the government from the humiliation suffered by Gladstone in 1893. The seeming imminence of Home Rule gave added authority to Redmond's hitherto rather hesitant leadership, and the seventy-three members of his party elected to the House of Commons in December 1910 became a diligent and formidable political unit. Admittedly, Redmond still failed to win universal support even among constitutionalists, with most of the ten dissident nationalist members advocating more active conciliation of landlords and loyalists. This strategy, vigorously pursued by the All For Ireland League founded in 1910 by William O'Brien of Mallow, Co. Cork, gained strong support in Munster but little elsewhere. Redmond's tone—judicious and unembittered, increasingly warm in its depiction of Ireland's future within a reformed empire, conciliatory towards Irish Protestants in words if not specific commitments—sounded the characteristic public notes of pre-war constitutionalism. Seldom had Irish nationalism seemed less revolutionary than in 1912.

The popular organization and interlocking networks of

nationalism had marked similarities to those of Ulster Unionism. The Irish Parliamentary Party had no formal branches,
instead depending upon several organizations and fraternities
representing overlapping interests. Its 'official organization'
after 1900 was the United Irish League, whose initial social
radicalism was soon thoroughly tamed under the stewardship of
Joseph Devlin from West Belfast. Devlin's main network,
however, was the Ancient Order of Hibernians, a Catholic
fraternity with 'divisions' and rituals loosely resembling those of
the Orange Institution. He reorganized most Irish Hibernians
under the 'Board of Erin' in 1905, the order being restricted to
practising Catholics and committed to the pursuit of nationality
through Home Rule. The Hibernian symbols (shamrocks, round
towers, wolfhounds, snakes, sunbursts, harps) conducted a
vigorous visual tussle with those of Orangeism (lilies, walls of
Derry, white horses, ladders, guiding stars, crowns). The colourful and noisy Hibernian processions on St Patrick's Day and
Lady Day (15 August) matched those of the Orangemen and
Blackmen in high summer.

The Hibernians, being an avowedly sectarian body committed
to defending Catholic interests against Protestant menaces, were
far more numerous and active in Ulster than elsewhere. Like the
Orangemen, they were drawn from a wide social range: registers
for Cork between 1911 and 1918 indicate over-representation of
packers and stone-cutters as well as general dealers, drapers,
clerks, accountants, and skilled tradesmen.[3] The Hibernian order
had only about half the membership of the United Irish League,
though it acquired a vast auxiliary force of benefit-holders upon
becoming an approved society for administering National Insurance after 1911. The United Irish League's membership of
130,000 in 1913 represented about a seventh of Catholic adult
males, the proportion being markedly higher in Connaught and
mid-Ulster.[4] These organizations dominated the local electoral
conventions for nationalist candidates, though many other interest groups, cultural societies, and fraternities were entitled to
send delegates. In fact, as in the Unionist case, most selections
were skilfully fixed at headquarters by Devlin and his colleagues

in the League's National Directory. In between elections, local activity was sustained by committee meetings in innumerable tap-rooms, and public demonstrations under the watchful but reassuring chairmanship of the parish priest. The two major Irish parties were far ahead of their British allies in their combination of discreet central control with impressive popular mobilization at parish level.

Republicans and Gaels

Republican opposition to the constitutional strategy was feeble and diffuse by 1912. The absorption into the Home Rule movement of many cultural revivalists and former rebels or agitators had left a seemingly ineffectual rump of dissenters in scattered cells, circles, and societies. The conspiratorial tradition of Fenianism was maintained by the Irish Republican Brotherhood (1858), an oath-bound fraternity whose avowed aim was the armed overthrow of British rule in Ireland and its replacement by a republic of unspecified constitution. This grand design had been disabled since 1873 by the caveat that they should 'await the decision of the Irish nation, as expressed by a majority of the Irish people, as to the fit hour of inaugurating a war against England'.[5] Meanwhile, the president of the 'supreme council' was assigned the unmandated but ethereal duty of also presiding over 'the Irish republic' as proclaimed in 1867. Once numbering one or two women and over 30,000 men, many of them armed and drilled, the Brotherhood had been reduced to a few hundred fierce-spoken elderly stalwarts, often shopkeepers or artisans. Two Belfast republicans, the Quaker journalist Bulmer Hobson and Denis McCullough, a Catholic piano tuner, tried to rejuvenate the organization through recruitment from militant youth groups modelled on the Protestant Boys' Brigade. Nevertheless, Hobson himself attested that in 1912 there were only about 1,500 sworn brothers on the island, half of them in Dublin.[6]

The leaders and members of the reorganized Brotherhood were prominent in a complex network of nationalist societies, devoted ostensibly to innocuous objectives. These included Arthur Griffith's Sinn Féin (1905), Douglas Hyde's Gaelic League (1893), and Michael Cusack's Gaelic Athletic Association (1884). Although none of these bodies was merely a 'front organization', all were vulnerable to manipulation or takeover by republican schemers posing as passive resisters, linguists, or sportsmen. Sinn Féin (signifying 'we ourselves') had long since failed in its ambition to unite nationalists in a non-violent campaign of self-help, to be crowned by the withdrawal of nationalist members from Westminster to Dublin to establish an Irish parliament giving allegiance to an Irish monarch (identical in person to the British incumbent). Only one member had done so, being heavily defeated in the consequent by-election for North Leitrim in 1908. Thereafter, Sinn Féin and its few branches worked to revive the Irish language, encourage Irish manufactures, denounce military recruiting, calumniate Redmond and his party, and convert the General Council of County Councils into 'the nucleus of a National authority'.[7] By 1912, and for four inglorious years thereafter, the words 'Sinn Féin' generated ridicule rather than admiration or fear.

A more formidable potential challenge to constitutionalism was posed by the Gaelic League, the GAA, and other societies devoted to the regeneration of the Gaelic spirit rather than the creation of an Irish-governed state. Under the presidency of Douglas Hyde, son of a Roscommon rector, the Gaelic League avoided overt political commitment in order to maximize its capacity to organize language classes, lectures, céilithe (dances), and feiseanna (festivals of song and dance). Hyde's executive was often embarrassed by the political militancy of the metropolitan Keating branch, through which future revolutionaries such as Cathal Brugha (candlemaker and cricketer, baptized as Charles William St John Burgess) pursued an integrated campaign for Gaelic revival and republican revolution. The Keating branch eventually embraced many future organizers of the IRA, IRB, and Dáil ministry, providing useful cover for conspiratorial meetings before and after the Easter Rising of 1916. Much of the provincial work of the Gaelic League was done by National Teachers, often using schoolrooms for evening classes. The League had about 1,000 branches by 1905, and was quite successful in promoting the use of Irish in higher education and in the state-funded National Schools (both as an extra subject and as a medium of instruction). Its greatest triumph (against powerful opposition from the Catholic hierarchy) was the inclusion of Irish as a compulsory element of matriculation for the National University of Ireland, inaugurated in 1909 to provide tertiary education on terms acceptable to the hierarchy through a network of affiliated colleges in Dublin, Cork, and Galway. Like Sinn Féin, the Gaelic League lost impetus in the years immediately preceding the Easter Rising, with scarcely 260 active branches by 1915.[8]

The GAA had an extensive network of branches (about 800 clubs by 1908), the focus of whose activities had shifted from athletics to hurling, and subsequently also Gaelic football.[9] Another 'native pastime' of enduring appeal to GAA organizers was politics, as manifested in bitter clashes between 'clerical' and 'Fenian' factions in the 1880s, and likewise in the exclusion from competition of policemen, servicemen, and pensioners (1903). Both Gaelic organizations, like Sinn Féin, had some success in recruiting from groups normally marginal to nationalism, such as women and Protestants; but the revived influence of the IRB was reflected in an increasingly militant and exclusive tone during the Edwardian decade. The 'cultural' challenge to the constitutional campaign was latent rather than manifest, and numerous 'Gaels' became involved in the Irish Party and its local organizations in the hope of guiding the forthcoming Home Rule state towards Gaeldom. The party, at first deeply suspicious of Gaelic zeal and unruliness, characteristically appropriated much of the rhetoric of Irish Ireland. Constitutionalism was eclectic and vital enough to retain the vigorous advocacy even of Patrick Pearse (founder of St Enda's Irish school and former editor of the Gaelic League's journal) until 1913. Militant nationalism, despite its revolutionary potential, still seemed as securely saddled by Redmond as by Parnell in his pomp.

Oppositions

Social conflicts always threatened to complicate the primary antagonism between nationalism and loyalism. In Ireland as elsewhere, the privileged classes were relentlessly assailed by their social 'inferiors'. Landlords and employers were confronted by ever more formidable combinations of tenants or workers; men became aware that there were women demanding equal rights. All of these oppositions tended to disturb the solidarity of nationalists and loyalists alike, since they cut across communal loyalties and solicited support without regard for religious affiliation. The major political organizations responded firmly and imaginatively by trying to stifle independent debate while offering conciliation within their own structures. The more urgent the national question seemed, the easier it was to secure postponement of social conflict until it had been resolved.

The supremacy of landlords had been shaken but not immediately shattered by the populist campaign of the Irish National Land League (1879–81) and its successors, together with the radical legislation by which both Liberal and Conservative governments had sought to avert social revolution. In fact, by some definitions, the effect of that legislation was to accomplish a social revolution. Initially focused on reducing rents through a system of 'dual ownership', the progressive reform of the Irish land code had the eventual effect of inducing most owners of tenanted property to sell out to the current occupiers. After several largely ineffectual land purchase acts, two crucial statutes were put through by the Conservative chief secretary George Wyndham in 1903, and his Liberal successor Augustine Birrell in 1909. Though flawed and cumbersome, these acts offered landlords sufficiently attractive bonuses to induce most to surrender their estates, leaving them in control of demesnes, home farms, and leasehold. More draconian measures applied to the poorest western and midland regions, where an ambitious programme of rural regeneration was conducted under the Congested Districts Board (1891). By early 1915, 72 per cent of all the land eventually transferred had been sold by the landlords, although only 58 per cent had so far been assigned to occupiers.[10]

The slow pace of transfer gave continued impetus to the United Irish League, whose local branches often handled negotiations with landlords (on occasion reinforced by threats and 'outrages'), in conjunction with the Catholic clergy. The struggle between tenant and landlord was easily portrayed as part of the nation's battle against alien oppressors, despite the awkward fact that some proprietors were Catholics of seemingly impeccable lineage while many tenants were Protestants and Unionists. In practice, the League restricted its agitation to the Catholic tenantry, so recognizing the futility of earlier attempts by the Land League and the Irish Tenant League (1850–3) to mobilize Ulster and southern farmers in a common campaign. More divisive within nationalism was the sometimes furious agitation for the division of grasslands, typically leased by landlords to shop-keepers who were often Catholic nationalists. This campaign, initiated by William O'Brien's United Irish League in 1898 and later championed by the maverick Laurence Ginnell (MP for North Westmeath from 1906), sometimes threatened to set prosperous nationalist investors against nationalist labourers and small farmers, enviously eyeing neighbouring tracts of pasture. The Irish Party excelled itself in defusing this menace, allowing leaseholders masquerading as populists to inflame the 'peasantry' against the claims of rival 'ranchers', only to soothe and discharge their followers upon securing possession themselves. Meanwhile, the party maintained its rhetorical assault upon the iniquitous class of graziers, without having to dispense with their services as local organizers and subscribers.

Discontent among employed workers was more difficult to subsume within nationalism (and likewise loyalism). Not only were employers typically of the same religion as their workers, but the rhetoric of socialism and militant trades unionism asserted the priority of class over religious or national affilations.

In Ireland, despite the fact that 55 per cent of occupied men were engaged in agriculture in 1911, the Labour movement was over-whelmingly urban. This was largely due to the predominance of family labour in Irish farming: an official report in June 1912 indicated that only 30 per cent of men engaged in agriculture were employed labourers, of whom 43 per cent were temporary hands.[11] Since many of these 'labourers' were in fact small farmers or their offspring seeking supplementary income, the rural proletariat was small, scattered, divided in its class identity, and very difficult to organize in collective actions. The grievances of permanent agricultural labourers had been somewhat pla-cated by the building of labourers' cottages at public expense, despite resultant grumbling about the rents due to local author-ities. Several nationalist organizations, including the United Irish League and the Land and Labour Association (1894), espoused the more moderate demands of rural labourers while urging them to subordinate their sectional interests to the national struggle. In Ulster, where landlords and large farmers had been far more active in providing adequate housing and sometimes estate villages for their dependents, the relatively small agricul-tural proletariat was even more quiescent than elsewhere.

Ulster, however, provided the theatre for Ireland's first major experiments in the 'new [trades] unionism', with its aspiration to organize unskilled workers as well as artisans and to incorpor-ate employees of all occupations in 'general unions'. Irish manu-facturing had become ever more concentrated in Belfast and in the 'linen triangle' to the south-west of the city, and a large and volatile proletariat serviced the engineering and shipbuilding trades as skilled artisans, labourers, carters, and dockers. The Belfast proletariat was itself increasingly stratified according to religion, with Catholics ever more confined to an underclass of temporary and manual workers. This was partly accountable to the influence of fraternal networks seeking preferential Protest-ant access to apprenticeships and skilled employment. Sectarian discrimination was bolstered by the periodic violent expulsion, most recently in July 1912, of nationalist and usually Catholic workers from the shipyards by their Protestant fellows. Seldom overtly condoned by police or employers, and fiercely opposed by liberal capitalists such as the Canadian-born William Pirrie of Harland & Wolff, these expulsions fatally subverted Labour's strategy of supplanting sectarian conflict by proletarian collective action.

This was nevertheless the mission of two immigrant organizers, James Larkin (born in Liverpool of Catholic stock from Armagh) and James Connolly (a lapsed Catholic and veteran of the Royal Scots from Edinburgh, whose parents had emigrated from Monaghan). Larkin's inspirational syndicalism, with its evangelical and moralistic tone, blended uneasily with Connolly's more analytical socialism to generate the Irish Transport and General Workers' Union (1908). Larkin's early success in 1907, when he mobilized Belfast dockers and later policemen of all religions in spectacular if sometimes ineffectual strikes, encouraged him to boast that 'the old sectarian curse had been banished for ever in Ulster'.[12] His militant campaign won support from the irrepressible Robert Lindsay Crawford, exposing further rifts within loyalism. However, the dream of uniting Catholic and Protestant workers through industrial struggle was soon spoiled. The focus of the 'new unionism' shifted to mainly Catholic Dublin, where Larkin and Connolly organized a massive but disastrous strike in 1913, leading to a ruthless lockout and eventual surrender without readmission of unionized workers. The Irish Trades Union Congress (1894) became ever more closely aligned with the Irish Parliamentary Party, so alienating Protestant workers and segmenting the Labour movement. The nominal creation by Congress of a 'Labour Party' in 1914 failed to generate significant independent activity. In Ulster, most organized workers adhered to unions affiliated to the British rather than the Irish Congress. Sectarian loyalties had once again overwhelmed the tenuous solidarity of 'class'.

Feminism offered a further challenge to conventional political divisions, as educated Irish women (and often men) began to apply the precepts and methods of English suffragism. As with socialism and syndicalism, the novelty and external genesis of feminist doctrine fostered the illusion that it might transcend the familiar sectarian polarities. Initially, Irish suffragism was a respectable cause espoused by middle-class Protestants such as Isabella Tod, the Edinburgh-born schoolmistress and fierce opponent of Home Rule who convened the North of Ireland (later 'Irish') Women's Suffrage Society in 1873. Her southern counterpart was the Quaker Anna Maria Haslam from Cork, who founded the Dublin (likewise, later 'Irish') Women's Suffrage Association in 1876. Its immediate aim was to extend the local government franchise to qualified women, and to enable them to stand for election. The accomplishment of this aim was mainly attributable to an organization claiming only about 650 members in 1911.

Meanwhile, a slightly more militant and emphatically more Catholic organization of similar size, the Irish Women's Franchise League, had been formed in 1908. Led by two graduates of the Royal University, the Dublin Catholic Hanna Sheehy-Skeffington and the Roscommon Methodist Gretta Cousins, the League organized meetings and lectures in country towns, lobbied parliamentarians, and established umbrella organizations aiming to co-ordinate the numerous local feminist societies. Though restricted to women, the Franchise League was vigorously publicized by male 'associates' such as the founders' husbands, the pacificist Frank Sheehy-Skeffington and James Cousins, a vegetarian theosophist from Belfast who had resigned from his Dublin Orange lodge in 1900. The Irish Party's mainly negative attitude to the enfranchisement of women for parliamentary elections induced many suffragists to denounce orthodox nationalism and seek support from socialists, syndicalists, and other political fringe-dwellers. Further marginalization occurred in 1912 when militant suffragettes, mostly visitors from England, began to burn buildings, assault politicians, and disrupt traffic on the English model. Once again, however, the division between nationalists and loyalists proved dominant, and much effective suffrage agitation was conducted by explicitly Conservative and Unionist bodies. The same applied to anti-suffrage agitation, whose chief organizer in Ireland was the mother of Northern Ireland's first governor, the 3rd duke of Abercorn.

Small though it was, the women's movement was fragmented and polarized as the crisis of 1912 unfolded. Issues of sex, like class, remained marginal to the demarcation of the revolutionary battle-lines.

Why?

Doctrines of Liberation

Every protagonist in Ireland's revolution proclaimed the ideal of liberation. Loyalists, nationalists and republicans, tenants, workers, and women: all felt that their entitlements were menaced or withheld by others. The ideal of liberation drew force from the conviction that these entitlements had been recognized and asserted in the past, before some ulterior and malign influence snatched them away. Vying visions of a golden age gave form and meaning to personal failure or discontent, weaving individual experience into the plot of a familiar historical melodrama.

For loyalists schooled in the Orange outlook, freedom was encapsulated in the Protestantism of the Glorious Revolution. The free-born subject, submissive to the rule of law but defiant of all its subverters, whether internal or external, had triumphed against the satanic forces of Romish superstition and arbitrary government. In origin, this was a defensive notion: liberty had been restored and guaranteed only after its betrayal by the very symbol of fidelity, James II, the reigning monarch. It followed that no subsequent monarchs or governments seemed intrinsically trustworthy, so that every affirmation of loyalty was conditional upon their continued profession of Protestantism. The Union, despite the disturbing impact of Catholic emancipation and Church disestablishment, was viewed as the constitutional form best designed to protect Irish Protestants from subjugation to a Catholic majority: by defining their nationality as British rather than merely Irish, the Union incorporated them within a broader Protestant majority. This status was clearly more defensible than adherence to an embattled Ascendancy vastly outnumbered by ever more fractious inferiors, and therefore driven to play havoc with the liberty of the subject. The morale of Ulster Unionists was further sustained by their impressive capacity to mobilize political, financial, and moral support throughout the English-speaking world. Ulster's international-ism was reinforced through incessant colonial and military service, emigration, and trade, being vigorously affirmed by sym-pathetic Protestant fraternities and churches in every country of settlement.

The Unionist conception of liberty was not purely defensive and reactionary. Since 1800, new tokens of freedom had become interleaved with the Protestant insistence that no human author-ity be permitted to interrupt the transmission of faith between God and the enlightened. The merchants and industrialists who dominated Ulster Unionism cherished freedom of trade with the same fervour as freedom of faith. The empire, transcending its cruder strategic and economic functions as an instrument of British power, was now pictured as a missionary force for spreading enlightenment and liberation; its wars were no mere exercises in realpolitik, but episodes in the interminable struggle of good against evil. The United States, despite a century and a half of political independence, was widely regarded by Ulster Unionists as the key element of Britain's cultural empire and a bulwark against the insidious advance of the Church of Rome. The fusion of seemingly incongruous elements in Union-ist ideology was eloquently expressed in 'Ulster's Solemn League and Covenant', signed by three-quarters of all Protestant Ulster-men over 16 on 28 September 1912. The very name evoked the Scottish parliamentary covenant of 1643, reminding signatories that loyalty to the monarch was subordinate to the defence of political and religious liberty. The covenanters concurred 'that Home Rule would be disastrous to the material well-being of Ulster as well as of the whole of Ireland, subversive of our civil and religious freedom, destructive of our citizenship and perilous to the unity of the Empire'.[1] For Irish Unionists, being 'British' was shorthand for remaining a part of God's chosen people, with all the spiritual and material privileges that this conferred.

Nationalism, like loyalism, drew inspiration from an idealized vision of the past, in which the nation had been free to pursue its chosen course until besieged and ravaged by alien forces of darkness. Belief in the existence of a Gaelic commonwealth, marked by piety, clan loyalty, and equity between the sexes and classes, was widespread among nationalists of all programmes and reinforced by the writings of nationalist historians such as Alice Stopford Green (a Meath Protestant) and Eoin MacNeill (an Antrim Catholic). The supposed institution of a kingship governing the entire island was also the first of several 'proofs' that Ireland had been an integral nation-state which, if recreated, must apply to all thirty-two counties. Many of the proclaimed inheritors of this medieval nation demanded the freedom to pursue a distinctively Gaelic destiny, rather than freedom of individual or even of majority choice. The nation, including its dead and its unborn, was entitled to freedom; those claimed for the nation as its living citizens had the duty to pursue that abstract liberation.

Since successive invasions and migrations had mingled the races until 'pure Celtic blood' became as rare and dubious as a four-leaved shamrock, modern 'Gaels' required an unambiguous badge of identity. A small but growing élite used language to attest their nationality: as cultural nationalism struggled to break free from conventional alignments, the ability or desire to speak in Irish became a proof of citizenship in the republic of the spirit. The exchange of greetings in Irish had functions similar to a masonic handshake or an Orangeman's sign, promising access to a protected world governed by trust and peopled by the enlightened. For most nationalists, however, Catholicism remained a sufficient qualification for claiming a share in the 'native' inheritance. Gaeldom was more important in defining a shared past than in shaping the future for the Irish nation. Indeed, constitutionalist leaders from O'Connell to Parnell, and then Redmond, hoped that freedom from English exploitation would enable the Irish nation to modernize its social and economic organization according to the English model. Even so, in their search for nationalist solidarity pending Home Rule,

Redmond's rhetoricians were typically careful to avoid narrow prescriptions for freedom. In the words of Tom Kettle (MP for East Tyrone from 1906 to 1910, poet, drinker, political economist, and casualty at Givenchy on the Somme in September 1916): 'Constitutional freedom is not the fifth act of the social drama in modern times, it is rather . . . the theatre in which other ideas that move men find an arena for their conflict.'[2] The ultimate character of freedom was something better not discussed.

In affirming its constitutional goals, Redmond's party confined its programme to a few simple and abstract slogans. Home Rule, like the Union of the Orangeman's dream, was a catchcry evoking visions of freedom and harmony, bearing little connection with political practicalities. Unlike Unionism, however, it was not shackled by constitutional precedent. Advocacy of Home Rule as a first step was consistent with many futures, ranging from a republic to a loyal dominion within a brotherly commonwealth or federation. So long as Home Rule was a demand rather than a fact, the latent tensions between republicans and imperialists, and between social groups with conflicting economic interests, could be suppressed in pursuit of the common goal. Redmond's party, like Parnell's, embraced many former Fenians and advocates of physical force who supported parliamentary action—so long as it promised results. Redmond's successor as leader in 1918, John Dillon from Mayo, continued in later life to hanker sentimentally for direct action as practised by his father (John Blake Dillon) in 1848, without deviating from pragmatic attachment to constitutionalism. In 1917, Dillon claimed never to have uttered 'one word against physical force when it was used in a just cause and with some hope of success'.[3] The adherence of ex-fighters, and the regular commemorations of past rebellions, reinforced loyalist suspicions of the Irish Party's deceitfulness and hypocrisy. Yet these very ambiguities were the foundation of its predominance in nationalist Ireland. Imprecision and inconclusiveness were essential to the appeal of Home Rule: like the flapping signpost at an Irish country crossroads, it could point towards any destination.

As republicanism supplanted constitutionalism after 1916, the

ideologists of the renascent Sinn Féin reformulated the rhetoric
of liberation, reaffirming Patrick Pearse's demand for a republic both Gaelic and free. Six months before his execution as
'President of the Irish Republic' of 1916, Pearse had rejected
'limited freedom' as promised under Home Rule, instead requiring 'absolute freedom, the sovereign control of Irish destinies'.[4]
This achievement would however be worthless unless exercised
to restore Gaelic culture: freedom must be permitted to point
towards one destiny alone. Adherence to this doctrine, no less
intolerant of individual dissent than its loyalist counterpart, was
prerequisite for post-Rising Sinn Féiners, who in many districts
were ordered to attend Irish classes as part of their education in
nationalism. The pursuit of 'Irish Ireland' was coupled with a
naïve but venomous loathing for England and her culture: as the
mother of a future taoiseach (premier) had boasted to G. B.
Shaw in November 1914, 'I am bringing up my small son with
the sound traditional hatred of England and all her ways—you
should just hear him say Sasanach, the concentrated hatred in
his voice is worthy of Drury Lane.'[5] Faith in a Gaelic destiny was
the crucial discriminant between constitutionalism and republicanism: 'self-determination', the national slogan between 1917
and 1921, entailed liberation from 'alien' control in order to
impose a particular ideology upon the 'natives'. The authoritative exposition of this claim was an open letter addressed to
President Wilson in October 1920, signed by Eamon de Valera
as 'President of the Republic of Ireland'. This affirmed 'that the
people of Ireland constitute a distinct and separate nation, eth-
nically, historically, and tested by every standard of political
science; entitled, therefore, to self-determination'.[6]

Despite its insistence on the Gaelic distinctiveness of the Irish
nation, the rhetoric of Sinn Féin was by no means parochial.
Arthur Griffith, like Michael Davitt and other cosmopolitan
proponents of Home Rule, viewed Irish nationalism as part of a
broader struggle against the exploitation of subject peoples by
colonial powers. Republicans and Home Rulers alike searched
the world for precedents, parallels, and potential partners among
foreign nationalist movements. The constitutionalists had found

particular inspiration in the South African and Indian struggles for freedom, observing with interest the relative effectiveness of their respective techniques of guerrilla warfare and passive resistance. Arthur Griffith had urged Ireland to emulate the Hungarian campaign of non-violent obstruction which led to the *Ausgleich* with Austria in 1867 and the creation of a 'dual monarchy'.[7] The pursuit of practical co-operation with overseas movements, especially in Egypt and India, was a major preoccupation of the Dáil's foreign ministry in 1919–21. By drawing upon foreign models and feeling fraternity with other oppressed nationalities, Irish nationalists warded off the spiritual isolation of fighting a lonely battle in defence of a unique ethnicity. Nationalism, in Ireland as elsewhere, was an internationalist ideology.

Sinn Féin's strategy for achieving independence was based on the belief that Britain could be induced to bend to the world, if only the world could be converted to Ireland's cause. The appeal of the term 'republic' was mainly derived from its romantic associations in America, France, and other republics which were regarded as potential allies. Following Unionist and constitutionalist precedent, Sinn Féin selected a simple and unqualified slogan for foreign ears, in the hope of maximizing the political, diplomatic, and financial response to its international propaganda. In advocating a republic, Sinn Féin's revised constitution of October 1917 presented this as a pragmatic device for winning international support, after which the Irish people might select any form of government (even monarchy) by referendum. As its new president, de Valera, explained to a rather bemused ard fheis (convention): 'It is as an Irish Republic that we have a chance of getting international recognition. . . . We do not wish to bind people to any form of government.'[8] The point of this liberality was to encourage constitutionalists and others wary of separatism to find a place within the new nationalism, and also to be enumerated as fellow-advocates of 'self-determination'. De Valera's characteristically perverse essay in compromise was part of a broader search for consensus among nationalist factions, using the very techniques lately applied by Redmond.

Moreover, as the prospect of international recognition for the republic receded, while the possibility of a partial settlement became manifest, the constitutionalist strategy of accepting half a loaf grew ever more appealing. Unwavering adherence to the republican slogan had lost its strategic utility, whereas compromise with Britain promised prompt and tangible benefits. By December 1921, when Michael Collins defended the Anglo-Irish treaty as giving 'not the ultimate freedom which all nations hope for and struggle for, but freedom to achieve that end', the rhetoric of self-determination and of Home Rule had become virtually indistinguishable.[9]

The forms of liberation sought by potential social revolutionaries were likewise influenced by various visions of history. The campaigns for tenant right and land purchase assumed that the current occupiers of land were entitled to recognition as proprietors, on the ground that their ancestors had been expropriated by planters and forcibly reduced to the status of insecure tenants. In most cases, of course, it was impossible to demonstrate that a particular farmer was indeed the descendant of a former occupier under Brehon law, or that one such claim was superior to another. The assertion of entitlement therefore applied in effect to a class rather than a set of individual claimants: all those currently managing land as occupiers were entitled to some modern equivalent of the rights enjoyed by Gaelic landholders. The rhetoric affirming communal sovereignty over 'the Nation's soil and all its resources' was a commonplace of radical nationalists from Davitt to Pearse, attaining its barren apotheosis in Dáil Éireann's Democratic Programme in 1919.[10] Nevertheless, no serious demand was made for the restoration of communal ownership, or for the banishment of occupying tenants with demonstrably non-Gaelic origins (though 'land-grabbers' profiting from recent evictions were to be displaced by the descendants of those evicted). Nor did the United Irish League and its predecessors pay much attention to the claims of those who worked the land without managing it. Agricultural labourers, though scarcely less likely than current tenants to hold an ancestral entitlement, were allowed only a secondary claim through the campaign for division of grasslands. These anomalies by no means negated the historicist rhetoric, which served an essential function in asserting that the land movement was a national rather than a sectional enterprise.

Since the ideologies of Irish feminism and socialism were fractured and faction-ridden, it would be inappropriate to attribute a single, coherent doctrine of liberation to either movement. The entitlement of women to citizenship, or of workers to a fair share in the product of their labour, was usually grounded in some doctrine of universal human rights rather than a vision of the Irish past. In Ireland as elsewhere, much of the passion and energy of feminists and socialists was consumed by arcane doctrinal disputes of foreign origin. Nevertheless, strenuous attempts were made by republicans to show that these demands had been anticipated in Gaelic Ireland. James Connolly's *Labour in Irish History* found parallels with primitive communism in the communal ownership of land; and feminist republicans such as Kathleen Clarke (widow of Thomas, the former dynamitard executed in 1916) lauded the system enabling Gaelic women to retrieve their property after marital breakdown, and to pursue professional careers.[11] These attempts to nationalize social struggle were far less influential than the more mundane appeals of moderate trades unionists and suffragists, who drew inspiration chiefly from their English and American counterparts. The freedom to vote, to belong to a union of fellow-workers, and to secure higher wages and better conditions, were demands made forcefully and sometimes effectively in Ireland as elsewhere in Europe. This intrusion of 'foreign' ideas posed a disconcerting challenge to both nationalist and Unionist ideologies, in which liberation was but a means towards a predetermined end.

Pursuits of Power

For every major participant in the Irish conflict, the rhetoric of liberation served to purify and ennoble the pursuit of power. Through a prolonged process of collective self-justification, often without conscious hypocrisy, the paths of virtue and self-interest became indistinguishable within each ideology. The resultant note of righteousness, equally strident in nationalism and loyalism, had the negative effect of encouraging opponents to dismiss each other's claims as fraudulent propaganda devised for gullible external audiences. This cynicism was only partly justified, despite the undeniable propagandist benefits of invoking justice and equity when grasping for power. The Orangeman who denounced 'the fatal errors and doctrines of the Church of Rome', while promising in the same breath to abstain 'from all uncharitable words, actions, or sentiments, towards his Roman Catholic brethren', was zealous but not necessarily disingenuous. After all, the Catholic who converted to Protestantism was welcome to share the rewards of enlightenment and even, on occasion, to join the Orange Institution.[12] By contrast, most Unionists cared nothing for the liberties demanded by Catholics and nationalists who rejected the Union, except (often grudgingly) to admit their existing legal rights as 'British' citizens.

The extent to which Unionist pursuit of Protestant power threatened Catholic liberties depended on the territory within which the Unionist claim was asserted. In loyalist theory, this was the entire island; but by painful degrees the claim espoused by most Ulster Unionists was eventually restricted to six Ulster counties alone. This respecification was already under way before 1914, as Unionist leaders toyed with proposals for excluding part or all of the province from a southern state under Home Rule. As Bonar Law asserted in 1912: 'Ireland is not a nation; it is two nations. It is two nations separated from each other by lines of cleavage which cut far deeper than those which separate Great Britain from Ireland as a whole.' He concluded that every argument supporting 'separate treatment for the Irish Nationalist majority' within the United Kingdom applied 'with far greater force in favour of separate treatment for the Unionists of Ulster as against the majority of Ireland'.[13] For contemporary readers, the term 'separate treatment' would have signified not self-government, but Ulster's exemption from Home Rule and its unqualified retention within the United Kingdom.

The revision of Ulster's claim was sealed in 1920 when Carson and Sir James Craig, the Belfast stockbroker who succeeded him in the following year as Ulster Unionist leader, accepted and popularized the government's novel proposal to create a separate government for six northern counties under Home Rule. This notion had in fact been raised five years earlier by Alfred Perceval Graves (anthologist of sentimental Irish verse and father of Robert), in private discussion with Carson.[14] Despite the obvious objection that loyalists had long claimed that any form of devolution would destroy the Union and imperil the empire, the Unionist leaders defended their apparent apostasy by affirming that devolution would be safe in their hands, and that partition would give Protestants an unassailable demographic and economic advantage within their own territory. The acceptance of partition confirmed that their primary concern was with the consolidation of Protestant power, rather than the defence of liberty throughout the United Kingdom. Overriding the anguished protests of many southern loyalists abandoned to an uncertain future, and largely indifferent to the fears felt by nationalists trapped in the northern state, the chosen people of Ulster prepared to fulfil their destiny.

In principle, nationalist and loyalist rhetoric had agreed that the territory of the nation should be undivided, the 'nation' being defined respectively as Ireland and the United Kingdom. As constitutional change became a practical possibility, many nationalists likewise allowed the desire for power and possession to compromise their ideal of national indivisibility. Demography ensured that this compromise would be far more painful for nationalists, since any viable form of partition or exclusion would leave a much larger Catholic minority under Ulster or British rule than the corresponding Protestant minority under nationalist rule. During the tortuous negotiations over Home Rule between 1912 and 1918, Redmond's party contemplated every variation short of permanent partition, including 'Home Rule within Home Rule' for part or all of Ulster, and eventually (after the Easter Rising) temporary exclusion of six counties from the new nation-state. Permanent division was as yet publicly undebatable, since the nationalist conviction that all inhabitants of Ireland had a duty to conform to the nation remained sacrosanct.

This rationalization of the national claim was all the more essential in face of the practical restriction of nationalism to Catholics (with the exception of a few intellectuals claiming the inheritance of Presbyterian radicalism; a medley of high-spirited rebels against the conventions of their family, class, or community; and some well-meaning Protestant patricians who felt that *noblesse oblige*). However convenient the political alliance of constitutionalism and the Catholic hierarchy might be for both parties, it undermined the genuine desire of Redmond and at least some of his colleagues to spurn sectarianism. Nationalist rhetoric therefore emphasized the racial admixture of the inhabitants, the tendency of successive invaders to become more Irish than the Irish, and the prominence of Protestants in previous insurrections and campaigns. Hugh Alexander Law from Donegal, a rare Protestant in Redmond's party who had however converted to Catholicism in 1912, offered a subjective definition of nationhood with a decidedly modern ring: 'That people is a Nation which feels itself to be a Nation, and those rightly belong to a Nation who desire to belong to it. Sometimes, as is the case of the Southern Slav, a common racial origin is the foundation of national sentiment. But quite as often it has nothing whatever to do with it. There have been many famous Irishmen—Parnell was such a one—Irish to the fingertips—who were no more Celts than they were Choctaws.'[15] Law's formulation left one problem unposed: how would a nation-state deal with those inhabitants who did not desire to belong to the nation?

The triumph of republicanism over constitutionalism owed much to public indignation at Redmond's 'betrayal' in accepting Lloyd George's futile proposal of May 1916 for immediate Home Rule with supposedly 'temporary' exclusion of six counties. Sinn Féin, still a small organization and so far untainted by compromise, declared the attainment of a united Ireland to be its fundamental and distinguishing national demand. De Valera's letter to President Wilson reaffirmed the hybrid origins of the people of Ireland, claiming 'that there is no district in Ulster where the inhabitants could, with any degree of accuracy, be termed a different race from the people of the rest of Ireland'. Conscious that Ireland's claim to nationality appealed to its 'ethnic' (as distinct from racial) integrity, de Valera dismissed any counter-assertion of Ulster's cultural distinctiveness by explaining 'that the supposed progressiveness of Ulster is a myth, pure and simple'. The 'Ulster question', if any, was restricted to Belfast, and posed no serious threat to national organization: 'A free Ireland will have no difficulty solving its minority problem. It can solve it much more easily, in fact, than most countries have been able to solve similar problems.'[16] Protestants were welcome to subscribe to the Irish nation, and would surely do so once pig-headedness had given way to the pursuit of enlightened self-interest.

Having reiterated precisely the assumptions of their constitutionalist predecessors, republicans soon found themselves following a similar path towards acceptance of some form of partition on the optimistic assumption that it would not last. When offered control over a Free State of twenty-six counties with the vague hope that Northern Ireland would eventually be dismembered by a boundary commission, the majority of republican negotiators and legislators accepted partitition as the price of power. Given the manifest unfeasibility of promptly achieving a united Irish state, and the practical advantages of not having to manage a million refractory Ulster Unionists, the lure of limited territorial possession was irresistible. Even de Valera, in his initial attempts to secure rejection and renegotiation of the treaty, incorporated its provisions for Northern Ireland in his alternative document. Few indeed were the purists who rejected all forms of partition, although some deluded themselves that any division of Ireland would be easily reversible. Thus the bulk of republicans, like Ulster loyalists, settled for secure control of a section only of their promised land. The liberation of northern nationalists would have to wait a while.

As republicans and loyalists prepared to administer their

assigned territories, the problem of catering for discontented subgroups became acute. Both movements presented themselves as upholders of equity between classes, sympathetic to the underdog when engaged in conciliation. The Ulster Unionist leaders, though conservative to a fault on social and sexual issues, took care to provide separate loyalist bodies within which radical murmurings could be uttered, heard, and placated. Women played an active if emphatically subordinate part in Unionist political and military organization, co-ordinated by the Ulster Women's Unionist Council (headed, like the anti-suffrage campaign, by the duchess of Abercorn). This body, with its hierarchy of duchesses and dowagers dictating to middle-class secretaries, was still more reactionary than its male counterpart. The female role in loyalism was comically evident in the formulation of the 'Women's Declaration' of 1912, which gained 229,000 signatories in Ulster (an excess of 10,000 over the male covenant). A fortnight before Ulster Day, the Women's Council was still under the impression that their declaration was to be 'prepared by the men, and that we have nothing to do with this matter'. Richard Dawson Bates, secretary to the Ulster Unionist Council (the Belfast lawyer who became Northern Ireland's first minister for home affairs), hastily replied that the declaration had indeed been drafted by Craig, but that the women were solely 'responsible for settling what Declaration they wish to issue'. The resultant document blushingly left reasoned argument to the male covenanters, declaring that the signatories 'desire to associate ourselves with the men of Ulster in their uncompromising opposition to the Home Rule Bill'.[17]

This deferential attitude resurfaced in January 1921, when the Women's Council decided not to nominate women for parliament. The executive committee resolved that 'the time was not yet ripe for this, and the essential thing in the first Parliament was to preserve the safety of the Unionist cause, that much organisation and construction work would be necessary for which perhaps women had not the necessary experience'.[18] In Comber, Co. Down, the recent formation of a women's Orange lodge had been 'considered by some as a huge joke'; but the worshipful mistress insisted that 'all women Unionists, whether Orange women or not, must make themselves a force to be reckoned with and vote only for men of sterling character, whose integrity and loyalty were above suspicion'.[19] Yet it would be wrong to dismiss female participation in loyalism as ludicrous. Women's groups were active and effective in propaganda as well as electoral campaigns, and Ulster Unionists had raised no objection against extending female suffrage to Northern Ireland. The varied participation of women in the Ulster Volunteer Force by comparison with the British army was remarked upon by Wilfrid Spender, who had served as a staff officer in both bodies before becoming Northern Ireland's first cabinet secretary. The UVF included many 'women who not only enrolled as nurses but also performed most efficiently much of the clerical work and those supplementary services which rather late in the Great War were allotted to women's organisations'.[20] By encouraging active female participation to a degree unusual in Irish affairs, Unionist leaders blunted the appeal of more radical feminist demands.

Republicanism was equally successful in disarming feminism by enrolling women in political and military organizations, with the half-promise of female emancipation once the republic had been created. Redmond's party had made less effort than Ulster Unionism to mobilize women, their part being largely confined to the Ladies' Auxiliary of the Ancient Order of Hibernians. Unlike the United Irish League, Sinn Féin never excluded women; although a stray police return indicates that less than a tenth of Limerick's Sinn Féiners in 1921 were female.[21] The formation of the Irish Volunteers in November 1913 was followed within six months by that of Cumann na mBan (Society of Women), an ancillary body which aimed 'to assist in arming and equipping a body of Irishmen for the defence of Ireland'.[22] It eventually played a major part in nursing, signalling, sabotage, and intelligence during the War of Independence. Despite the belated creation of a formally separate, hierarchy, in practice the organization remained firmly under the control of male officers at every level from company to general staff.

Many old suffragists and new feminists viewed Cumann na mBan with suspicion, both for its subservience to male leaders and for its insistence that pursuit of the republic had priority over female emancipation. But the radical rhetoric of Constance Markievicz (daughter of a Protestant landlord from Lissadell, Co. Sligo, Easter rebel and candidate Joan of Arc), and the active involvement in Sinn Féin of no less a suffragist than Hanna Sheehy-Skeffington, persuaded most feminists to suspend independent agitation until the republic had been accomplished. The assimilation of feminism was sealed on 'Women's Day' in June 1918, when the Irish Women's Franchise League joined Cumann na mBan and other societies in pledging their members not to take up posts vacated by conscripted males, subsequently declaring that coercion had 'rendered the carrying out of suffrage activities impossible'.[23] Such responses paralleled the decision of most Unionist and British suffragists to shelve feminism for the duration of the war. Feminist patience brought tangible rewards when Markievicz became the first female parliamentarian, spurning her seat at Westminster but eventually becoming minister for labour in Dáil Éireann. Despite some cavils, the constitution of the Free State proclaimed universal franchise regardless of sex, several years before that extension was accomplished in Britain or Northern Ireland. Helping republicans to take power raised the hope, soon to be disappointed, that women would share in the exercise of that power.

The taming of Labour, potentially a more serious distraction from the struggle over Irish nationality, was accomplished with panache by both nationalists and loyalists. Militant trade unionism seemed a spent force after the collapse of the not-quite-general strike in Dublin and the advent of European war. The triumph of William Martin Murphy and his fellow employers left Larkin's Transport Union penniless and discredited, while the advent of war caused many trade unionists to enlist in the services. By early 1917, current membership scarcely exceeded the number alleged by a prominent union official to have joined the colours.[24] After initial economic disruption, the war proved unexpectedly beneficial to those on the 'home front', causing reduction of unemployment in most sectors, unprecedented protection of wages and hours of work in war-related industries, controls on prices for consumers, and extension of state provision for the welfare of mothers and children. Despite wartime restriction of labour mobility and consumer choice, the net effect was to reduce the grievance of workers against their masters. Although relatively few Irish workers were constrained by the 'Treasury agreements' of March 1915, whereby many major unions suspended strikes for the duration of the war, extensive industrial disruption did not resume until 1918.

Over the following three years, however, Irish Labour was more active than ever before, with more strikes over a wider range of issues, affecting ever more occupations and localities. Employers, shocked by the scale and solidarity of these collective actions, showed unaccustomed eagerness (so long as prosperity lasted) to reach rapid settlements. The renewal of heavy unemployment and economic disruption after the armistice benefited all varieties of Labour organization, including the English-based 'amalgamated' unions which fought off the Transport Union's challenge in most of Ulster. That union, however, was the major beneficiary of Labour's growth, its membership rising from about 5,000 in April 1916 to 25,000 in December 1917, exceeding 100,000 three years later.[25] The 'one big union' broadened its intake to embrace shop assistants, clerks, farm labourers, and even domestic servants, until it could fairly claim to represent virtually every category of 'wage-slave' in accordance with the syndicalist programme. Its phenomenal growth was only partly achieved through the absorption of existing unions and trade associations, such as the constitutionalist Land and Labour Association. More profoundly, it signified the rapid diffusion among workers of a limited but pugnacious consciousness of the power of their class.

The recrudescence of industrial unrest aroused fears of class conflict within Ulster Unionism, and a prescient initiative from Carson. The Belfast Trades Council, though circumspect in politics as befitted a body representing a divided workforce, was dominated by Home Rulers and inclined to support the

London-based Independent Labour Party. The eventual return of ex-servicemen to civil employment raised the further prospect of tussles between loyalist veterans and entrenched workers. The Ulster Unionist Council therefore created its own Ulster Unionist Labour Association in mid-1918, with Carson as president and, as chairman, John Miller Andrews (a linen manufacturer from Comber, great-grandson of the United Irishman William Drennan, second prime minister of Northern Ireland, and ultimately grand master of the Council of World Orange Institutions). Despite this characteristically unabashed assertion of paternalism, the Association provided a significant conduit for working-class participation in loyalist politics. Three representatives were elected to Westminster in December 1918, and the Association provided five of the forty Unionists elected to the first northern House of Commons in May 1921. All rival Labour candidates in Belfast were defeated, including five nominees of the Belfast Trades Council or the Independent Labour Party in 1918, and four Independents in 1921. By giving workers a distinct voice in Unionism, Carson averted repetition of the disastrous split which had caused so many loyalist proletarians to join the Independent Orange Institution after 1903.

Labour was less successful in securing formal recognition within republicanism, although Sinn Féin proved no less adept than the Ulster Unionist Council in undermining Labour's potentiality as an independent political force. James Connolly's involvement as Dublin commander in the 1916 Rising, along with the conspicuously bloody part played by his tiny vigilante force, the Irish Citizen Army, ensured that the Transport Union would long remain identified with republicanism. Indeed, during the conscription struggle in 1918 and the guerrilla campaign of 1920–1, Connolly's successors such as William O'Brien and Cathal O'Shannon played an essential part in maintaining republican organization and propaganda. By contrast, the Free State's future Labour leader, Thomas Johnson (a Liverpool Unitarian formerly based in Belfast as a commercial traveller), worked assiduously to distance Labour from republicanism and restore its political independence. Five months after the Rising,

as chairman of the Irish Trades Union Congress, Johnson fear-
lessly declared that he remained a Home Ruler who supported
the Allied cause, despite his admiration for the heroism of Connolly and his colleagues. Johnson accurately observed that 'as a
Trade Union Movement we are of varied minds on matters of
history and political development'; though the rift between
northern and southern Labour was by then so severe that his
ecumenical appeal was largely directed towards constitutional
nationalists rather than loyalists.[26] Johnson had not yet lost hope
that the post-war British government would move to avert social
revolution by introducing state socialism, with the implication
that Irish Labour should attempt to promote that outcome. By
February 1918, however, even he was publicly contemplating a
revolutionary partnership against British rule. In his article 'If
the Bolsheviks Came to Ireland', Johnson mused that the
Russian soviets had 'their Irish equivalents in the trades councils, the agricultural co-operative societies, and—dare we say
it?—the local groups of the Irish Republican army. An Irish
counterpart of the Russian revolution would mean that these
three sections, co-operating, would take control of the industrial,
agricultural and social activities of the nation.'[27]

Though most republican rhetoricians welcomed Labour's
incorporation in the national struggle, few went so far as to
encourage Labour's representation in elected bodies. Congress,
newly transformed into the Irish Labour Party and Trades Union
Congress, made a botched attempt to put up independent candidates in the general election of 1918, only to withdraw them
under strong central and local opposition from Sinn Féin. This
was a prudent decision, since both Labour organizers and police
analysts doubted whether any Labour candidates would have
prevailed against republican hostility and intimidation. No
nominees of the Irish Labour Party contested either northern or
southern constituencies in May 1921. Nevertheless, Labour's
fairly impressive performance in the industrial struggle gave
it a considerable potential following in politics, as demonstrated
at the first post-war municipal elections, held throughout
urban Ireland in January 1920. Labour candidates of various

affiliations gained nearly a fifth of votes cast, compared with a seventh for the constitutionalists, and just over a quarter for both Sinn Féin and the Unionists. Labour's support in urban Ulster only slightly exceeded that in each of the other provinces. This was Labour's only significant success in achieving public representation outside Ulster, and most of the Labour councillors eventually formed alliances with republican representatives.

In the absence of an electoral mandate, Labour did its best to influence Sinn Féin and the republican administration to espouse its policies. The proudest outcome of this strategy was the Dáil's Democratic Programme of January 1919, drafted by Labour leaders but drastically censored by the Dubliner Seán T. O'Kelly, the zealously Catholic librarian and Gaelic Leaguer who would eventually succeed Douglas Hyde as President of Éire in 1945. The Programme stitched together Sinn Féin's social policy with radical-sounding demands by Pearse for land nationalization; Labour was wooed by an enigmatic promise of 'social and industrial legislation' designed to improve the lot of 'the working classes'. Whatever radical elements the Programme might be deemed to contain were firmly suspended by de Valera on his accession to presidency of the Dáil in April 1919, when he regretfully explained that little effect could be given to the social programme so long as 'they had the occupation of the foreigner in their country'.[28] In practice, the republican administration tended to favour employers when called upon to conciliate Labour's claims, while the intensification of revolutionary conflict made it ever more difficult for Labour to secure an independent hearing. For all their misgivings, the key organizers of southern and northern Labour found it impossible to stand aside from the central conflict between nationalism and loyalism.

Despite the political polarization of Labour, the economic reversal of 1920–1 threatened briefly to precipitate class warfare. For many observers, the 'red menace' seemed no less terrifying than the prospect of republican takeover. Demobilization of servicemen had created a violent increase in unemployment, the effects of which were mitigated by introduction of a temporary dole in November 1918 and by the unexpected prolongation of agricultural prosperity. By mid-1920, the decline in exports and collapse of wartime industry had generated renewed and worsening unemployment, accompanied by reductions in prices and still more markedly in wages. In the brief interval before unemployment undermined the bargaining power of trades unionism, the menace of economic collapse after the wartime boom encouraged frenzied collective protests. As conventional strike activity lurched towards the creation of 'soviets' whereby discharged workers took over the management of creameries and other plants, the fear of social revolution in Ireland became widespread. Agricultural labourers showed unprecedented aggression, transforming branches of the Transport Union into companies of 'Red Guards', which seemed likely to come into armed conflict with the shadowy Farmers' Freedom Force, a militant offshoot of the normally respectable Irish Farmers' Union (1917). The prospect of renewed rural conflict involving landless labourers added to the confusion caused by the collapse of civil government. With the police immobilized and the civil service on retreat, there was little to prevent acquisitive labourers and landholders alike from seizing pastures and leaseholds, compulsorily expropriating landlords, and performing agrarian outrages on a scale unknown since the 1880s. Anticlimax followed in the autumn of 1920, partly because of republican action against agrarian offenders, and also in response to the declining returns from land occupancy as the recession deepened. The Red Guards and the Freedom Force vanished; the seizure of land and division of estates were restrained by the Dáil; and economic collapse created a new solidarity of impotence among employers and workers. As the spectre of social revolution faded, the national issue resumed its accustomed pre-eminence.

HOW?

The Ulster Crisis, 1912–1914

The preceding chapters have outlined the contending forces in Ireland's revolutionary epoch, the ideologies which justified their conduct, and the contradictions between the rhetoric of liberation and the practical pursuit of power. These elements help to explain Irish responses to the political opportunities and challenges of the period, but they alone cannot account for the actual course of change. Each phase of the revolutionary process was circumscribed and moulded by external factors such as British party politics, world war, and the post-war reorganization of Europe, which combined to generate a fatal cycle of response and counter-response, resistance and coercion. The outcome of violent conflict giving rise to partition was therefore a by-product of forces largely beyond Irish control. This chapter examines the process by which outside influences and Irish responses interacted to yield revolution.

The lurch towards revolution began with Asquith's introduction of the third Government of Ireland bill in April 1912. British as well as Irish Unionists interpreted this proposal as an assault upon Britain's unwritten constitution: prompted by Asquith's dependence on nationalist support in a hung parliament, made practicable by the Parliament act of 1911 with its 'unconstitutional' usurpation of the power of the peers, and calculated to fragment the United Kingdom as established in 1801 and 'for ever after'. For British Unionists, the conflict over Home Rule presented an opportunity for embarrassing and perhaps bringing down a government deemed dangerously 'radical' in its social programme. The impassioned defiance of Irish loyalists was a useful bonus in inflaming British public opinion, and

Bonar Law's opposition exploited that bonus with skill and relish.

In Ireland, however, opposition to Home Rule was no mere device for scoring political points at Westminster. The Ulster Unionist Council was confident that it could actually prevent application of the measure, at least to most of Ulster. This could be achieved by three possible means: inducing Asquith to drop or emasculate the bill; forcing the resignation of his government in face of 'diehard' Ulster opposition; or, in the last resort, establishing a provisional government to defend the homeland from British and Irish foes alike. The focus of the Ulster Unionist campaign was propaganda, designed to intimidate the government and encourage the opposition to concentrate on Ulster rather than social issues. The propaganda campaign was slickly professional, involving lecture campaigns using pre-circulated speech notes, mobilization of sympathetic British academics and public figures, discreet canvassing of editors, and a barrage of picture postcards, leaflets, newsletters, and treatises. Further support was secured from sympathizers throughout the dominions, often mobilized through the Imperial Grand Orange Council and its affiliates, so reinforcing Ulster's claim that Home Rule was an imperial rather than a narrowly Irish problem. The culmination of the campaign outside Ulster was the 'British Covenant' of March 1914, whereby (allegedly) almost 2 million opponents of Home Rule declared themselves 'justified in taking or supporting any action that may be effective to prevent it being put into operation, and more particularly to prevent the armed forces of the Crown being used to deprive the people of Ulster of their rights as citizens of the United Kingdom'.[1] This echoed and reinforced the grim message of the pledges offered eighteen months earlier by half a million men and women in Ulster itself.

The main theme of Unionist propaganda was Ulster's intransigence and refusal to compromise, as demonstrated by a sequence of ever more formidable collective demonstrations. The Ulster covenant carried the implicit threat of violence in its pledge to use 'all means which may be found necessary to defeat the present conspiracy to set up a Home Rule Parliament in

Ireland'. Orangemen had already been mobilized in legal drilling, a process leading to the formation of the Ulster Volunteer Force in January 1913. Top-heavy with retired army officers, it was commanded by Lieutenant-General Sir George Richardson, celebrated for having ransacked Peking's Temple of Heaven in 1901. Advised by Field Marshal Earl Roberts, and applauded by members of the general staff, the Ulster Volunteers rapidly became a formidable and well-disciplined army complete with signallers, motor cyclists, service corps, and intelligence officers. The police knew of 85,000 members by May 1914, representing almost a third of Ulster's adult male Protestants. Protestant mobilization in the force was particularly intense in counties with large Catholic populations (such as Cavan and Tyrone), though relatively sparse in Donegal as well as in Belfast and the north-east.[2] These regional variations roughly replicated the distribution of Orange lodges, a major source of personnel and inspiration for the new organization.

The growing strength and bellicosity of the UVF provoked indignant nationalist demands for its suppression, but its supporters in the war office schemed ingeniously to ensure that no test of strength would occur. Ulster's most ingenious and influential military ally was the director of military operations, Sir Henry Hughes Wilson from Edgeworthtown, Co. Longford (CIGS during the Anglo-Irish war and subsequently, until his assassination by London republicans in June 1922, military adviser to the government of Northern Ireland). On 20 March 1914, most officers of the 3rd cavalry brigade at the Curragh, Co. Kildare, were induced by a superfluous ultimatum from the officer commanding in Ireland (Sir Arthur Paget) to declare that they would resign rather than enforce Home Rule in Ulster. Instead, those who resigned were the secretary for war, the adjutant-general, and the CIGS (the future viceroy of Ireland, Sir John French). Their assurances that the refractory officers would not be ordered to serve in Ulster were repudiated by the cabinet, so forcing their removal and demoralizing the army command scarcely four months before the outbreak of European war. The major Irish outcome of the 'Curragh mutiny' was to make the government even less inclined to contemplate military enforcement of the Government of Ireland act or suppression of the Ulster Volunteers. The militarization of the UVF was crowned by the illegal importation in April 1914 of 25,000 German, Austrian, and Italian service rifles, each with a hundred rounds of ammunition. With considerable finesse and without police interference, these were smuggled by sea to Larne, Co. Antrim, and also to Bangor and Donaghadee, Co. Down. The UVF was now clearly superior to any regular force likely to be available for deployment in Ireland.

Meanwhile, the Ulster Unionist leaders elaborated their contingency plans for establishing a provisional government, disabling the police, and taking control of communications and supplies. Already in September 1913, Carson had announced his readiness to assume control of such a government upon implementation of Home Rule, and the Ulster Unionist Council had given its authority and support to that proposal. After Asquith's abortive attempt to amend Home Rule by allowing for the temporary exclusion of parts of Ulster under 'county option', the provisional government actually convened in Belfast on 10 July 1914, although negotiations leading to a conference at Buckingham Palace postponed the moment of collision. Despite nationalist sneers that Ulster's militancy was mere sabre-rattling, there is little reason to doubt the willingness, readiness, and in some cases eagerness of Ulster loyalists to assert control over 'their' province. The logic of 'conditional loyalty' made it perfectly appropriate for Ulstermen to seize local power if betrayed by the government and ultimately, through the granting of royal assent, by the monarch. By August 1914, the seemingly irreversible Liberal commitment to Home Rule left only two likely outcomes: armed conflict between the Ulster Volunteers and the police (bereft of military support), resulting in a speedy *coup d'état*; or Asquith's resignation. Either outcome carried the obvious risk of provoking nationalist violence, whether in the form of sectarian civil war or of armed insurrection.

The vigour and apparent effectiveness of Ulster militancy inspired nationalists with a mixture of outrage, admiration, and envy, culminating in imitation. The Ulster example showed the feasibility of raising private armies with impunity, and the propagandist value of backing one's constitutional demands with the threat of violence. These lessons were soon pointed out by radical analysts such as the schoolmaster and nascent republican, Patrick Pearse, and the vice-president of the Gaelic League, Professor Eoin MacNeill. In his article 'The North Began', published in the journal of the Gaelic League in November 1913, MacNeill not only advocated creation of a nationalist counter-force, but affirmed the latent fellowship of loyalists and nationalists in their shared hostility to the government. Whereas MacNeill hoped that the mere threat of force would ensure implementation of Home Rule, Pearse exulted in the prospect of a general bloodbath: 'I am glad that the Orangemen are armed, for it is a goodly thing to see arms in Irish hands. . . . We must accustom ourselves to the thought of arms, to the sight of arms, to the use of arms. We may make mistakes in the beginning and shoot the wrong people; but bloodshed is a cleansing and a sanctifying thing.'[3] Pearse's vision of 'The Coming Revolution' was focused on the slaughter of opponents rather than self-sacrifice, the quasi-Christian motif which later became so emotive an element of republican propaganda. The immediate outcome of these reflections was the launching on 25 November 1913 of the Irish Volunteers, with MacNeill as president and a provisional committee dominated in practice by the Irish Republican Brotherhood. That committee included Patrick Pearse.

The initial identification of the Irish Volunteers with the small-scale, urban-centred, and cabalistic IRB aroused the distrust of constitutionalist leaders, and inhibited its growth. However, the alarm caused by the 'Curragh mutiny' and the Larne gun-running encouraged enlistment by many local activists in Home Rule organizations, eventually persuading Redmond and Devlin to authorize and take control of the Volunteers. From May 1914 onwards, the Hibernians were urged to join local companies and provide their halls for drill; in June, Redmond induced the provisional committee to accept twenty-five nominees from his party, so securing nominal administrative control of the Irish 'National' Volunteers. The party's intervention was reflected in the growth of reported membership from 50,000 in late May to 100,000 in mid-June, and 150,000 a month later. Though determined to restrict the force to bellicose gestures and 'defensive' organization against an unspecified antagonist, the constitutionalist leaders collaborated in acquiring weapons to replace the wooden rifles and hurleys initially used for drill. On 26 July and 2 August, boatloads of arms from Germany were landed illegally at Howth, Co. Dublin and Kilcoole, Co. Wicklow. This mimetic response to the spectacular feat of the Ulster Volunteers three months earlier had limited military value, supplying only 1,500 venerable Mausers along with 30 rounds per rifle of explosive ammunition (which Pearse chivalrously declined to distribute). Even after Redmond's secretive but legal acquisition of 6,000 additional rifles in the early months of war (when restrictions on importation were relaxed), the force was hopelessly ill-equipped and ill-trained for any military conflict. Though the Irish Volunteers, like the Ulstermen, were mainly drilled by British army veterans, their 'route marches' sometimes began and ended at the commanding officer's public house.[4] The organizers were a strange medley of shopkeepers, Gaelic athletes, republican brothers, and a sprinkling of retired army officers, headed by Colonel Maurice Moore of Moore Hall, Co. Mayo (a choleric Catholic landlord and brother of George, the novelist). By comparison with the UVF, the Irish Volunteers were an amateur army indeed.

Though cumbersome as a military force, the Irish Volunteers fulfilled Pearse's hope by instilling a military outlook in countless labourers, farmers' sons, and shop assistants, even in the most remote districts. Their more immediate achievement was to revive popular interest in the Home Rule movement, and to mobilize up to 190,000 men in a relatively disciplined exhibition of collective determination. At their peak as reported by the police in September 1914, the Volunteers incorporated nearly a fifth of all Catholic men in Ireland, the proportion being highest in Ulster and lowest in Munster and Dublin. The heaviest concentrations of Irish as well as Ulster Volunteers were mainly found in the religious borderlands, support in Belfast and the Protestant-dominated north-east being relatively sparse. The coincidence of intense loyalist and nationalist militarism in much of Ulster enhanced the risk of sectarian conflagration between the two private armies. Reflecting upon the inauguration of the provisional government in July, a loyalist editor anticipated 'a long and bloody conflict' if the constitutional question were not speedily resolved. Admitting that the Irish Volunteers had the numerical advantage and 'much fine material', he gloated about their inferiority in training, equipment, and leadership: 'Were the issue left to be decided between the two rival bodies, there is small doubt but that the Ulstermen could not only hold their own, but establish a military hegemony over the whole of Ireland.'[5] The war office declined to prepare any plan for dealing with such a collision, informing the cabinet that all available home forces and probably general mobilization would be required, so risking unrest in India and Egypt and encouraging 'trouble' from 'certain countries in Europe'.[6]

Redmond's exhibition of militancy did not lead to the collapse of his parliamentary strategy, or to the severance of his working alliance with the Liberal Party and government. As chief secretary, the benevolent Augustine Birrell was determined to 'govern Ireland according to Irish ideas', to avoid coercion and render 'Home Rule inevitable', and to involve the constitutionalist leaders in ever more aspects of policy, administration, and patronage as the moment of emancipation approached.[7] Dublin Castle and the RIC were dismissive of the military potential of the Irish Volunteers, and Birrell condemned the heads of the Dublin Metropolitan Police for employing troops in a bloody but ineffectual attempt to disarm the Howth gun-runners at Bachelor's Walk on the Dublin quays. Despite the countervailing influence of many diehard loyalists in the civil administration, Birrell's warm relations with the nationalist leaders caused outrage and alienation among Ulster Unionists, who felt themselves excluded from the administrative process to an unprecedented extent. 'Ulster ideas', as so often in the chronicle of British government in Ireland, were neither solicited nor comprehended.

Ireland and the War, 1914–1916

Germany's invasion of Belgium on 3 August 1914 provided a further external shock, which was to transform Irish politics through a complex and unpredictable chain of effects. For Britain, its immediate consequences included the declaration of war; general mobilization followed by massive military enlistment; suspension of civil liberties and extension of state economic controls; and an informal 'truce' between the major political parties, whereby electoral contests and parliamentary divisions were to be avoided in the national interest. In Ireland, the sudden conflagration in Europe offered an unexpected opportunity for avoiding or at least postponing conflict at home. Carson and Redmond, whose private armies had so recently been supplied with German weapons, both declared their support for the allies. Both hoped to obtain political rewards for securing the loyalty and military mobilization of their followers, and used the two volunteer forces as bargaining counters while seeking face-saving compromises over Home Rule. On 3 August, Redmond had already proposed that the Ulster and Irish Volunteers should collaborate in defending the coast of Ireland, so releasing regular forces from duty in a country which since 1908 had had no militia infantry for home service (apart from reserve battalions), and where no Territorials had been formed. Scores of elderly colonels and majors stirred in their big houses, thrashed out their greatcoats, and prepared to assume their proper part as leaders of the peasantry in the defence of Ireland's shores. After initial murmurs of approval from Asquith and Paget, Redmond's offer was ignored by the war office, partly because of military scepticism about the efficiency and dependability of the Irish Volunteers, but also because of the rapidly increasing demand for recruits to serve overseas.

Although prepared to collaborate in home defence if so requested, Carson concentrated upon securing the suspension of

Home Rule and the eventual incorporation of the Ulster Volunteers into Kitchener's New Armies. On 3 September, he 'unconditionally' offered 35,000 members of the UVF for overseas service, whereupon a well-disposed war office approved formation of the 36th (Ulster) division whose enlistment, initial training, and officer corps were closely controlled by the UVF command. All told, nearly 31,000 Ulster Volunteers were enrolled in the wartime army, including over 4,000 reservists who typically had served as drill sergeants or instructors. The energies of the remaining two-thirds of the force, along with its service units and female auxiliaries, were largely redirected to providing moral and practical support for the Ulster division. The reconciliation of Ulster Unionism with Asquith's wartime administration was sealed by Carson's appointment as attorney-general in the coalition government of May 1915.

The price of Ulster's loyalty was not the abandonment but the suspension of Home Rule, which was duly accomplished with remarkable deftness on 15 September. Asquith offered Carson the tangible benefit of an act suspending Home Rule for a year in the first instance (with provision for extension to 'the end of the present war'), together with the rather indeterminate assurance that the eventual Irish settlement would incorporate special but undefined provision for Ulster. For Redmond's party, he provided the purely rhetorical satisfaction of giving legal status to the unamended Government of Ireland act, which duly received royal assent on 18 September. All parties accepted the impracticability of either implementing or amending Home Rule while war continued: the unresolved conflict which had threatened civil war a few weeks earlier was deferred indefinitely. Redmond now attempted to secure an 'Irish brigade' equivalent to the Ulster division, having greeted the compromise of 15 September by promising the House of Commons that he would instruct his fellow-countrymen 'that it is their duty, and should be their honour, to take their place in the firing line in this contest'.[8] Redmond thereupon enjoined qualified Irish Volunteers to enlist for overseas service, and himself took an active part in recruiting meetings and propaganda. The party's commitment was symbolized by the military enrolment of several past or present parliamentarians, such as Tom Kettle, the Protestant essayist Stephen Gwynn, and John Redmond's brother William, the veteran MP for East Clare (who, like Kettle, was killed in action).

Once again, despite support from Asquith, Redmond's proposal for military embodiment of the Irish Volunteers was rejected. Although two 'Irish' divisions were formed, Redmond exercised little influence over their development. The 10th division formed part of Kitchener's first New Army in August 1914, and was shattered by the loss of three-quarters of its members in its first campaign, at Suvla Bay (Gallipoli) in August 1915. The 16th division was created in September 1914 as part of the second New Army, and after experiencing a gas attack at Hulloch at the time of the Easter Rising it reached the Somme shortly after the decimation of the 36th. Its heaviest casualties were spread out over three major bloodbaths (Guillemont and Guinchy in September 1916; 3rd Ypres in August 1917; and the German spring offensive of 1918). Although Redmond eventually secured fife and drum bands for each battalion, Hibernian mascots (three wolfhounds named Benburb, Grania, and Zoe), and the odd commission for associates including his son William Archer Redmond, the division was organized and officered with scant regard for the nationalist interest. Its commander during home training, Sir Lawrence Parsons from Parsonstown, King's Co., patronizingly rejected many applications from 'socially impossible' candidates, 'men who write their applications in red or green ink on a blank bill-head of a village shop'.[9] Parsons reluctantly surrendered his command to Brigadier-General William Bernard Hickie, a Catholic from a minor landed estate near Borrisokane, Co. Tipperary. Yet scarcely one officer in five was a Catholic, although that proportion was roughly doubled in two of the division's twelve battalions.[10]

As in the case of the 36th division, the appalling losses of 1916 and diminished recruitment made it impracticable to maintain the fiction of ethnic integrity, and from October 1916 the enrolment of non-Irish soldiers (already dominant in the service units) was officially sanctioned. In the chaos of war, national and religious distinctions quickly became blurred, and Irish Protestants, Irish Catholics, and British soldiers were obliged to live, obey orders, fight, die, and endure imprisonment together. Although national and sectarian animosities occasionally surfaced, the shared experience of war more often generated mutual if grudging respect. Yet the comradeship of the trenches proved evanescent, and Redmond was to be disappointed in his conviction that the outcome of shared service 'must inevitably be to assuage bitterness, and to mollify the hatred and misunderstanding which have kept them apart'.[11] Sadly, it was simpler for Irish nationalists and loyalists to die together in war than to live together in peace.

Despite Redmond's bitterness over his failure to control the administration of the 16th division, a failure which he considered disastrous for recruiting, even more Irish Volunteers than Ulster Volunteers served during the war. The police reported the enlistment of 32,000 Irish Volunteers, including 7,600 reservists mobilized in August 1914. Although this represented only a sixth of peak membership compared with over a third for the Ulster Volunteers, the discrepancy was partly accountable to the greater participation of juveniles and older men in the nationalist force. Ireland's Volunteer forces thus contributed massively to wartime military mobilization, which altogether involved the raising of over 200,000 men in Ireland (of whom about three-fifths were Catholics).[12] Although well below the rate of enlistment in Britain, this represented the most massive military mobilization in Irish history. Irish militarism, so it seemed, had been safely exported to foreign battlefields.

The advent of war brought Birrell and the constitutionalists still closer together, since Birrell regarded himself as Redmond's caretaker now that Home Rule had been enacted. Discreet but regular meetings were arranged between Birrell's talented under-secretary, Sir Matthew Nathan, and party leaders such as Dillon and Redmond. Birrell and Nathan did their best to blunt the Irish edge of wartime restrictions, securing preferential terms for the Irish liquor trade and ameliorating the impact of the draconian Defence of the Realm legislation. The Consolidation act of November 1914 generated a wide range of regulations purporting 'to prevent the spread of false reports or reports likely to cause disaffection to His Majesty', enforcible by courts martial and courts of summary jurisdiction. An amending act in March 1915 allowed those accused of serious offences to demand trial by jury rather than courts martial, although civilians might still be tried by military courts in areas where a state of 'special military emergency' had been proclaimed.[13] The increasing bellicosity and bravado of a militant minority of pro-German nationalists goaded the Castle into penalizing anti-recruiting propaganda and other disloyal expressions through arrests, summary convictions, deportations, and suppressions of 'seditious' journals. Yet Birrell continued to prefer ridicule to repression as an antidote to republicanism, avoiding systematic coercion and dismissing the protests of the Ulster Unionists and many of his military and police advisers. By declining to make martyrs of the militants, he hoped to deflate their popular appeal and maintain the predominance of constitutional nationalism until the war's end.

This strategy grew increasingly strained as the war dragged on, since the major nationalist organizations had been robbed of their customary practical functions. The military enlistment of the most active Volunteers left the residue moribund; the virtual suspension of land purchase and the absence of electoral contests enfeebled the United Irish League; and the receding prospect of sectarian conflict reduced the urgency of Hibernian vigilance. Nevertheless, loss of vitality did not inevitably entail loss of popular approval for the constitutionalists. In Protestant Ulster, after all, orthodox Unionism maintained its sway throughout the war despite the quiescence of the residual Ulster Volunteers and the curtailment by the Orange Institution of its customary marches and pageantry. Until April 1916, Birrell's policy of non-provocation seemed remarkably successful. The growth of militant nationalism was modest; and until the accession of Carson and the Unionists as minority partners in Asquith's coalition, Birrell was able to defend nationalist against loyalist claims in the vital matter of patronage. His influence was thoroughly discredited only in April 1916, when the key post of attorney-general for Ireland was granted to Sir James Campbell (the diehard Dublin loyalist and chancellor of the ecclesiastical courts who, as Lord Glenavy, was to become the first and most acerbic chairman of the Free State's Senate). Even without an Easter Rising, such appointments would probably have severed the uncertain but productive alliance between the Castle and the constitutionalists.

For the IRB and romantic nationalists, reared on the fallacy that England's difficulty was Ireland's opportunity, the outbreak of European war seemed to promise an end to their isolation and unpopularity. The supposition of wartime vulnerability was initially confirmed by the rapid extinction of the regular army and reservists in the first British Expeditionary Force (about a tenth of whom were Irish). Republican optimism was also fostered by the virtual withdrawal of the Irish 'garrison', which by November 1914 could muster a striking force of only 2,000 infantry, 400 cavalry, and four machine guns.[14] Thereafter, the rapid assembly of an army of millions, of whom tens of thousands were normally in training or on leave in Ireland, rendered the possibility of military victory by republicans even more remote than before the war. Still more depressing was the evidence of almost universal nationalist support for the allied cause, unenthusiastic though that support might seem. The provincial press and the clergy, both Protestant and Catholic, were virtually united in condemning Germany. Republican organizers such as Desmond FitzGerald (the London-born Imagist poet who became director of propaganda in 1919 and minister for external affairs in 1922) bemoaned the apparent triumph of Anglicization over the Gaelic spirit. Following the course of the war from the west Kerry gaeltacht (Irish-speaking district), FitzGerald concluded that Ireland had been 'spiritually and nationally absorbed by England. The Irish nation had shrunk to a small corner in the West.'[15] Republicans observed with disgust the complacency of Irish farmers, prospering from rising prices as the disruption of international shipping drove their competitors from the British market. The eventual reduction of unemployment reduced proletarian discontent, and Catholics showed little disinclination to join the army. For revolutionaries in the making, the impact of the war was profoundly disconcerting.

The frustration of militant nationalists was worsened by the decay of their organizations, with the exception of the IRB. The Transport Union and its vigilante force, the tiny Irish Citizen Army, were virtually inert after the collapse of the Dublin general strike in January 1914. The Irish Volunteers, despite republican domination of the original provisional committee, were firmly under Redmond's control. Shortly after his exhortation to fight wherever the firing line might extend, the republicans managed to split the organization and retain its title, together with about a fifteenth of the membership (concentrated in Munster). The remaining 170,000 followed Redmond's instructions by adhering, at least nominally, to the new 'National Volunteers', under Colonel Maurice Moore. However, the anti-war minority controlled a disproportionate part of the available armament, and trained actively under IRB direction. The commander of the dissidents remained Eoin MacNeill, who neither belonged to the IRB nor trusted its conspiratorial methods. Like most secretive societies, the Brotherhood was itself factionalized, and even the president of the 'supreme council' (Denis McCullough) was excluded from the deliberations of the sinister 'military council' established in mid-1915. This cabal had been assigned the task of planning an eventual insurrection, as mooted by the supreme council in September 1914. Its members included Pearse and other zealots such as Joseph Mary Plunkett and Éamonn Ceannt, later joined by Seán MacDermott and Tom Clarke.

The more blood was shed in Europe, the more ecstatic Patrick Pearse became. In December 1915, he rejoiced that 'the last sixteen months have been the most glorious in the history of Europe. . . . It is good for the world that such things should be done. The old heart of the earth needed to be warmed with the red wine of the battlefields. . . . When war comes to Ireland, she must welcome it as she would welcome the Angel of God.'[16]

James Connolly, on the point of being initiated into the military council, expressed revulsion at the carnage of war but urged revolutionaries to join in the grim game while it lasted: 'Our rulers reign by virtue of their readiness to destroy human life in order to reign; their reign will end on the day their discontented subjects care as little for the destruction of human life as they do.' Having prophesied that in wartime 'the spilling of a torrent of blood in the city streets would cause the ruling class no more compunction than the slaughter of game on their estates', Connolly set about securing this outcome for his adopted city.[17]

Often depicted with hindsight as the culmination of a process of nationalist radicalization stretching back to the fall of Parnell in 1890 and accelerated during the war, the Easter Rising was in fact, as it seemed to most contemporaries, an unpredictable aberration. It was the enduring popularity of constitutionalism, not its failure, that led a motley band of frustrated militants to abandon the Queensberry rules of conventional nationalism. Only through provocation of a distracted government into insensate coercion might the carefully nurtured *modus vivendi* between nationalist Ireland and 'Liberal England' be ruptured. Republican visionaries further hoped that the shock of civil conflict would awaken some latent Gaelic pride, and encourage deluded constitutionalists to fling off their English vestments. Like every 'peace process', Birrell's policy of reconciliation depended on the reasoned calculation of self-interest by people of goodwill, being therefore sadly vulnerable to the fanatic's shot in the dark. As Birrell ingenuously observed in his memoirs, 'in my wildest dreams I never contemplated the possibility of what actually happened'.[18]

This failure of imagination was not due to lack of surveillance: the Castle was quite well informed about the conspiracy, including American fund-raising and the abortive importation of 20,000 German rifles and machine guns. It followed with interest the mediations of John Devoy, the pro-German leader of the American Clan na Gael (a Fenian fraternity founded in 1867); and Sir Roger Casement, the Protestant-reared humanitarian and former British consul, raised in Antrim, who travelled to

Germany to raise a 'brigade' of Irish prisoners of war and secure German military intervention. Devoy and Casement appear to have actually believed that military victory was the intended outcome, therefore assuming that no insurrection would be attempted without manpower as well as massive material help from Germany. Convinced that German support was inadequate for a successful Rising, Casement hitched a lift to Kerry in a U-boat in order to confirm its cancellation. Casement was arrested before he could do so (being subsequently hanged for High Treason at Pentonville prison); but the Castle was reassured to learn that the gunboat carrying the German armaments had been scuttled by her captain on 22 April after interception by a naval patrol. The military council's admission of deception and skulduggery had in any case induced MacNeill, as chief of staff of the Irish Volunteers, to countermand Pearse's orders for mobilization and 'manœuvres' on Easter Sunday, 23 April 1916. Not without reason, the Castle looked forward to rounding up the demoralized conspirators after holiday Monday.

Instead, Pearse and six associates declared themselves on Monday morning to be the 'provisional government' of an Irish Republic, which was 'entitled to, and hereby claims, the allegiance of every Irishman and Irishwoman'.[19] After frenzied efforts by the military council to negate MacNeill's countermand, about 1,600 rebels (scarcely an eighth of the number of anti-war Volunteers in 1916) were induced to turn out in Dublin, with sporadic backing from a few provincial units which attacked police barracks or patrols. The planning and conduct of the Rising provided chilling confirmation that military victory was not its primary objective. No serious attempt was made to provide strategic support for the Dublin campaign, beyond issuing an enigmatic instruction to western units to 'hold the line of the Shannon', without indicating whether enemy forces were to be prevented from crossing eastwards or westwards.[20]

In Dublin, the rebels occupied a medley of public buildings, shops, and factories, in accordance with a crude plan devised by the poet Joseph Mary Plunkett (whose father George Noble, a papal count and Trinity graduate, was director of the National

Museum until his internment and dismissal after the Rising). By placing detachments on roads or bridges lying between the various military barracks and the centre of town, Plunkett imagined that the enemy could be held at bay. The key administrative buildings were virtually ignored, apart from a brief and unauthorized incursion into Dublin Castle by over-zealous members of the Irish Citizen Army, who killed one of the two unarmed sentries. The rebels also failed to secure Trinity College, whose fortress-like walls and central site overlooking the Liffey were to provide an ideal vantage-point for British artillery pounding rebel positions. Instead, Pearse and Connolly barricaded themselves in the General Post Office in O'Connell (Sackville) Street, a building without notable strategic, administrative, or symbolic importance. By raising their tricolour in the centre of the main shopping area and close to Dublin's north-side slums, the rebels ensured massive human and material losses once their position was attacked. It is difficult to avoid the inference that the republican strategists were intent upon provoking maximum bloodshed, destruction, and coercion, in the hope of resuscitating Irish Anglophobia and clawing back popular support for the discredited militant programme.

After a brief delay while troops were marched up from Kildare and other outposts, and ferried in from Britain, the government obligingly set about blasting the insurrectionaries out of their lairs and destroying much of Dublin in the process. As Connolly had predicted, the army under General Sir John Maxwell (taking over from the hapless Lovick Friend) treated Dublin as an enemy city, without regard for loss of civilian life or property. As the familiar streetscape disintegrated, not all Dubliners reacted with horror. Wartime wildness coloured the response of Olive Armstrong, a young Trinity graduate who heard of the Rising in Killarney, Co. Kerry: 'The latest is that a Gun boat came up the Liffey and shelled and destroyed Liberty Hall, which is simply topping.' After returning to Dublin, she remarked wistfully that the ruins were 'really dreadful. We got a nice jarvey and drove through what was poor Sackville St. The thing that struck me most was the smallness of it, now that the height is gone.'[21] After provoking six days of senseless destruction, mostly attributable to British firepower, Pearse surrendered unconditionally in a purportedly humanitarian gesture. Most of the 450 deaths and 2,600 casualties involved civilians caught in crossfire: some 250 civilians and 132 soldiers or policemen were killed, whereas only about 64 rebels died in action in addition to the 15 executed in Ireland. Among the dead civilians was the suffragist Frank Sheehy-Skeffington, murdered by a crazy officer from a landed family in Cork. Though horrific, these casualties were minuscule if compared with Irish deaths in the war (between 25,000 and 30,000).[22] Before 1914, such an insurrection would have been scarcely imaginable; in wartime, it slotted easily into the gruesome catalogue of futile slaughter.

The link between the devastation in Dublin and Europe became more pointed on 1 and 2 July 1916, ten weeks after the Rising, when the Ulster division offered its own collective sacrifice at Thiepval on the Somme. This initial engagement, which left 2,000 Ulstermen dead and thousands imprisoned or wounded, became part of Ulster's mythology as rapidly as the Rising was incorporated into the nationalist litany of loss. As popular drama, the two events had significant parallels. In each case, the combatants performed with conspicuous bravery and recklessness against overwhelming odds, seizing positions that were ultimately indefensible. Just as the republicans could blame MacNeill's countermand or German recalcitrance for their defeat, so the Ulstermen justifiably exonerated their own officers while blaming the generals who had failed to provide the promised support and relief forces. Defeat was accepted with dignity, as the Ulstermen made a notably disciplined if belated retreat, and the republicans marched proudly to their doom after surrender. Neither action resulted in any perceptible military gain, despite the appalling losses. The emotive power of both episodes lay in the affirmation of personal courage untainted by pursuit of self-interest—the essential rhetoric of liberation. The victims acquired the sanctity of martyrs, whose willing sacrifice instilled a stronger faith into the living. Both nationalist and loyalist necrologies were already studded with stories of heroic suffering and savage punishment. By venerating the dead of 1916, the survivors joined them as a part of history's procession. Commemoration was almost instantaneous, memorial services and press eulogies of the martyrs soon being joined by 'favours', relics, and postcards—whether depicting the 'Easter martyrs' or the sons of Ulster buried near the Somme. Jarring notes (looting; the casual murder of five unarmed reservists in the Dublin Veterans' Corps; the involuntary 'sacrifice' of hundreds of civilians) were not permitted to spoil the Easter melodrama. Likewise, the sordidness of life in the trenches, with its itching and trembling and nightmares and malingering and petty treacheries, could not diminish the exalting image of daredevil Ulstermen yelling 'No Surrender' before going 'over the top'.

Being unpredictable according to conventional calculation, the Rising (like the war) may usefully be treated as an extrinsic shock, disturbing established attitudes and alignments. Its effect on government was to cause a temporary but disastrous abandonment of political logic, in favour of military efficiency. Martial law was declared not only in Dublin (25 April) but throughout Ireland a few days later; its administrator, Sir John Maxwell, executed rebels and even one of their brothers (simple Willie Pearse) without heed to the civil consequences; 3,500 recognized 'troublemakers', Gaels and republicans were arrested, mostly in districts unaffected by the Rising; over half of these were interned in Britain; and the burden of Maxwell's martial law was not lifted until November (although the frequency of raids, searches, and proclamations declined sharply after May). The resignation of Birrell and his senior advisers, and the absence of a chief secretary until the arrival of the moderate Unionist Henry Edward Duke in August, immobilized the Castle administration during a vital period of political flux. This alone would probably have ensured the failure of Lloyd George's proposal for immediate Home Rule, with its ambiguous stipulation for exclusion of six counties. The nationalist press and Catholic clergy were initially almost united in condemnation of the Rising, though often attributing selflessness as well as folly to the rebels. The effect of long drawn-out coercion, mainly affecting non-combatants, was to shift the balance of sin until still greater indignation was felt against the repressors than the insurgents.

The constitutionalists, having collaborated closely with Birrell and furiously denounced the Rising, could not throw off the taint (however unjustified) of having colluded with coercion. Redmond cabled an American newspaper in early May that 'it was not so much sympathy for Germany as hatred of Home Rule and of us which was at the bottom of the movement'.[23] In a sense, he was right: the Rising had been designed to shatter nationalist complacency and to reverse Anglicization, both being symbolized for republicans by the supremacy of the Old Party with its wily Westminsterish ways. For Ulster loyalists, the Rising demonstrated the unregenerate disloyalty and treachery of Catholic nationalists (Fenians, croppies, moonlighters) once the veneer of constitutionalism had been blasted off. Maxwell's iron hand also somewhat restored loyalist belief in the government's capacity to maintain the United Kingdom, a belief reinforced by the removal of Asquith and the predominance of Unionists in Lloyd George's coalition of December 1916. Within six months, the theatrical gesture of a coterie of poets and plotters had undermined the assumptions of Irish politics.

The Bequest of the Rising, 1916–1918

The impact of the Rising on popular nationalism was neither immediately obvious nor unambiguous. No single organization could claim to represent all of the participating groups; none of the surviving leaders were prominent public figures; no clear policy had been affirmed by the rebels, beyond the establishment of a republican government through an election under universal suffrage; and the future role of physical force had not even been debated. The political bequest of the Rising might therefore have assumed many alternative forms. Nor was it inevitable that the discrediting of Redmond's party would give rise to the repudiation of its policy, if pursued by others under a less tarnished name than Home Rule. For the inheritors of the Rising, the process of formulating a policy and shaping an alternative organization took nearly eighteen months, during which innumerable leagues, journals, and public meetings were assembled to celebrate the new spirit and hammer out a new orthodoxy. This process began in British prisons and internment camps, sometimes termed 'nurseries' or even 'universities' of revolution, where a bizarre mixture of about 1,800 radical nationalists and cultural revivalists foregathered, fraternized, learned the Irish language, played Irish games, and polished their anti-English rhetoric. Under the surprisingly benevolent regimes imposed by governors and warders relieved to be dealing with decent rebels instead of common criminals, a formidable revolutionary élite crystallized during the six months before the release of the last internees at Christmas. The 145 convicts had the advantage of a further six months' training before their sentences were truncated in June 1917.

Within the new élite, a recognized hierarchy soon emerged, reflecting the relative prestige of the surviving rebel leaders. Eamon de Valera, an American-born schoolteacher raised in Bruree, Co. Limerick, was widely though not universally regarded as the most effective commander after his performance at Boland's bakery. De Valera, and a few other conspicuous fighters such as Cathal Brugha, pointedly repudiated the conspiratorial strategy by leaving the Irish Republican Brotherhood. Despite this setback, the IRB played a crucial part in promoting brotherly contacts within and beyond the camps and prisons. Quite obscure participants in the Rising were able rapidly to achieve influence through the organization's manipulation of nationalist committees and societies. These included Michael Collins from Clonakilty, Co. Cork, who had returned from London after a decade of employment with the post office savings bank, the board of trade, and city firms. His financial expertise, in combination with his wide-ranging fraternal connections as an emigrant Gael, soon made Collins a key figure in every republican organization. Not yet a public figure, Collins received the lowest vote of any of the thirty Sinn Féiners elected to the new executive in October 1917. The separatist élite already had its share of apparatchiks as well as heroes: over the next five years, the two elements were often to collide and occasionally to reverse roles.

The emerging republican leadership faced formidable difficulties in finding an appropriate form of organization. None of the major anti-war groups whose members fought in 1916 had authorized that participation; yet all had been thrown into disarray by the conflict and subsequent repression. The Irish Volunteers soon resumed local drilling without central direction, attracting increasing enlistment from the almost defunct National Volunteers (whose last public endeavour had been to assist the police in rounding up suspected rebels). The IRB, with its military council executed and its former president (McCullough) humiliated, was reformed by Collins and his circle. By mid-1917, it was reported that the Brotherhood had 3,000 members in 350 circles, still a modest achievement by comparison with its strength a quarter of a century earlier.[24] Co-ordination between the prisoners and republican bodies in Ireland and overseas was handled by the Irish National Aid and Volunteers' Dependents Fund (May 1916), also organized by Collins along with a legion of women sympathizers (mostly mothers, sisters, widows, or wives of rebels). The impoverished Transport Union suffered further setbacks through the shelling of its headquarters (Liberty Hall), the removal of its leaders, and the impounding and destruction of many of its records. The Gaelic Athletic Association, whose sporting clubs were sometimes almost interchangeable with IRB circles and Volunteer companies, found it increasingly hazardous to organize competitions in the face of restrictions on Sunday excursion trains and public meetings.

Arthur Griffith's Sinn Féin, once the main open political forum for anti-Redmondites, had likewise been disrupted by the arrest of Griffith and most of his associates (in spite of Griffith's exclusion from the conspiracy and his party's advocacy of non-violent collective action leading to institution of a 'dual' monarchy). Though well aware that Sinn Féin was not responsible for the Rising, the government, the police, the Irish Party, Unionists, and the press had appropriated its name in order to cast scorn and ridicule upon the rebels. Use of the term quickly became universal, so that even republicans began to describe themselves as Sinn Féiners—a source of much irritation to independent organizers like Count Plunkett, whose Liberty Leaguers kept forgetting their official designation. Long before the new organization emerged, it had acquired a name.

The reconstitution of Sinn Féin was not achieved until the ard fheis of October 1917, which followed six months of trafficking between new radical bodies such as the Liberty League, the Anti-Partition League and the Irish Nation League, as well as the Dublin Trades Council, sympathetic Catholic priests, and the familiar array of 'Irish Ireland'. The creation of an open organization not committed to violence, representing a broad coalition of nationalist factions, was an astonishing sequel to a violent and conspiratorial insurrection. Eamon de Valera was largely responsible for marshalling the veterans of Easter Week towards political struggle, despite the sanctification of violence in republican propaganda and the understandable impulse of bellicose survivors like Brugha to have another innings. While still in Lewes prison, de Valera had followed Arthur Griffith's example by envisaging the eventual peace conference as an instrument for achieving international recognition of the Irish republic. Soon after his release, de Valera set about discouraging further insurrection, seeking instead to secure the wide popular support that republicanism had hitherto lacked. Republicans should mobilize and demonstrate their popularity by fighting elections, with the intention of 'abstaining' from Westminster and eventually establishing an alternative assembly by courtesy of government-paid returning officers.

When campaigning successfully in the East Clare by-election occasioned by William Redmond's death near Messines in June 1917, de Valera used his long experience with the clergy to win over Bishop Michael Fogarty of Killaloe and the majority of Catholic curates (most parish priests being slower to change affiliation). He paraded the pious and well-connected MacNeill

as a mascot of Catholic respectability, and called upon republicans to use passive resistance, boycotts of police, and propaganda
to achieve the republic. Impregnable behind his military record,
de Valera repeatedly expressed admiration for the rebels, and
preference for violent action whenever this had 'a good chance',
'a fair chance', nay, 'a ghost of a chance' of success.[25] This theme
was elaborated at Sinn Féin's ard fheis in October, when he persuaded the delegates that they should postpone the glorious
moment of getting rid of alien rule 'by physical force'. Reciting
the conditions for justified rebellion in Catholic theology, he sor-
rowfully explained that, for the time being, a second insurrection
would be futile and therefore sinful.[26] The insurrection had been
wonderfully effective in reinvigorating republicanism and
destroying the old politics; but the government could scarcely be
expected to respond to a second gesture of defiance with the
same counter-productive crassness as in 1916.

The outcome of the ard fheis was de Valera's election as president of Sinn Féin, and the approval of a constitution reaffirming Griffith's social programme, calling for the creation of a
national assembly derived from Westminster elections, and initiating a campaign of international propaganda. Like the Ulster
covenant, the constitution insinuated that violence might be
employed under undisclosed circumstances, the organization
being directed to 'make use of any and every means available to
render impotent the power of England to hold Ireland in subjection by military force or otherwise'.[27] With characteristically
forked tongue, de Valera left the reader to decide whether the
option of 'military force' applied to English subjection or Irish
resistance. Challenged by a priest to qualify the constitution's
sanction of 'any and every means available', which 'might cover
anything from pitch and toss to manslaughter', de Valera indig-
nantly replied that ' "available means" means "justly available"
in the minds of all Irishmen'.[28]

The installation of Griffith as a vice-president was not merely
a gesture towards old-fashioned radicalism, but an acknowledgement of two significant concessions by the republicans.
First, Sinn Féin's aim of a sovereign republic was qualified by

the provision for a 'referendum' to determine the form of future government, monarchy being mentioned as a practical option by de Valera (already dubbed the 'king of Ireland'). Second, Sinn Féin implicitly accepted Griffith's advice that it should become a political party, unashamedly exploiting the expertise and munificence of organizers who had 'worked as generously in former times for the Parliamentary Party'. Griffith's pragmatism was obliquely defended by de Valera, who declared that 'we should have got beyond the stage when we regard politics as roguery and a politician as a rogue'.[29] Shocking though this seemed to many zealots, raised on rhetoric equating politics and the Old Party with corruption and obsolescence, the politicization of Sinn Féin brought further comfort to wavering Home Rulers and to most of the clergy at the convention. The latter may have been further reassured by the election as joint vice-president of Fr. Michael Flanagan, a curate in Roscommon who turned out to be a remarkably free and troublesome spirit both within and beyond the church.

With astonishing vigour and professional skill, the new party reapplied the organizational techniques of its predecessor. Though very few constitutionalist members secured re-endorsement as Sinn Féiners, innumerable publicans and 'respectable' citizens serving as local councillors and guardians were welcomed to the new movement upon publicly repudiating Home Rule. This was typically done without apology or explanation, beyond the incantation that de Valera, not Redmond, was now the accepted leader of the Irish race at home and abroad. With the major exception of the Hibernian divisions in Ulster, the branches of constitutionalist societies decayed or dissolved, their organizers often emerging as officers of the new cumann (Sinn Féin club). The Catholic clergy continued their rapid movement from chair to chair, as approbation of Sinn Féin became consistent with the long-standing prohibition of clerical involvement in politics likely to divide the parish. Once most of the Catholic people had changed their allegiance, it was the priest's duty either to fall silent, or to catch up with and resume guidance of his flock.

By November 1919, police returns suggested that Sinn Féin had almost 1,500 clubs with 120,000 members (more than any pre-war Home Rule organization except the United Irish League and the Irish Volunteers), while Sinn Féin organizers predictably claimed a much larger membership.[30] As with the United Irish League, participation was most intense in the borderlands of south Ulster and north Leinster, and especially in Connaught. Rural support was enhanced by Sinn Féin's initially enthusiastic involvement in the agrarian agitation of 1917–18, though its campaign for stoppage of food exports, and for sale of cheap potatoes to the poor, temporarily threatened the interests of large farmers and shopkeepers. The police returns indicate that participation in Sinn Féin was relatively sparse in the vicinity of major cities such as Dublin, Belfast, and Derry. Even so, its mobilization of nationalists of all ages and social classes was a triumph of organizational efficiency as well as sheer enthusiasm. Innumerable resolutions were passed, press reports published, leaflets distributed, demonstrations organized, and 'Irish' entertainments provided through concerts, dances, lectures, and festivals. The political culture of nationalist Ireland re-emerged, draped in a tricolour that barely obscured the outline of a golden harp.

While the war persisted, Sinn Féin lacked focus for its republican campaign. No general election would be held in wartime, and the triennial elections for county and district councils (due in mid-1917) were repeatedly postponed. Pending the expected post-war peace conference, foreign propaganda was largely directed towards fund-raising for the dependants of republican prisoners, and publication of sympathetic resolutions by Irish organizations overseas. However, three external factors created ample opportunities for popular mobilization at home. A sequence of parliamentary by-elections between February and August 1917 enabled separatists to test their popular support against Home Rule candidates, resulting in victories for Count Plunkett in North Roscommon and the prisoner Joseph McGuinness in South Longford (with the slogan 'put him in to get him out'), as well as de Valera in East Clare. The first urban success, in Kilkenny city, went to William Thomas Cosgrave, a Dublin alderman who served as the republican minister for local government, eventually becoming the first president of the Free State's executive council, a papal knight, and even a master of hounds. These defeats left the constitutionalists humiliated and depressed, although three successive victories in 1918 (in South Armagh, Waterford city, and East Tyrone) showed that the party's decomposition was less complete than many had believed.

A further stimulus to republican organization came from the sporadic but provocative exercise of coercion, and the progressive suspension of normal law, in response to growing social, agararian, and political disorder. Hundreds of Volunteers and Sinn Féiners were summarily convicted for possession of weapons, unlawful assembly or seditious utterances, creating superb opportunities for theatre in the courtroom and the prison hospital. Each major eruption of local disorder provoked the temporary proclamation of military government in surrounding districts, resulting in a flurry of raids, searches, arrests, and courts martial; prohibition of fairs, markets, and sporting matches; suppression of newspapers; and consequent alienation of any remaining advocates of the British connection. These annoyances, clumsily juxtaposed with concessions and attempts at conciliation, allowed public indignation to be maintained and intensified despite the early release of the Easter insurrectionaries. The government seemed to have lost the will to uphold the rule of law in Ireland, reverting instead to the familiar and repulsive apparatus of colonial coercion.

The most momentous external intervention was the introduction on 9 April 1918 of a Military Service bill, providing for the extension of conscription to Ireland by a royal Order in Council. One of the most gratifying outcomes of the Rising, from the nationalist viewpoint, had been the last-minute exclusion of troubled Ireland from the second phase of conscription, enacted for Britain in late May 1916. By April 1918, however, the appalling losses on the western front during the German spring offensive (which further ravaged the 16th and 36th divisions) had impelled the government to raise extra manpower regardless of the political cost. Despite warnings to the contrary from the Irish administration, the war office persuaded Lloyd George that more men could be raised in Ireland than would be required to enforce the measure. This decision led to the resignations of the chief secretary (Duke); the lord lieutenant (2nd Baron Wimborne, who had mysteriously resurfaced after the Rising); and Maxwell's successor as army commander (Sir Bryan Mahon, a Galway gentleman who had relieved Baden-Powell at Mafeking and commanded the 10th division at Suvla Bay, crowning an adventurous life by conversion to Catholicism).

The threat of conscription signalled the end of the attempt to settle Ireland's constitutional future through the utterly futile Irish Convention, which had first met in July 1917 and reported on 5 April 1918. Its sole practical function was to suggest to Britain's American and imperial allies that the attempt to resolve Ireland's constitutional future had not been completely abandoned. The Convention produced no less than eight reports and notes, one for every twelve of its members, who did not however include official representatives of Sinn Féin or most other radical nationalist groups. The Ulster Unionists were steadfast in rejecting any all-Ireland settlement, though their more vulnerable southern brethren in Midleton's Irish Unionist Alliance belatedly moved towards compromise with the increasingly impotent constitutionalists. The conciliatory policy of the 9th Viscount Midleton, a former war secretary and a Surrey landlord with property in Cork, led to a 'diehard' takeover of the Alliance and Midleton's rival formation of an Anti-Partitition League (January 1919). The Unionist rift was not, however, reflected in significant division over conscription, despite the launching of a Protestant Anti-Conscription Movement by Nelly O'Brien, Gaelic Leaguer and granddaughter of the aristocratic rebel William Smith O'Brien.

With conscription presaged but not proclaimed, nationalists of all degrees were presented with a focus of common indignation. The Irish Party, though favourable to allied aims and military recruiting, had always strenuously opposed compulsion in the absence of an Irish parliament fit to legitimate it. By 18 April, when the Military Service bill became law, representatives of Sinn Féin, several factions of constitutionalists, the Trades Union Congress, and other interests contracted a remarkable alliance at Dublin's Mansion House (seat of the lord mayor). Instructed by de Valera, a deputation from the conference induced the united Catholic hierarchy to direct all parish clergy to announce the public administration of a pledge loosely based on the Ulster covenant: 'Denying the right of the British Government to enforce compulsory service in this country, we pledge ourselves solemnly to one another to resist conscription by the most effective means at our disposal.' The bishops added a wily and ambiguous exegesis, observing 'that conscription forced in this way upon Ireland is an oppressive and inhuman law, which the Irish people have a right to resist by all the means that are consonant with the law of God'. The hierarchy thus avoided rejection of conscription in principle, their brothers in Britain having firmly endorsed its imposition. The final caveat implicitly left it up to the infallible judgement of the bishops, subject only to papal appeal, to determine whether or not the conditions existed for just rebellion, and hence for the use of physical force.[31] This issue generated lively theological debate, long outlasting the crisis, with various Jesuits justifying rebellion; whereas Walter McDonald, a Maynooth professor of dubious orthodoxy, not only refuted this argument but defended the government's right to conscript its Irish citizens.[32]

The conscription crisis reinvigorated the strategy of violence, almost quiescent since the Rising despite the death of one policeman during a Dublin riot in June 1917. In October 1917, de Valera had been elected president of the reconstituted Irish Volunteers as well as of Sinn Féin. The organization acquired further commanders in March 1918 with the appointment of Brugha as head of the 'resident executive' and, as chief of staff, Richard Mulcahy (a Waterford-born postal engineer responsible for the death of eight policemen at Ashbourne, Co. Meath, in 1916). The Volunteers, though kept in a state of simmering excitement by dark hints of future 'stunts', had so far concentrated on drilling, parading, soliciting arrest, refusing to recognize 'British' courts, hunger-striking, and other collective assertions of irrepressibility. The use of hunger-strikes to secure privileges for 'political' prisoners was eventually effective, after further public outrage had been aroused by the forcible feeding and consequent death of the new president of the IRB, Thomas Ashe, in September 1917. Assaults and riots occurred ever more frequently, and innumerable raids, robberies, and forced sales augmented the armoury of the Volunteers with shotguns, revolvers, and sometimes rifles. Nevertheless, few policemen or Volunteers killed each other before the armistice, although an attack on a Kerry police barracks in April 1918 resulted in the death of two Volunteers and the attempted killing of those held responsible for their deaths.

Headquarters determined to resist conscription by force, should attempts be made to capture or disarm the Volunteers. Ernest Blythe (a Presbyterian Gaelic Leaguer from Antrim who was to become republican minister for trade and commerce and later Cosgrave's skinflint minister for finance) published a baleful appeal for 'ruthless warfare' in the Volunteers' clandestine journal. Blythe wrote from prison that all those assisting 'the enemy must be shot or otherwise destroyed with the least possible delay. In short, we must show that it is not healthy to be against us.'[33] Military preparations were complicated in May 1918 by the arrest of most of the republican leaders for involvement in a fictitious 'German plot'. Several key Volunteer organizers, including Brugha, Mulcahy, and Collins (by now adjutant-general), escaped arrest; but the removal of activists like Blythe, as well as de Valera, Griffith, and the politicians, meant that the organization of popular protest passed mainly to Labour leaders. While the IRB and the Volunteers co-ordinated their ragged forces and equipped their arsenal, Thomas Johnson and William O'Brien prepared an elaborate scheme for 'passive resistance'. This entailed strikes, interference with railways and exports, takeover of food supplies, and withdrawal of bank deposits by well-heeled nationalists.[34] Furthermore, the

techniques of civil disobedience developed by Britain's con-
scientious objectors (a category virtually unknown in Ireland)
were annotated and adapted for use in Ireland, should the police
eventually thump at the door.

Membership of Sinn Féin and the Volunteers soared during
the protracted crisis over conscription, as hitherto unorganized
districts followed the lead of those already activated through by-
election campaigns or agrarian agitation. Meanwhile, the Irish
Party attempted to retrieve its losses under John Dillon, who had
succeeded Redmond upon his death in March 1918. The party
proclaimed its renewed militancy by withdrawing from Westminster during the first two months of the crisis, but its revival
was probably inhibited rather than otherwise by the collaboration with Sinn Féin against conscription. There had already
been some reactivation of the Ancient of Order of Hibernians,
particularly in Ulster, where two of the three by-election victories between February and April 1918 were secured. Nevertheless, the main beneficiary of the alliance against conscription was
non-violent republicanism. To the chagrin of the wild men and
women, and the relief of most parties to the Mansion House
committee, the campaign of passive resistance and collective
affirmation was successful. The pledge and Labour's one-day
strike on 23 April were considered brilliantly effective, despite
the indifference of Belfast workers to the strike, the rejection of
the pledge by loyalists, and the failure of Sinn Féin organizers
to count the number of signatories.

The administration headed by the new Liberal chief secretary,
Edward Shortt, backtracked awkwardly in face of popular defiance. Shortt's retreat was complicated by his uneasy relationship
with Field Marshal Viscount French of Ypres and of High Lake,
Co. Roscommon, who had succeeded Wimborne as viceroy and
mistakenly believed that he had been granted plenary powers as
Ireland's 'military governor'. French remained convinced that
the Irish 'race' was 'peculiarly liable to be influenced by their
immediate environment', so that Irishmen had only to be freed
'from the terrorism of the few self-seeking hot-heads and the
majority would make excellent soldiers'.[35] Yet conscription was

postponed repeatedly, pending failure to achieve a set of ever-diminishing local quotas for voluntary enlistment, until the armistice of November 1918 allowed the government quietly to bury the iniquitous measure. The ruthless warmongers chafed at the bit, but did not yet bolt.

Irish Consequences of the Peace, 1919–1921

The end of hostilities in Europe administered a further external shock to Irish politics. After more than four years of deadlock, the rapidity of Germany's collapse seemed as disconcerting as the sudden plunge into conflict in 1914. Even so, all protagonists in Ireland had long since drawn up contingency plans for peace. An amended Government of Ireland act was still expected to come into force at the end of the conflict, although the technical prolongation of the state of war pending American ratification of the peace treaties in August 1921 made possible still further prevarication.[36] The resumption of party conflict at Westminster did not entail return to the stark polarities of 1914, since Lloyd George and Bonar Law jointly endorsed the principle of 'self-government' for Ireland in their manifesto for the 'coupon' election of December 1918. They also concurred that 'there are two paths which are closed—the one leading to a complete severance of Ireland from the British Empire, and the other the forcible submission of the six counties of Ulster to a Home Rule parliament against their will'.[37]

Ulster loyalists, as well as their southern brethren, became alarmed that the long experience of wartime coalition had sapped partisan intransigence. As Wilfrid Spender ruminated shortly before the election, even Carson had 'handicapped himself by an appearance of tolerance, probably from a feeling of loyalty to his own associates, which is bewildering to the onlooker'.[38] Equally bewildering for both loyalists and the government were the shifting allegiances of nationalists, for most of whom Home Rule was no longer an acceptable option. For republicans, the armistice offered a novel opportunity to seek a settlement through international pressure rather than domestic compromise. In January 1918, both Lloyd George and President Wilson (in his 'Fourteen Points' for world peace) had proclaimed the entitlement of small European nations to statehood. Griffith and de Valera argued that the post-war peace conference might fruitfully be used to advance Ireland's analogous claim to self-determination. Thus nationalists and Ulster loyalists prepared to reassert their demands for liberty, addressing different audiences whose responses could not easily be anticipated.

The general election, though rigged to avoid a test of strength between the major British parties, was crucial in securing mandates for Ulster Unionism and republicanism. The outcome was rendered somewhat unpredictable by the extension of suffrage to adult males, young servicemen, and mature women, though the enfranchisement of women and soldiers was widely expected to bolster conservatism. In Ireland, where most constituencies were usually uncontested, there were elections for 78 of the 105 seats, enabling over a million people to cast votes. The outcome was consolidation for the Ulster Unionists, humiliation for the constitutionalists, and undeniable triumph for the republicans. Sinn Féiners, again pledged to abstain from Westminster, received just under half of votes cast, including three-quarters in Connaught and over two-thirds in Munster and Dublin. In Ulster, where the relative strength of the nationalist parties was obscured by Cardinal Michael Logue's rather maladroit electoral pact, Sinn Féin obtained 24 per cent of votes compared with 16 per cent for Home Rulers. Though anti-republican nationalists gained 23 per cent of the contested vote overall, they were virtually eliminated from parliament. Unionists of all shades increased their share of votes actually cast in Ulster from 52 to 60 per cent, so slightly exceeeding the Protestant component of the population. Six nationalists from Ireland (and Liverpool's T. P. O'Connor) remained to debate Irish issues at Westminster along with twenty-six Ulster Unionists, even more than in the bumper crop of 1880. Over half of the Ulster Unionists were merchants or lawyers. These were joined by three workers from the Ulster Unionist Labour Association, six army officers and a single landed gentleman (representing the class which had held the majority of Unionist seats up to 1892). Meanwhile, the seventy-three Sinn Féiners prepared to fulfil their pledge by convening an alternative parliament in Dublin.

The absence of effective nationalist representation at Westminster enhanced the influence of the Ulster Unionists in shaping a settlement. Athough Carson no longer belonged to the government, having twice resigned from wartime cabinets, his eventual successor Sir James Craig retained minor ministerial posts until April 1920. Ulster Unionist views were well aired in the cabinet's Irish committee, convened in October 1919, and chaired by Carson's predecessor as Ulster Unionist leader, Walter Long. Reassured by the Unionist majority in Lloyd George's coalition, the Ulster leaders did not at first find it necessary to mobilize mass support as in 1912. Lloyd George had dismissed Asquith's proposals for a dominion settlement, and Ulster's immunity from compulsory Home Rule seemed unchallengeable. Nevertheless, Carson warned on 12 July 1919 that 'if any attempt were made to interfere with the rights and liberties of Ulster he would get the Ulster Volunteer Force into activity again'.[39] Within a year, as unrest intensified and the government pressed for a constitutional settlement, the force was indeed reorganized under Wilfrid Spender, mastermind of the Larne gun-running. Its former chief of staff (Sir William Hacket Pain) had transferred his loyalties to administering the police forces in Belfast, after a stint as army commander for the northern district. The UVF was reinforced by hardened ex-servicemen, of whom about 100,000 were demobilized throughout Ireland during 1919. Its reappearance offered nationalists the same menacing message as in 1914.

Membership of the loyalist orders also rose markedly after 1918, particularly in the hitherto unruly and disorganized region of Belfast. Over the next two years, the number of Belfast Orangemen and also Blackmen increased by nearly half, leaving both orders far stronger than in even the year of the covenant (1912).[40] The loyalist cause was further promoted by international propaganda directed towards the 'Scotch-Irish' and the Protestant churches in Australasia and America. The Irish

Presbyterian, Methodist, and Anglican churches combined to send a delegation of six clergymen to twenty-four north American cities, between November 1919 and February 1920. The clergymen were accompanied by William Coote, MP for South Tyrone, a Presbyterian elder and manufacturer of woollen yarns and hosiery.[41] This visit, self-consciously replicating a familiar nationalist device, resulted in the creation of a 'loyal coalition' to safeguard Anglo-American relations and counteract Irish nationalist agitation in the United States. With characteristic relentlessness, discipline, and showmanship, Ulster Protestants asserted their entitlement to British citizenship in recompense for serving the empire.

While loyalists reconstructed their pre-war barricades within Ulster and beyond, Sinn Féin attempted to transform nationalism and the nation by incorporating an Irish republic. The initial function of the Dáil was not to establish a republican administration, but to provide a mandate for Sinn Féin's campaign of international propaganda. The first meeting of the Dáil on 21 January 1919, ignored by all non-republican members and also lacking the imprisoned half of the Sinn Féin party, was therefore devoted to approving French, English, and Irish versions of three grandiloquent declarations. These comprised a 'Declaration of Independence' with obvious American resonance, a 'Message to the Free Nations of the World', and a 'Democratic Programme' primarily addressed to the forthcoming Berne meeting of the Socialist International. The hope for recognition of the republican claim at the Paris peace conference, inaugurated three days before the Dáil, was either naïve or disingenuous, since the triumphant allies could not reasonably be expected to carve up each other's empires by analogy with those of Germany and Austria. Not surprisingly, republican emissaries were excluded from the conference and the parallels between Ireland and emerging 'nations' such as Czechoslovakia and Poland were ignored. All expectation of success ceased on 28 June 1919, with signature of the principal peace treaties between Germany and the victorious allies.

Meanwhile, the Irish claim was skilfully disseminated among

potential sympathizers in the United States and most other countries, the rhetorical effect of its appeal to Wilson's principles being enhanced by the manifest hypocrisy of the Versailles settlement. De Valera and his team of expert propagandists gave priority to winning political and financial support, through mobilization of Irish emigrants and their descendants, in the hope of eventually securing diplomatic intervention. This strategy, unlike the appeal to the peace conference, was not entirely fanciful. The 'Irish vote', though less cohesive than often asserted, was a significant element of party politics not only in America, but in the dominions such as Australia. Its power had been somewhat reduced by the slackening of emigration since 1900 and its virtual suspension during the war, resulting in the reduction of America's Irish-born population from nearly 2 million in 1880 to just over a million in 1920. In compensation, however, the number of descendants identifying themselves as 'Irish', and the relative wealth and social status of that group, were rapidly increasing. In focusing its propaganda on the Irish overseas, Sinn Féin was reiterating the long-established practice of the Irish Party, which since the 1880s had been largely financed by American and Australian organizations linked to the United Irish League and the Ancient Order of Hibernians. Likewise, the old IRB had depended heavily on arms, money, and personnel supplied by Devoy's Clan na Gael and other Fenian bodies. The novelty of Sinn Féin's strategy was the belief that ethnic support could be translated into government policy and effective diplomatic pressure upon Britain.

The propagandist campaign was a triumph of style, being promoted by an ever multiplying network of emissaries and 'consuls' throughout the world, co-ordinated by Count Plunkett's department of foreign affairs. Foreign journals were supplied with largely factual if highly coloured Irish news through the *Irish Bulletin*, produced from November 1919 by Desmond FitzGerald's publicity department. After his arrest in February 1921, FitzGerald was succeeded by the still more resourceful Erskine Childers (an Anglican Englishman reared in Wicklow, and a former Home Rule theorist and gun-runner, who had served as a clerk in the House of Commons and as a wartime intelligence officer in the air services). The proof that propaganda was the central element of republican policy came in June 1919, when de Valera (recently elected as president of the Dáil) began an American mission which was to keep him out of revolutionary Ireland for eighteen months. Though unable to induce the ailing President Wilson to press Ireland's claim with his heavily indebted British ally, and unsuccessful in winning significant commitments from either party in the conventions preceding the presidential election in 1920, de Valera proved to be a superb money-raiser. His main triumph was to secure nearly 6 million dollars through two issues of 'republican bonds' in January 1920 and October 1921, a far greater sum that that raised in Ireland itself through the Dáil's 'internal loan'. Though nearly half of these payments were retained in America because of factional squabbles and the 'split' over the Anglo-Irish treaty, enough reached Ireland to make possible a functioning republican administration and to pay for substantial purchases of arms. Another 5 million dollars were collected for relieving victims of the Irish conflict, while Devoy's 'victory fund' yielded a further million.

In his as yet unauthorized role as 'President of the Irish Republic', De Valera conducted a tireless round of American lectures and pseudo-'interviews'. In one of these he shocked republicans at home and in America by suggesting that Ireland's future status with respect to Britain might resemble Cuba's strategic dependency on America under the Monroe doctrine. Though de Valera spent much of the rest of his long life explaining that he had not intended to countenance the creation of a British protectorate maintaining British bases in Ireland, his apparent repudiation of the demand for full independence provoked furious and damaging denunciations from John Devoy and Clan na Gael. Having further splintered the existing Irish-American organizations and encouraged their leaders to tear each other to pieces, de Valera created a tame American Association for the Recognition of the Irish Republic (November 1920). His key assistant was Harry Boland, the Dublin hurler and former president of the IRB whose intimacy with Michael Collins was soon to be shattered by their common pursuit of Kitty Kiernan, the celebrated publican's daughter from Granard, Co. Longford. Boland, as energetic and ebullient as Collins himself, deployed his charm and persuasive skills to ensure that the Chief's solemn pronouncements were implemented. Headed by a corrupt Californian oil magnate (Edward L. Doheny), the American Association eventually claimed half a million members.

By comparison with American assistance, British political and financial support for the Dáil was meagre. The Dáil's most effective political ally was a 'purely English movement' established in October 1920 to combat coercion and reprisals. Brilliantly organized by the imperial historian Basil Williams, who had once campaigned with Childers for Home Rule, and Oswald Mosley, the future Blackshirt leader, the Peace With Ireland Council was crucial in generating the political will for a settlement. The Irish Self-Determination League, co-founded in March 1919 by the London-born Gaelic Leaguer Art O'Brien, never dared to declare itself republican and failed to win significant support in centres of Irish settlement such as Liverpool and Glasgow. The League's 40,000 members contributed less than a pound a head to Irish causes.[42] In Britain, as less markedly in both Australia and America, the fraternal networks associated with the Home Rule movement remained influential among Irish emigrants. The success of republican propaganda was further qualified by the fact that no government or major international organization formally recognized the republic (though Russia, and both the Socialist and Communist Internationals, came close to doing so). Even so, the panache and profitability of the Dáil's campaign were astonishing for so inexperienced a party, far outpointing the performance of subsequent republican front organizations such as Noraid in America.

The creation of a ministry in January 1919 had been a rhetorical gesture, lending further *gravitas* to the Dáil's assertion of national sovereignty. Sympathetic foreigners, whose knowledge of Ireland often went little beyond the stories disseminated by the publicity department, were no doubt willing to accept de Valera's claim to Wilson 'that the National Congress thus assembled elected and set up a government, which government is, on democratic principles, the de jure, and has ever since been functioning as the obeyed, de facto government of Ireland'.[43] Yet de Valera and his colleagues at first assumed that no rebel administration could function under British rule, despite the cumulative effect of 'passive resistance' in immobilizing elements of the existing administration (especially the police and the courts). The Dáil's early forays into administration were mainly elaborate propagandist gestures, such as the ponderous but impotent Commission of Inquiry into the Resources and Industries of Ireland (September 1919). Its secretary was the eccentric and egocentric Dubliner Darrell Figgis, importer of tea, nonpractising Protestant, early advocate of Sinn Féin, gun-runner, and suicide. In such hands, the administrative revolution would have had no more substance than Figgis himself, 'strolling dapperly down O'Connell Street in smartly cut clothes, with his red hair gleaming like newly polished boots'.[44]

The demand for practical innovation came from local republicans who had taken the Dáil's rhetoric at face value and discovered ingenious methods of applying it. In June 1919, the Dáil had decreed a scheme for local arbitration courts (which though extra-judicial were not intrinsically illegal), so reapplying an old idea of Griffith's with precedents in the Land War and the Repeal struggle. No systematic effort was made to put the decree into effect, this being a risky and expensive option without obvious propagandist value. In Connaught and Munster, however, republican organizers were under popular pressure to assume judicial functions. This demand was prompted by the diminishing competence of the police to detect or pursue offenders, and the growing fear that social disorder and contempt for private property would shatter republican unity by setting neighbours at each others' throats. As agrarian outrages, land seizures, and other offences multiplied, local Volunteer companies and Sinn Féin clubs began to set up illegal tribunals, charged respectively with punishing criminals and enforcing civil decrees. A detailed scheme for civil courts, complete with guards in each parish to 'preserve the peace', was devised for West Clare by the sentimental poet Brian O'Higgins. Encouraged by the popularity and apparent effectiveness of such experiments, the Dáil belatedly drew up instructions for a network of parish, district, and superior courts handling both civil and criminal cases (August 1920). In the same month, as part of its campaign to restrain and regulate agrarian unrest, the Dáil established a Land Commission more concerned with preventing than executing transfers.

Despite the formidable difficulty of creating, administering, and gaining public respect for a rival judicial system, the handful of republican lawyers devised a quirky but surprisingly effective apparatus, administered mainly by shopkeepers and priests as justices and by Volunteer officers as registrars and clerks. Certain technical matters such as pub and dog licences were left to the enemy courts; imprisonment was usually avoided because the republicans had no prisons or warders; execution or forced emigration (often soon followed by clandestine return) were the only convenient remedies for punishing serious criminals and 'informers'. Even so, the courts enforced a great many small decrees for unpaid rent or debts, and demonstrated that in most parts of Ireland respect for the republic was sufficient to induce many offenders to endure punishment. This achievement was widely praised even by the remaining resident gentry, whose disgust at the collapse of civil administration sometimes outweighed their political aversion to republicanism.

Local initiative was equally crucial in developing the republican system of local government, whose effrontery appalled but impressed Lloyd George's cabinet. In July 1919, Sinn Féin had drawn up elaborate plans for contesting the local elections postponed since 1916; these were finally activated in January and June 1920. January's municipal elections demonstrated the relative weakness of republicanism in the towns, as Sinn Féin won only a quarter of the vote and could not always prevent the control of urban councils by coalitions of Labour and constitutionalist representatives. Five months later, however, republican candidates took command of virtually every county and rural authority outside Protestant Ulster. The new councillors were mainly Volunteer officers, as in Clare, where the new and enterprising chairman of the county council was the resourceful and already legendary Michael Brennan. One of three brothers who rotated control of the East Clare brigade, he was to become commander of the 1st western division in 1921, a key figure in negating 'Irregular' resistance in 1922, and chief of staff of the national army between 1931 and 1940. Cosgrave's department of local government had arranged for the new councils to convene, pass republican resolutions for circulation in various languages, and await official penalties. Few doubted that local administration would thereupon be plunged into anarchy, as a result of the imposed or voluntary dissolution of the rebellious councils. This outcome, ideal for foreign propaganda, threatened to alienate local residents from Sinn Féin, whose administrative legacy would have been potholed and filthy roads, unlit streets, unstocked dispensaries, beggars starved of poor relief, and labourers' cottages with leaking roofs. The *Irish Bulletin* would doubtless snarl that Britain was responsible, but Irish ratepayers were more likely to blame their defaulting councillors.

This fear, fortifying the social conservatism of many republican leaders, induced the new Clare county council to resolve upon maintaining local services despite its repudiation of Sir Henry Robinson's local government board. Once again, a Clare initiative was eventually taken up by the Dáil, which promulgated an elaborate scheme for local government in September 1920. Since four-fifths of the income of county councils came from rates rather than grants or loans, reduced services might be continued with the co-operation of ratepayers. Robinson, pragmatically dismissive of republican manifestos and determined to avoid anarchy, worked skilfully to postpone irrevocable conflict with the local councils. Despite Bonar Law's insistence that grants and loans should be withheld from councils refusing to promise submission to the next audit, and despite the failure of many ratepayers to pay any of the rival collectors, the republican councils managed to beg, bully, bludgeon, or borrow enough money to stay in business until the truce of July 1921. Brennan was one of many republican organizers who found themselves responsible both for destroying roads by night and repairing them by day, often employing the same people for both tasks. For practical republicans, the 'constructive' element of revolution was essential to its popular appeal.

The constructive campaign, and the social disorder that prompted it, were by-products of a cycle of violence and counter-violence which steadily intensified during 1919 and 1920. The most conspicuous early 'engagement' was the murder of two policemen escorting a cart of gelignite, at Soloheadbeg, Co. Tipperary, which coincided with the first meeting of the Dáil on 21 January 1919. Though almost universally depicted as the 'first shots of the War of Independence', this escapade by Seán Treacy, Dan Breen, and other desperadoes of the 3rd Tipperary brigade was unauthorized, unoriginal, and initially unimitated, being also unpunished by Mulcahy's headquarters staff. Attacks on barracks and policemen had occurred sporadically during 1918. Though more numerous in 1919, such armed clashes continued to be locally inspired, as Volunteer companies grew increasingly bold in taunting, defying, humiliating, and disarming the police and occasionally the army. Only about 16 members of the 'crown forces' were killed during 1919, compared with 44 in the first half of 1920, 171 in the second half, and no less than 324 before the truce in 1921. The republican 'roll of honour' indicates a continuous annual decline in republican deaths between 1916 and 1919, when only 8 fatalities were ascribed to service against Britain. That number rose to 32 in the first half of 1920, 228 in the second half, and 182 up to the truce in 1921. No reliable figures exist for civilian losses, although the official outrage returns attributed 196 civilian murders to 'Sinn Féin', of which 154 were perpetrated in 1921. It thus appears that at least 1,200 people died as a result of the Anglo-Irish conflict, casualties being relatively infrequent until mid-1920.[45]

The Volunteers of 1919, like MacNeill's force, were most densely organized and most heavily armed in Munster, which was to remain the epicentre of revolutionary violence until 1923. The cat-and-mouse game of pursuits, arrests, and escapes continued, although after early 1918 the Volunteers had been less inclined than before to court imprisonment. Since the anticlimax over conscription, no coherent military policy had been developed to complement the propagandist and administrative campaigns. Headquarters remained a shadowy institution, its influence largely exercised through the fraternal web of the IRB, spun by Collins and his associates in Dublin. Despite an increasingly elaborate hierarchy of brigade and battalion staffs, company officers and support services, most of the local companies were still loose bands of neighbouring adolescents as in 1914. The early captains were not commissioned but elected by companies, typically being chosen for their social status or sporting prowess rather than shooting skills. However, as Soloheadbeg showed, an informal élite of more robust and adventurous fighters was springing up in small units throughout the country, gradually developing *esprit de corps* as they went 'on the run' to evade arrest. These bands, dependent on 'safe houses' and sustained from day to day by the need to acquire weapons, whether by purchase, burglary, or ambush, were the nucleus of the 'flying columns' of 1920–1.

As with all post-war military organizations, the membership and soldierly expertise of the Volunteers were bolstered by enrolment of ex-servicemen with itchy fingers, often careless of human life and innocent of political ideology. For demobilized Catholics reared in the shadow of Home Rule, Sinn Féin's Ireland was a strange and threatening environment. By October 1919, 35,000 ex-servicemen were receiving the out-of-work donation in Ireland, an unemployment ratio of 46 per cent compared with only 10 per cent in Britain. After temporary alleviation, heavy unemployment resumed during the recession, and over 23,500 veterans were listed on the 'live register' by mid-January 1921. The proportion of ex-servicemen without employment was proportionately much higher in south-western Munster and north-western Connaught than in Ulster. This probably signified local hostility from organized Labour and republican employers, and the weakness of the ex-servicemen's associations in regions of relatively low enlistment.[46] One path of adjustment for alienated veterans was that taken by Tom Barry of Bandon, Co. Cork, a policeman's son who had served in the Mesopotamian Expeditionary Force. After demobilization he returned to Bandon and joined one of the competing associations for veterans. By 1920, Barry had decided to switch allegiance to the Volunteers, becoming one of the most feared guerrilla fighters as commander of the West Cork flying column. In his ever-popular memoirs, he backdated his conversion to 1916 in Mesopotamia, where he claimed to have been 'awakened to Irish Nationality' by news of the Easter Rising. By contrast, his motives in joining the British army in 1915 had been 'to see what war was like, to get a gun, to see new countries and to feel a grown man'.[47] For an adventurer like Barry, involvement in the Volunteers provided further opportunities for manly gun-toting, with the added gloss of being at one with the new politics of most of his neighbours.

The increasing unruliness of the Volunteers led to desperate but ineffectual efforts to repress sedition and improve the performance of the army and police. After the appointment in January 1919 of another tough-talking Liberal chief secretary, Ian Macpherson, coercion again became the core of government policy. Many punitive regulations under the Defence of the Realm act were maintained or amplified long after their withdrawal in Britain. Further attempts were made in 'disturbed areas' to apply military law, followed by curtailment of fairs and markets, curfews, and other interferences with daily and nightly life. In April 1919, as briefly in mid-1918, all meetings, assemblies, and processions in public places were prohibited throughout Ireland, the entire country being deemed to be in a state of military emergency. Sinn Féin and even the Gaelic League, as well as the Volunteers and Cumann na mBan, were 'proclaimed' as illegal organizations in Tipperary (July 1919), Cork (September 1919), and throughout Ireland (November 1919). The Dáil itself achieved the status of 'dangerous association' in September 1919. The progressive abandonment of civil rights facilitated a massive campaign of public intrusion into Irish private lives, involving thousands of nocturnal raids designed to secure intelligence as well as to capture suspects and intimidate communities. In 1919, the balance of terror was decidedly weighted in favour of its official practitioners.

Each act of coercion stimulated further bellicosity among the Volunteers, increasingly restive after three years of restraint and ever less confident in the political strategy of seeking international recognition. The cycle of violence was further accelerated by 'reprisals' for republican attacks, the first of which occurred at Fermoy in September 1919. Local shops were burned and ransacked in retaliation for an ambush of soldiers on their way to a Methodist service, which had resulted in one death and several injuries. This attack by the 2nd Cork brigade was led by Liam Lynch, a Limerick-born hardwareman, member of the IRB's supreme council, and later chief of staff of the Irregular IRA until killed by national soldiers in April 1923. Coercion and counter-violence were further stimulated by the attempted assassination of Viscount French at Ashtown, near his viceregal residence in the Phoenix Park, in December 1919. Mulcahy and his staff were bombarded with imaginative plans for 'all-out war', including a proposal in November for an Easter-style rising in Cork to be followed, after its inevitable military failure, by a similar conflagration in Galway. Though this wild scheme was rejected, headquarters purged Volunteer frustration by sanctioning several large-scale attacks on occupied police barracks in January 1920.[48] The proponent of the rejected strategy was Terence MacSwiney of the 1st Cork brigade, a romantic playwright and former commercial teacher who was briefly to serve as lord mayor of Cork, before dying after seventy-three days on hunger-strike in October 1920. MacSwiney was almost universally bemoaned by republicans, priests, and foreigners as a Christlike man of peace who had sacrificed himself for the people. The episode was to be replayed in 1981, with the widely publicized hunger-strike and death of the poet and republican militant Bobby Sands.

In March and April 1920, the Irish administration was extensively overhauled in the hope of restoring both civic order and civil government. A bullish Canadian Liberal, Sir Hamar Greenwood, replaced Macpherson as chief secretary, Viscount French having already become a mere figurehead despite his admission to the cabinet in October 1919. The head of the civil service (Sir Warren Fisher) made imaginative attempts to revivify the archaic Castle executive by introducing a team of outstanding and unconventional officials, led by Sir John Anderson (subsequently governor of Bengal and wartime chancellor of the exchequer). For the first time since the Union, expenditure on Irish services could now be sanctioned on the spot. While Greenwood thundered maledictions against the republicans, his offsiders made informal or clandestine contact with a wide range of political interests. In May 1920, raids, arrests, and searches were briefly suspended in the hope of securing peace and a new constitutional settlement. The attempt at conciliation soon collapsed, in the face of republican rejection of compromise and public indifference to parties urging moderation. Despite misgivings in the embattled Castle, the focus of the government's Irish policy reverted speedily to coercion. The distinction between the various 'crown forces' became ever more blurred. The militarization of the RIC was symbolized by the choice of Major-General Sir Henry Hugh Tudor as chief of police; while a former commissioner of the Metropolitan Police in London, General Sir Nevil Macready, became army commander. However, the associated reorganization failed dismally to retrieve efficiency, discipline, or co-ordination among the forces in Ireland.

By the end of 1919, it was already obvious that the armed services in Ireland were incapable of 'maintaining the peace' or 'restoring law and order'. The antiquated armament of the Royal Irish Constabulary was designed to overawe rather than kill the population; its elderly personnel, their number depleted by wartime wastage, could not adjust to the novel rigours of living amidst an aggressive and hostile people. Foot and cycle patrols were abandoned and hundreds of outlying barracks were vacated, only to be burned by Volunteers throughout southern

Ireland in an orgy of arson concentrated in April 1920. Following an overdue improvement in wages and conditions of employment, active recruitment to the police resumed at the end of
1919, and 300 Irishmen enlisted in the first two months of 1920.
Meanwhile, the regular police were beginning to be reinforced
by ex-servicemen termed 'temporary constables', whose motley
uniform caused them to be nicknamed 'Black and Tans' after a
pack of hounds in Co. Limerick. An élite force involving about
2,300 ex-officers, ranked as temporary police sergeants in the
'Auxiliary Division' but with an independent structure of
command, was inaugurated in July 1920. The enrolment of ex-
officers to defend police barracks had first been sanctioned on
a small scale in March 1920, being progressively extended
despite reiterated protests from the treasury.[49] The subordination of the Auxiliaries to the police and army commands was
never satisfactorily achieved, and individual companies
remained impervious to directions and reprimands from the
divisional staff. Until early 1921, the Auxiliaries' unruly commander was Brigadier-General Frank Percy Crozier, who
(though a Limerick man) had served with the UVF and the
Ulster division at the Somme. The supplementary police forces
embraced an unsavoury medley of adventurers and unemployed
fighters from Britain, America, Australasia, and Ireland herself,
where 700 Black and Tans were raised during the year before
the truce of July 1921. Although greatly outnumbered by the
10,000 or more non-Irish 'temporary constables', the intake of
Irish police recruits exceeded the annual rate during and even
before the war. The strength of all full-time police forces never
exceeded 17,000, being steadily eviscerated by some 3,000 resignations (in 1920–1) as well as numerous dismissals, premature
retirements, deaths, suicides, and murders.

The new recruits paid scant respect to their officers, relishing
the absence of military discipline and their ready access to
weapons and civilian targets. Republican killings and attacks
were routinely 'punished' by reprisals against alleged accom-
plices, as raging and often drunken policemen looted shops and
pubs, burned houses and particularly creameries, murdered

'Shinners', and roamed the roads by night in masked gangs. Hundreds of such incidents are recorded in the official returns of outrages, often being attributed to the nebulous 'Anti-Sinn Féin Society'. An ambush at Rineen, Co. Clare, in which six policemen were killed in September 1920, resulted in the burning of three small nearby towns and six more deaths, including the fortuitous incineration of an ambusher as he rested in a pub after his endeavours. The Auxiliaries gained the reputation of being more systematic and efficient, but also more vicious, than the Black and Tans. Though never a declared policy of Lloyd George's government, the campaign of violent reprisals was applauded by Churchill at the war office and condoned at every level of administration, notwithstanding mild expressions of regret for the understandable excesses of men under intolerable pressure. Even General Macready, ever ready to punish military hotheads and to deplore police indiscipline, told a Castle official 'that if a policeman put on a mackintosh and a false beard and "reprised" on his own hook he was damn glad of it'.[50]

Official restrictions on the use of weapons were relaxed, the police being encouraged to shoot and kill suspected armed rebels after a perfunctory challenge. It was probably these innovations, not the unverified legitimation of reprisals, which drew the comment from one divisional commissioner, in June 1920, that 'I have been told the new policy and plan and I am satisfied, though I doubt its ultimate success in the main particular—the stamping out of terrorism by secret murder. I still am of opinion that instant retaliation is the only course for this.'[51] This remark suggests that it was not the architects of the 'new policy' but the commissioner who favoured reprisals ('instant retaliation'). According to an alternative reading, however, this statement refers to the secret murder of (rather than by) terrorists and so confirms the alleged use of secret servicemen to pursue and assassinate rebel 'ring-leaders'. The horrific record of reprisals prompted a powerful international campaign. Commissions representing the British Labour Party and Irish-America toured the country and collected damning evidence of misgovernment and brutality, confirmed by numerous foreign

journalists (expertly briefed by the Dáil's publicity department).
Though equally strong objections to reprisals were expressed
privately by both civil and military administrators in Dublin, the
crown forces seemed uncontrollable.

Macready repeatedly urged the government either to reach a
settlement or to exercise ruthless coercion, through imposition
of martial law by a vastly expanded army. Yet, as his friend Sir
Henry Wilson made clear when CIGS, military resources were
already overstretched with increasing trouble in the empire and
the Welsh minefields. Although there were some 50,000 troops
in Ireland by early 1921, only 15,000 were considered capable of
'offensive action'.[52] The primary responsibility for suppressing
the 'rebellion in Ireland' therefore remained with the paramilitary police. Additional facilities for search, arrest, summary jurisdiction, execution, and internment were provided by the
Restoration of Order in Ireland act (August 1920), which
renewed and extended the emergency powers provided by the
expiring Defence of the Realm legislation. In November 1920
the government set out to intern all known Volunteer activists
in Ballykinlar, Co. Down, and subsequently in other Irish and
English camps and prisons. Five thousand suspects were incarcerated, including a substantial part of the republican élite.
Despite this achievement, and the appointment in March 1920
of police divisional commissioners to liaise with each army
command, the army, police, and Auxiliaries remained hopelessly
uncoordinated. Martial law was eventually proclaimed in eight
counties, stretching south from Galway to Kerry and Waterford,
near the end of 1920. This enabled the local army commanders
to assert formal control over the police and to exercise rough
justice in military courts, leading to the execution of two dozen
prisoners. An attempt was made to regulate retribution by introducing 'authorized reprisals', whereby military parties burned
buildings and furniture, but not bodies, after notifying their
owners. Some 150 such punishments were carried out under
martial law between January and June 1921. Macready's fearful
alternative of universal martial law was often discussed but
never implemented.

The character of republican violence was mainly determined by the powers and conduct of the crown forces, which were in turn affected by the conduct of the republicans. The immediate republican objective was typically to acquire arms and defend them, rather than put them to offensive use. Despite frenzied attempts to secure weapons through the black market and foreign purchase, headquarters only managed to import six machine guns and about 100 rifles in the year up to July 1921. Another 50 machine guns and 300 rifles were imported between July and December. Even in November 1921, the reported arsenal of the Volunteers amounted to a mere 3,300 rifles, nearly half of which were held in Munster and less than a tenth in Connaught.[53] As police and military arsenals became better protected, through consolidation and sandbagging of barracks and the use of armoured motor transport, the arms-hungry Volunteers increased the scale of their 'stunts' from minor raids to attacks on barracks, and eventually to ambushes involving dozens of armed men. The bloodiest of these was Tom Barry's massacre of seventeen Auxiliaries at Kilmichael, Co. Cork, in November 1920. In the following month, the killing of an Auxiliary at Dillon's Cross provoked the razing of central Cork, entailing two further fatalities and loss of property worth several million pounds. As the divisional army commander remarked: 'Our own preliminary [inquiry] is not very good reading. The Auxiliary Company seems to have been all over the place.'[54] Several other fatal ambushes occurred during late 1920 and the first half of 1921, mainly in Munster and north Leinster. Yet improved security and intelligence made 'hits' less and less frequent, as Volunteer parties hovered behind ditches day after day in anticipation of convoys that never passed. The monthly diaries sent to Mulcahy by brigade and battalion commanders indicate an experience of frustration and stalemate comparable to that of soldiers on the western front four years earlier.

Volunteer tedium was however alleviated by development of the 'flying columns', whose initial *raison d'être* was the need for wanted men to 'go on the run'. The effective qualification for inclusion in these units was possession of a rifle, and the first duty of the column man was to protect his rifle from capture. Most ambushes were conducted by flying columns rather than regular Volunteer companies, though local Volunteers, and members of Cumann na mBan and the Fianna Éireann, were assigned the ancillary but indispensable tasks of signalling and intelligence. In between stunts, the flying columns had ample diversion as they moved from house to house, securing free bed and board from more or less willing residents. Released from the social constraints of life in their own neighbourhood and parish, the column men could smoke, drink, fraternise, brandish their rifles, strut like heroes, and inspire fear, admiration, or lust among their hosts. These were the cavalry or aviators of Ireland's rebel army; the poorly armed local Volunteers were the humble infantrymen sweating in the trenches. Tales of life in the column soon became part of Ireland's historical romance of incessant militarism, matching the glory of the United Irishmen, the Fenians, and the men of 1916. The casual and sponanteous genesis of the columns, and their self-sufficient ethos, made them resistant to both central and local discipline. Indeed, it was not until September 1920 and April 1921 that headquarters called for the attachment of regular columns to all brigades and battalions, respectively. Mulcahy's staff struggled gamely to assert control over the myriad local columns and Volunteer units by establishing ever more elaborate structures of inspection and discipline, culminating in the creation of sixteen divisions during early 1921. The result was to increase the co-ordination but not the submissiveness of the army's constituent parts. The independent spirit of column leaders like Barry and Breen was to outlast the truce, helping to tear the IRA apart in 1922.

The struggle for arms was supplemented by a more concerted campaign to immobilize the administration. This entailed cutting communications, raiding mails, stealing old-age pension payments, robbing banks, destroying public buildings, and terrorizing or killing 'enemy agents'. The cycle of mimetic violence was formalized in June 1921 by the introduction of systematic counter-reprisals against 'enemy' property. The most spectacular incidents involved the slaughter of fourteen alleged secret servicemen on 21 November 1920, and the burning of the Dublin Custom House on 25 May 1921. The first action, conducted by night marauders from Collins's 'Squad', mistargeted several ex-officers without intelligence assignments. It also provoked reprisals causing fifteen deaths ('Bloody Sunday'), and the massive reimposition of internment. The destruction of the Custom House (at de Valera's urging) was equally counter-productive, as a hundred members of the Dublin brigade were captured in exchange for the loss of a fine building and some departmental files.

During 1921, Collins's systematic elimination of unarmed magistrates, policemen, and civil servants in Dublin inspired ever more frequent provincial emulation, as armed targets grew less vulnerable. But for the cessation of fighting in July 1921, Collins would doubtless have succeeded in launching 'a regular, all round, well thought out onslaught on all the Departments' (with exceptions such as the post office, former employer of both Collins and Mulcahy).[55] As it was, the intimidation of unpaid magistrates was sufficient to cause the majority to neglect their duties and hundreds to resign their commissions, further immobilizing the conduct of justice. In addition, several hundred supposed 'informers' were murdered, sometimes in gruesome fashion, their bodies being buried in bogs or dumped in the sea. Though many of the dead had indeed tipped off the police or the Castle, others were the victims of rumours or paranoic assumptions. Adulterers, homosexuals, tinkers, beggars, ex-servicemen, Protestants: there were many dangerous and potentially lethal labels for Ireland's inhabitants in the revolutionary period. The increasing use of assassination discomfited the many Volunteers who regarded themselves as military men bound by the code of war—a code which in other armies had disappeared almost without trace during the carnage of the Great War. The purity of the fight had been sullied, even in republican consciousness, well before the truce.

As violence and bitterness intensified, Sinn Féin and the Dáil struggled to avoid contamination of the nationalist cause by social and sectarian rivalries. The republican administration, as indicated in the previous chapter, proved surprisingly effective until late 1920 in defusing class conflict through its courts, tribunals, and local councils. Thereafter, industrial and agricultural recession diminished both the allure and the practicability of collective action by workers or peasants. Sectarian animosities, however, were not so easily controlled. The line between sectarian and social conflict was always indistinct, since Protestants dominated the landed gentry and were heavily over-represented in banking, business, and manufacturing. Attacks on wealthy loyalists and their property might therefore be ascribed to political or economic motives rather than religious antipathy. Loyalist propaganda invariably attributed such outrages to sectarianism, an accusation deeply damaging to the republic's claim to universal allegiance from Irishmen and Irishwomen of every creed. Even more dangerous was the renewed antipathy between Belfast's Catholic and Protestant proletarians, their livelihood threatened by post-war recession in the engineering and shipbuilding industries upon which Belfast's prosperity depended. As unemployment loomed, competing groups of insecure workers faced each other across the familiar barricades of religion.

The predictable outcome, in July 1920, was yet another expulsion of workers mainly from Belfast's shipyards, affecting 5,500 Catholics and some 1,900 Protestants suspected of socialist or nationalist sympathies. A quarter of the victims were women, a slightly larger proportion were not unionized, and a substantial minority were skilled workers. Perhaps 700 Catholic ex-servicemen were expelled, having been 'poisoned by Sinn Féin propaganda' after demobilization; as one Protestant veteran informed a cheering crowd at Ballymacarrett, their places had been filled by 'over five hundred loyalists, most of them exservicemen'.[56] Redmond's dream of solidarity among fellow-sufferers in the Great War was finally shattered on the grimy pavements of Queen's Island and York Street. Within three months, eighty-two deaths resulted from the consequent riots and unrest. Some employers collaborated in this 'pogrom' by demanding a formal repudiation of republicanism from workers seeking reemployment. The expulsions facilitated a massive and permanent reduction in the shipyard workforce, and long after the creation of the province of Northern Ireland the army of unemployed 'expelled workers' remained a social and political embarrassment for the Unionist government.

The bitter confrontation of summer 1920 epitomized the peculiar character of sectarian conflict in Ulster, where the social gulf between combatants was often inconsiderable. Most Ulster Protestants as well as Catholics were wage-earners or small farmers, even though Protestants were more likely to secure higher wages and larger farms. Whenever economic hardship threatened, religious affiliation provided the most convenient discriminant for assembling rival factions in the scramble for scarce benefits. In political rhetoric, however, the consequent collisions were usually ascribed to non-economic motives. Loyalists asserted, and often believed, that the expelled Catholic workers were Sinn Féin infiltrators who had migrated from the south in order to undermine Protestant security. Republicans, desperate to deny irreversible antagonism between Ulster's Catholic and Protestant masses, ascribed the confrontation to religious bigotry on the part of Protestant employers.

This analysis justified the Dáil's imposition in August 1920 of a 'Belfast Boycott', whereby the Volunteers and the courts were mobilized against wholesalers, retailers, and even purchasers of goods produced by Belfast (and then Ulster) firms, in reprisal for the failure of Belfast employers to protect their Catholic workers. This boycott was accompanied by a demand for the withdrawal of deposits from banks based in Belfast. As usual, the decree was prompted by a local initiative, in Tuam, Co. Galway. The most furious advocate of a general 'embargo' upon Belfast was Seán MacEntee, the Belfast Catholic engineer and deputy for South Monaghan who was to become tánaiste (deputy premier) to Seán Lemass between 1959 and 1965. Equally vehement in opposition was the Dáil's token Ulster Protestant, Ernest Blythe, who warned that such a blockade would 'destroy for ever the possibility of any union'. Though Griffith secured a more selective boycott, its impact was sufficiently widespread to force closure even of the bagpipe factory run by Denis McCullough, former president of the IRB.[57] Though unwelcome to a few republicans like Blythe for its implication that Ulster was external to Ireland, the boycott was quite effective in reducing trade between north and south, and also in reinforcing Protestant conspiracy theories. Orange and loyalist organizations responded with a shadowy 'Southern Boycott' of uncertain impact, and the Dáil added an ineffectual 'English Boycott' for good measure.

The bloody collisions between Catholic and Protestant workers in Belfast had been preceded in June by sectarian riots in Derry, and were compounded by ever more frequent raids, attacks, and assaults against neighbours of different religion. So intense was the conflict in Ulster that in mid-1920 it seemed at least as menacing as the republican guerrilla campaign in Munster or Dublin. After a relative lull in early 1921, violent conflict resumed with even greater ferocity during the year after the Anglo-Irish ceasefire in July. The Dáil and the Volunteers could not avoid embroilment in the struggle, despite their determination to confront Britain rather than Protestant Ulster. The Volunteers, though weaker, less active, and more poorly armed in Ulster than in any other province except Connaught, enhanced their popularity by presenting themselves as defenders of Catholic civil liberties. In their rhetoric, if not their actions, they were at one with the still powerful Hibernians and the Catholic church. As in the campaign for civil rights in 1967–70, northern Protestant belligerence helped unify southern Catholics in righteous indignation, so providing a welcome distraction from the moral quandaries of the Anglo-Irish struggle.

Even without that surge of sympathetic emotion, however, the confluence of nationalist and sectarian conflict in Ulster could scarcely have been avoided. In September 1920, well before the enactment of partition, the English Unionist Sir Ernest Clark had been appointed assistant under-secretary in Belfast. This appointment reassured loyalists that Ulster would be shielded from the baneful influence of Sir John Anderson's fellow under-secretary in Dublin, James MacMahon (a Belfast Catholic, intimate with Cardinal Logue of Armagh). Clark remained in Northern Ireland as secretary to the treasury. In November, in a controversial attempt to mobilize civilians in defence of public order, the government commenced recruitment for a Special Constabulary with three divisions, involving different duties and levels of commitment. Recruitment to the new force was mainly assigned to the Ulster Volunteer Force (revived in June 1920), whose officers were routinely transferred to the Special Constabulary just as their predecessors had been recommissioned in the 36th division. Inevitably, ex-servicemen were predominant. Though not initially restricted either to Ulster or to Protestants, the bulk of the Special Constabulary was in practice the UVF reconstituted under an official name. For General Macready, this signified the 'raising of Carson's army from the grave'.[58] No more disciplined or law-abiding than the Black and Tans, the 'B Specials', in particular, methodically abused their privileges and powers in victimizing Catholic 'suspects'. The gentlemanly old guard of rural Orangeism, its influence waning fast, predictably deplored the wanton violence and unruliness of Protestantism's new plebeian protectors, themselves protected and armed by the government. By contrast with the regular constabulary, which in Ulster was predominantly Catholic and deeply unpopular among loyalists, the new force embodied Britain's belated blessing of bigotry. Long-standing communal rivalries, inflamed by armed gangs in various uniforms and disguises, ensured that in Ulster the 'Anglo-Irish' conflict began to take the shape of a sectarian civil war.

By late 1920, the prospect of retrieving peace in Ireland through further coercion seemed remote. Draconian legislation and unlawful 'reprisals' had failed to suppress militant republicanism, instead driving it underground and transforming ragged idealists into ever more efficient and ruthless terrorists. Since the greater sin always seemed to lie with the government and its agents, the effect of repression was to reinforce Catholic support for the Dáil and the Volunteers. Although the republicans failed to secure sufficient money, arms, or skills to gain military control

over most regions, their guerrilla campaign and immobilization
of the civil administration made it intolerably costly for the
crown forces to maintain their footing. Equally demoralizing
and politically damaging was the slide towards civil war in
Ulster, as the nightmare of 1914 approached realization. It was
the urgency and imminence of that threat which prompted
Lloyd George's government to seek a political settlement
through the partition of Ireland.

Partition, 1921–1922

The (Better) Government of Ireland act, passed in December
1920, provided for the creation of separate parliaments to
administer Home Rule in the six counties of Northern Ireland
and the twenty-six counties of Southern Ireland. With various
modifications, the division of services proposed under the
dormant act of 1914 was reapplied to the two proposed bicameral legislatures, each of which would be subordinate to the
imperial parliament and formally responsible to a lord lieutenant representing the monarch. Irish constituencies would
retain some parliamentary representation at Westminster, so signifying the continued adherence of both states to the modified
Union. Subject to the familiar constraints upon religious discrimination, each parliament would control domestic services
including education, local government, justice, social welfare,
economic agencies, and eventually policing. Westminster was to
retain control over foreign policy, external trade, the armed services, coinage, and the post office. Major sources of revenue such
as income tax, customs duties, and excise duties on manufactures
would continue to be paid into the consolidated fund of the
United Kingdom, and an imperial contribution would be levied
on each province.

The 'Partition act' broke with precedent by applying Home
Rule to Northern Ireland, instead of simply excluding six counties from Dublin's jurisdiction, or else creating a Belfast assembly subordinate to Dublin and thence to Westminster. Those
options no longer seemed viable, having formed the basis of

repeated and fruitless negotiations in 1914 and 1916, not to mention the Irish Convention of 1917–18. Partition, though no less repellent to nationalists than exclusion, had compelling advantages for northern loyalists as well as for the government. It offered Unionists power over a restricted territory, while absolving the British government of direct responsibility for the application of that power. These arguments were sufficiently forceful to secure the agreement of Carson and Craig, and general if unenthusiastic acquiescence among their followers in Ulster. For northern Catholics, an embattled minority sidelined by all the major protagonists, subjection to northern Protestant control was an even less agreeable prospect than perpetuation of 'direct rule' under the Union.

The apparent equity in the treatment of Southern and Northern Ireland was a sham that deceived nobody. Instead of trying to induce nationalists to accept Home Rule in the form specified, Dublin Castle and the government dropped hints of a more favourable southern settlement once the northern crisis had been resolved. The act itself included provision for a Council of Ireland, which was eventually to administer railways, fisheries, and the control of animal contagions, and to which further services could be transferred by consent of both provincial parliaments. The powers of the Council might even be transferred to a united parliament, whereupon certain additional functions would be surrendered by Westminster. While the act pursued its leisurely course through parliament, Lloyd George's emissaries floated ambitious schemes for 'Dominion Home Rule', whereby a southern state would assume the superior status and some of the wide-ranging powers of Canada or Australia. Aside from earnest but unpopular lobbies such as Sir Horace Plunkett's Irish Dominion League (June 1919), no major political body expressed interest in such a compromise during 1920. Even so, the spiral of coercion and terrorism did not extinguish British attempts to identify reliable and representative parties with whom to negotiate. Agents such as Andy Cope dealt increasingly with Sinn Féin and Volunteer leaders instead of well-meaning worthies, abandoning bureaucratic etiquette in favour of casual

chats in republican tap-rooms. The search for a negotiated settlement was aided by mediators as diverse as Archbishop Clune of
Perth, the 17th earl of Derby, and the South African prime minister, General Jan Christiaan Smuts. In a touching if limp gesture
of pluralism, Viscount French was replaced in May 1921 by an
English Catholic and former Unionist chief whip, the newly
elevated Viscount FitzAlan of Derwent. Yet no public progress
towards peace was achieved before the appointed day for inaugurating Home Rule in both Dublin and Belfast.

Nominations for the southern House of Commons closed on
24 May 1921, coinciding with the election which inaugurated
Home Rule in Northern Ireland. In the north, as the wife of the
future cabinet secretary gleefully observed, the elections were
'an astonishing success, every single Unionist candidate who was
put up, being returned'. Lady Spender was delighted that peace
at the poll had been so firmly maintained by 10,000 dutiful Specials, although she regretted the rashness of a local yacht club in
'celebrating' the event with a volley of shots.[59] Almost nine-
tenths of the electorate cast their votes. The outcome was a
triumph of discipline for the Orange Institution, whose members
in Newtownards, Co. Down, had been sternly instructed that 'it
was their duty as loyal Orange men and women to see that the
official candidates for Parliament were returned. They must vote
and work for them, whether they liked them personally or not.'[60]
Northern Ireland's first prime minister was Sir James Craig, who
had replaced Carson as Ulster Unionist leader in February 1921.
When resigning in consequence as grand master of the Loyal
Orange Institution of England, Craig had memorably affirmed
that 'my heart is always in the Orange'.[61] Apart from the forty
Unionists, the new House of Commons contained six Sinn
Féiners and six constitutional nationalists who all 'abstained'
from attendance. With a single abstentionist exception, every
senator was a Protestant Unionist. George V therefore received
a loyal welcome when he opened the northern parliament on 22
June, although his appeal for peace and reconciliation (drafted
by General Smuts) did not arouse universal enthusiasm among
his Ulster subjects.

In southern constituencies, 124 abstentionist Sinn Féiners were elected unopposed, leaving the four 'Independent' but Unionist representatives of Dublin University to bemoan their insufficiency to form a quorum. In August 1921, the republican deputies and a single northern Sinn Féiner (Seán O'Mahoney) instead convened the Second Dáil, which drew authority from the presence of many of the most active guerrilla fighters. Even the nominated Senate succeeded in meeting only twice, and no government of Southern Ireland was ever constituted. This fiasco reinforced the demand for a settlement with Sinn Féin, the king's address providing an excuse for formerly diehard ministers to announce their conversion to open-mindedness. After nearly a year of abortive informal negotiation and constitutional stalemate, a meeting was arranged between de Valera and Lloyd George. General Macready and Volunteer representatives agreed to a ceasefire commencing on 11 July, the day before Southern Ireland was due to be declared a crown colony under martial law, by virtue of its failure to implement Home Rule.

The five months between the truce and the Anglo-Irish treaty were critical to the development of the two nascent states. Northern Home Rule was institutionalized at breakneck speed, as Sir James Craig and his Unionist ministry sought successfully to make the 'province' impregnable before the perfidious Welshman could seal a deal with Sinn Féin. After fruitless negotiations with de Valera in early May 1921, Craig had abandoned pursuit of any compromise with Sinn Féin. His ministers were mainly Orangemen with proud records of defiance in the pre-war UVF, the northern equivalent of service in the 1916 Rising. Sympathetic officials, co-ordinated by the cabinet secretary Sir Wilfrid Spender, achieved a fairly smooth and rapid transfer of administrative services to the new northern departments, despite recurrent rumours that Lloyd George was retarding the transfer of powers as a prelude to dismantling Northern Ireland. Unionist confidence was further shaken in November by Craig himself, when he urged an incredulous British cabinet to maintain equity between the two Irish constitutions by extending dominion status to the northern state. This bold if perplexing redefinition of Unionism had the presumably intended effect of securing Lloyd George's assurance that Northern Ireland's rights under Home Rule would not be abrogated without her consent.[62] Craig's domestic priority was to suppress disorder and outrage, a task mainly assigned to the remobilized B Specials while the army and the regular RIC sat out the truce. Over twenty deaths had occurred in northern riots during the week following agreement on the ceasefire, and disturbances recurred during the transitional months. The divisional commissioner of police in Belfast lived in trepidation of a republican invasion 'in the event of a break in the Truce'. The B Specials had therefore to be held ready for mobilization against any such 'sudden attack against the Northern counties'.[63] From late November, formal control of all police forces passed to the northern government, the regular police being reconstituted six months later as the Royal Ulster Constabulary. Having declined to participate in further constitutional discussions in Dublin or London, Craig methodically set about consolidating Protestant power in the new state.

Meanwhile, the republicans used the ceasefire to prepare for government, whether with or without an agreement. The Volunteers, now generally termed the IRA, were at last able to parade in public, recruit thousands of 'Truciliers' eager to show their patriotism at reduced personal risk, undertake systematic training, buy additional arms, and consolidate central control of the organization. By the end of 1921, Volunteer inspections had revealed a membership of over 70,000, concentrated as always in Munster.[64] The most convincing evidence of the IRA's assertion of central control was the effective implementation of the most critical element of the truce, only one policeman having been killed after mid-July. The army commander in Munster nevertheless complained that 'apart from the actual murder of members of the Crown Forces, the rebels have not complied with any of the terms of the agreement'.[65] Regardless of the continued prohibition of illegal assemblies, the republican administration was reactivated, enabling the courts and local councils to operate openly and quite effectively. The Second Dáil conducted its widely reported proceedings with increasing pomp and formality, giving added gloss to de Valera by at last appointing him president of the republic as well as the ministry (August 1921). Admittedly, the division of authority between the Dáil, the Volunteers, and the IRB remained unclear, despite the IRB's surrender of its claim to the presidency (September 1919), the widespread administration of an oath to the republic by the Volunteers (August 1920), and the Dáil's retrospective 'acceptance of a state of war with England' and responsibility for the guerrilla campaign (March 1921).[66] Public unity was secured by the ministerial activity of military and conspiratorial leaders such as Collins and Mulcahy, though the ministry's attempt to assert the Dáil's military supremacy by recommissioning the officer corps met with obdurate resistance from local chieftains. Nevertheless, de Valera was increasingly able to present himself as the accredited spokesman for all major republican interests, thus greatly enhancing his authority as a negotiator.

For many republicans, the truce initially offered a welcome opportunity for rest and regrouping rather than a pathway to constitutional settlement. Even without the *fait accompli* of partition, the promise of expanded Home Rule or dominion status would have seemed hopelessly irreconcilable with the republican demand. The failure of de Valera's meetings with Lloyd George between 14 and 21 July fostered further scepticism. The revolutionaries therefore sought to strengthen their administrative and military organization in preparation, not for peace, but for resumed conflict. As in 1917, De Valera's peculiar blend of superficial inflexibility with profound opportunism was crucial in gradually persuading republicans that an acceptable settlement was possible. The pressure for serious negotiation was strengthened by popular relief and delight at the end of hostilities, as churchmen, businessmen, and farmers rediscovered the conveniences of peace. As in all ceasefires, however, public opinion alone would not have prevented a resumption of fighting had this been sought by any major faction of the republican military élite.

After prolonged and awkward preliminary exchanges, the

ministry agreed in mid-September to send a deputation to London, which commenced two months of taxing discussions with senior British ministers on 11 October. Both parties proclaimed their internal unity and seriousness of purpose by selecting some of their most warlike leaders as negotiators. Lloyd George headed a cabinet delegation including Churchill (the belligerent colonial secretary) and his successor at the war office, Sir Worthington Lamar Worthington-Evans, 1st Bt. Lloyd George's six associates were evenly divided between Liberals and Unionists. Diehard Irish republicans were reassured by the selection of Collins, along with Griffith and the lawyers George Gavan Duffy and Eamonn Duggan. The remaining Irish delegate was Robert Childers Barton, a landed gentleman from Annamoe in Wicklow, cousin of Erskine Childers, and former army officer who had been commissioned on the wrong side in April 1916, only to become republican director of agriculture. De Valera himself cannily remained in Ireland to preside over the home administration, while confusingly instructing his 'plenipotentiaries' to submit any draft agreement for approval by the full ministry before signing it.

By unanimously agreeing to enter negotiations, the Dáil implicitly accepted the impracticability of immediately achieving either a united Irish dominion or a southern republic. Sinn Féin's acceptance of compromise depended on two hazardous calculations, concerning the potential for future constitutional evolution, and the severity of the penalties likely to result from failure to compromise. While virtually all revolutionary leaders could contemplate working towards a republic of thirty-two counties from an initial condition of restricted autonomy, there was no consensus as to the maximum endurable degree of restriction. Nor did republican strategists agree on the likelihood of resumed conflict, or on its probable outcome, should the negotiations collapse. The negotiations were framed by two proposals: the British government's offer of dominion status for Southern Ireland, and the Dáil's demand for a unified sovereign state linked to the empire by 'external association', symbolized by acknowledgement of the monarch as 'head of the Association'. Lloyd George maintained that formal subjection to the monarch, through a governor-general and an oath of allegiance, was a modest price for effective autonomy on the Canadian model. By contrast, de Valera proposed collaboration with the empire in matters of 'common concern', in return for the token recognition of Irish sovereignty. Each party was thus intent on deflecting accusations of apostasy by maintaining the desired forms, while offering significant concessions in substance. During the protracted, intricate, and often bitter discussions, only minor attention was given to modifying the practical restrictions associated with dominion status. By contrast, elaborate and ingenious formulas were devised to allow both parties to save face with their deeply suspicious constituencies. The oath of allegiance to the monarch was modified to one of fidelity, allegiance being reserved for the future constitution of the 'Irish Free State'. Most crucially, the future of partition was left unresolved.

On 6 December 1921, the Irish delegation unanimously if grudgingly accepted an amended form of the 'articles of agreement' for a 'Treaty between Great Britain and Ireland' (a remarkable form of words, designed to reassure republicans that sovereignty had not after all been surrendered). The autonomy granted by the treaty went well beyond Home Rule by granting fiscal autonomy without explicit insistence on free trade within the British Isles, allowing creation of a 'military defence force', envisaging future Irish involvement in coastal defence, and neglecting to reserve key services such as currency and the post office. Even so, the Irish Free State was submitted to several impositions unknown in the dominions, including continued control of various ports and harbours by the Admiralty, and liability to a share in the public debt of the United Kingdom. The provisions for Northern Ireland further diminished Irish sovereignty, despite the formal application of the treaty to the entire country. While republican pride was salved by an elaborate but irrelevant scheme for northern Home Rule within the Free State, loyalist interests were protected by the opt-out clause. Should the northern parliament so address the monarch within a month of ratification, its powers were to be perpetuated, subject only to the possible convening of the fanciful Council of Ireland and the creation of a boundary commission. Since that commission was charged only with determining the border 'in accordance with the wishes of the inhabitants, so far as may be compatible with economic and geographic conditions', there was no sound reason to expect that the casting vote of a British-appointed chairman would support any but the most minor alterations.[67] Even so, this judicious deployment of waffle proved remarkably effective in placating republican cavils and raising false hopes of future unification. Until the collapse of the boundary commission in December 1925, nationalists continued to predict the drastic contraction of the northern state and thence its disintegration.

Signature of the agreement was greeted with cautious but widespread acclaim in both islands, the promise of peace being of greater public concern than the constitutional forms. The coalition government had surprisingly little difficulty in persuading once intransigent Unionists to accept the treaty as the lesser evil, while northern Protestants paid little heed to a settlement that left their territorial interests undisturbed. The major objections came from within the revolutionary élite, for whom unflagging resistance to British oppression had become an accustomed and often exhilarating way of life. Many flying column leaders and local republican heroes were understandably loath to revert to civilian ordinariness or submit to the authority of any Dublin government. The strongest resistance came from Munster, where the guerrilla campaign had been most intense, effective, and therefore prestigious. Hardened veterans such as Tom Barry, Liam Lynch, and Liam Deasy were far more confident than their counterparts in less active regions of holding their own, should the conflict resume. The agreement was however supported by a majority of the headquarters staff, its advocacy by Collins being crucial in securing the support of many key fighters and IRB organizers. Even so, neither the IRA nor the Brotherhood was sufficiently disciplined to offer solid support. The supreme council maintained the façade of unity only by declining to assert its authority over sworn Brothers in the Dáil, while the already fractured Volunteers soon began to disintegrate. Corresponding divisions appeared in other republican bodies such as Sinn Féin, Cumann na mBan, and, most crucially, the Dáil.

The Second Dáil was largely composed of Volunteer officers who had achieved prominence before May 1921, and its protracted debates on the terms of agreement provide unrivalled insight into the varieties of militant mentality. The rhetorical focus of opposition was the formal abandonment of Irish sovereignty, exemplified by the oath of fidelity to the monarch. Among the most self-righteous defenders of the republic was Cathal Brugha, the minister for defence, whose power and celebrity had been cruelly eclipsed by the unorthodox Collins. Yet even Brugha was conscious of his own vulnerability to the charge that the cabinet, by entering negotiations and contemplating 'external association', had compromised the republican demand from the outset. He therefore insisted that the difference between external association and the terms of the treaty was that between 'a draught of water and a draught of poison'.[68] The purest expositions of republican faith came from those choosing to speak on behalf of the dead, who had been released from the temptations of compromise. These invocations came primarily from female deputies, whose nomination had in most cases resulted from the death of a husband, brother, or son. Even Constance Markievicz adopted a keening tone, in summoning forth the 'voices of men from the grave, who call on us to die for the cause they died for'. 'For God's sake and the sake of the dead let us keep together', cried Terence MacSwiney's sister Mary.[69] The widow of Michael O'Callaghan, the ex-mayor of Limerick murdered in March 1921, challenged any deputy 'to deny my husband's devotion to the Republic, a devotion he sealed with his blood'. Mrs Margaret Pearse refuted the speculation 'that Pádraig Pearse would have accepted this Treaty. I deny it. As his mother I deny it, and on his account I will not accept it.'[70] Though such invocations invited and prompted ridicule and misogynist sneers, they illustrate a significant element of Irish nationalist ideology. Since the nation embraced all Irish people, whether living, dead, or unborn, its fate could not properly be consigned to its living representatives alone. Yeats's 'dead men' loitered about the Mansion House, still stirring 'the boiling pot'.[71]

The treaty's leading opponent was no great-hearted if simple-minded guerrilla hero, but the Dáil's most celebrated casuist and tactician, President de Valera. His repudiation of the agreement split the cabinet and astonished most observers, permanently alienating de Valera from his closest crony in the Catholic hierarchy, Bishop Michael Fogarty of Killaloe. Though disingenuously presented as an unwavering defence of the sacred principle of external association against the dominion betrayal, de Valera's objection was neither pig-headed nor irrational. His primary concern was to offer substantial concessions to 'the enemy' without alienating the militant zealots and so splitting the republican movement. De Valera believed, perhaps falsely, that the ingenious formula of external association would be accepted by republicans as affirming Irish sovereignty in addition to promising practical evolution towards full independence. He further asserted that the British government could be persuaded to renegotiate the agreement on these terms, and that Lloyd George's threat of 'immediate and terrible war' had been a bluff which Griffith and Collins failed to call. De Valera's rambling addresses to the 'private sessions' of the Dáil indicate, however, that he was not fully confident in these assumptions. While he believed 'that with such a countermove war would not ensue', he gave priority to the maintenance of republican unity in case it should again be necessary 'to get the nation to fight'.[72] De Valera was probably correct in assuming that the treaty terms would have split the revolutionary movement, even without his own public opposition. He might also have succeeded, as at Sinn Féin's ard fheis of 1917, in persuading republican firebrands such as Cathal Brugha to accept the need for compromise. It seems unlikely, however, that Lloyd George's tottering coalition would have renegotiated the agreement, at least without a further burst of coercion under martial law and colonial rule.

The fact that de Valera's alternative proposals differed so little in substance from the treaty added further bitterness to the debates, since his objection was easily if misleadingly construed as a mere quibble. De Valera, like Griffith and Collins, was prepared to accept involvement with the empire in return for immediate possession of twenty-six counties, and the hope of future constitutional evolution. His initial acceptance of the retention of Northern Ireland, though soon severely qualified under republican pressure, prevented a clear division of principle over partition. Even in its qualified form, de Valera's document expressed the 'desire not to bring force or coercion to bear upon any substantial part of the province of Ulster', while denying 'the right of any part of Ireland to be excluded from the supreme authority of the Parliament of Ireland'. He further devised an ambiguous undertaking to provide 'that portion of Ulster' with 'privileges and safeguards not less substantial' than those in the treaty.[73] These 'safeguards' (specified in article 22) concerned the status of Northern Ireland should it adopt the unlikely course of accepting Home Rule within the Irish Free State. Republicans could equate the term 'privileges' with the innocuous 'safeguards'; whereas Britain might conceivably assume that those privileges included the option of preserving Northern Ireland within the Union. By such sleight of hand, de Valera seems to have supposed that he could conjure unity as well as peace.

While Griffith and Collins had likewise hoped to maintain national unity in favour of their agreement, their strategy once that unity had collapsed was to retain the support of key organizers, marginalize de Valera, and mobilize public opinion. Collins's argument was pragmatic and persuasive, carrying the authority of the republic's most admired military organizer. The Volunteers, dependent on about 3,000 rifle-bearing activists and still poorly organized and armed, were unfit to resume war; Britain, as indicated by its response to resistance throughout the colonial empire, was still capable of wrecking Ireland; the agreement offered the best obtainable terms, with the prospect of evolution towards broader sovereignty. The revolutionaries had not fought for a particular form of government, but for self-determination, or the freedom to achieve 'ultimate freedom'.

Though differing in their vision of 'ultimate freedom', most supporters of the treaty adopted the rhetoric of common sense
rather than ethereal principle. Eoin O'Duffy found the prospect
of peace rather daunting, since 'the only pleasure in freedom is
fighting for it'. Yet, as Mulcahy's deputy chief of staff, he
acknowledged 'a big responsibility' for averting further loss of
Irish manpower. The treaty was a 'stepping stone' towards the
republic—not, as de Valera maintained, 'a barrier in the way to
complete independence'.[74]

According to Kevin O'Higgins, soon to become minister for
home affairs and Cosgrave's steely vice-president until his assassination in 1927, 'the fact that we were willing to negotiate
implied that we had something to give away'. This view was
expressed more pithily by Seán MacEoin, the belligerent black-
smith of Ballinalee, Co. Longford, who became army chief of
staff in 1928–9 and twice failed to become president. Speaking
'as a plain soldier' who realized that 'if England goes to war
again she will wipe all out', Collins's wrestling partner declared
that 'there is not a man in the Dáil from the President down but
has eaten principles from the start (Hear, hear). There is not one
who has stood definitely for the ideal that was before us.'[75] In
the absence of simple divisions on principle, the split centred on
the relative risk of resuming the Anglo-Irish conflict in case of
rejection, or precipitating civil war among nationalists in case of
acceptance. Given the intricacy of these calculations, it is not surprising that the Dáil was almost evenly divided. The agreement
was approved by 64 votes to 57 on 7 January 1922, de Valera's
re-election as president being subsequently rejected by a slightly
smaller margin. The architects of the treaty were therefore faced
not only with creating a Free State of ill-defined constitution out
of the rubble of revolution, but also with stemming the drift
towards civil conflict.

The twin tasks of implementing the agreement and conciliating its opponents created extraordinary political and institutional confusion. The treaty required ratification not by the Dáil
but by the House of Commons of Southern Ireland, elected in
June 1921 but never convened, and equivalent in membership

to those representing southern constituencies in the Dáil. The Commons met only once, ratifying the agreement after its approval by the Dáil, and in the absence of its opponents. It also appointed a provisional government, charged with preparing a constitution, holding elections for the new parliament, and progressively taking over the machinery of administration. Collins became president of the provisional government, but Griffith replaced de Valera as president of the Dáil ministry in a gesture designed to reaffirm the essential republicanism of those supporting the treaty. This gave extra force to de Valera's sneer that 'you are voting for it because you don't mean to obey it',[76] a suggestion confirmed by Collins's abortive electoral pact with de Valera (May 1922) and the associated attempt to smuggle popular sovereignty into the draft constitution. Both the Dáil and its ministry soon fell into abeyance, practical responsibility being exercised by the provisional government. The transfer of administrative services and personnel got underway with startling haste, sometimes even before British ratification of the treaty. Dublin Castle, government offices, police, and military barracks were more or less ceremoniously surrendered, creating a lasting image of Michael Collins in military uniform as Ireland's latest janitor, jangling innumerable rusty keys presented to him by red-faced generals, star-struck police officers, and bashful bureaucrats.

Within six months of the signature of the treaty, the partition of Ireland was complete in all but form. On 13 March 1922, the northern cabinet had resolved 'to safeguard itself by exercising its option to vote out after the passing of the "Treaty" Bill'.[77] On 31 March, the treaty was ratified by a statute requiring that the 'Parliament of Southern Ireland' be dissolved within four months and replaced by a new assembly for the twenty-six counties, to which the provisional government would be responsible.[78] This 'provisional parliament' was elected on 16 June, a draft constitution having been accepted by the British government after drastic amendment of that initially proposed. In the midst of the civil war that followed, the constitution was approved by the provisional parliament on 25 October, and given statutory force at Westminster on 5 December. Next day, as the treaty required, the Irish Free State was formally inaugurated. The character of the two new states was profoundly affected by the turmoil following approval of the treaty, state authority being ruthlessly consolidated at the expense of individual liberty. That story, however, belongs to the 'legacies of revolution' analysed in Part II.

Yet, even before the bitter conflict and bloodshed of 1922, the priorities of Ireland's revolutionaries had been tested and exposed. Virtually all Ulster loyalists, and most Irish republicans, had set aside their respective principles in order to secure partial control over part of Ireland. Despite their mutual antipathy, loyalists and nationalists (both constitutional and republican) had conducted their revolutions along remarkably similar lines, imitating each other to the point of parody. Both protagonists had relied upon massive popular mobilization through fraternities and other networks serving social as well as political functions. Both had combined shrewd campaigns of propaganda with the menace of physical force, showing little respect for democratic niceties. Through the accident of world war in 1914, the Ulster Unionists had achieved their revolutionary settlement without the expected civil war. The same factor, compounded by the unpredictable shock of the Easter Rising and the consequent cycle of violence and counter-violence, had transformed the nationalists' long-running constitutional revolution into a bloody conflict. The possibility of accomplishing both revolutions without extensive bloodshed had always been remote, though many nationalists as well as loyalists had glimpsed that mirage in August 1914. The effect of partition was to reduce (but not to eliminate) the risk of renewed Anglo-Irish conflict, while leaving ample potential for civil wars and border wars in Ireland itself. Even today, that potential has not been exhausted.

PART II

Legacies of Revolution:
Ireland, 1922–1939

Civil Wars, 1922–1923

Like most political 'settlements', partition redirected but failed to resolve the antagonisms that engendered it. The terms of settlement left almost all parties more or less dissatisfied, while encouraging dissident groups to challenge the legitimacy of Irish rather than British authorities. Yet dissent occurs and endures in every society, erupting into violent confrontation only under abnormal conditions. The rational dissentient is unlikely to rebel if alternative mechanisms for political reform are available, or if the wherewithal for effective rebellion is unavailable, or if the repressive power of the state makes rebellion risky enough. An efficiently coercive state may succeed for long periods in averting armed rebellion, even if its antagonists are thoroughly alienated from the political process. Such was the case of Northern Ireland between 1923 and 1969, after a brief but bloody challenge to Unionist supremacy. By contrast, violence may all too easily engulf even a conciliatory and accommodating regime, if the agencies of control are sufficiently feeble. Where the state apparatus is undeveloped, both the risks entailed by rebellion and the benefits of peaceable political participation seem minor. It may be argued that these conditions applied in the nascent Irish Free State, whose founders faced the daunting task of restoring civic order in a country where revolution had thoroughly subverted respect for almost every instrument of authority. In the process of overcoming the armed republican challenge, the new government imitated its northern neighbour by rapidly creating a rough but all too ready engine of repression. The civil war of 1922–3 was at once the outcome of the state's initial weakness, and the origin of its subsequent repressiveness. The extent to which the democratic process in both states survived and recovered after these bloody initiations would be repeatedly tested over the two decades following the two civil wars.

In the first half of 1922, it was by no means obvious what forms of armed conflict, if any, would disturb the post-revolutionary settlement. Despite its head start in organizing a paramilitary police force and its access to British military support, the northern government initially seemed incapable of suppressing sectarian riots and guerrilla attacks by the renascent IRA. Having largely escaped civil war and civic breakdown during the Anglo-Irish conflict, the six counties belatedly faced that nightmare after the truce of 11 July 1921. As usual, the seasonal celebrations scheduled for the following day (the Twelfth) provided a focus for sectarian animosities already heightened by Catholic anticipation of Protestant persecution, and Protestant fear of Catholic subversion, following the creation of the northern government. Private armies on both sides ensured that tension was translated into violence and murder. With the police and army under restraint during the truce, the hitherto rather quiescent northern divisions of the IRA were flooded with recruits under the mistaken impression 'that we had been victorious and that the Specials and U.V.F. were beaten'. As the commanding officer in the Belfast region recollected nostalgically in mid-1922, 'the perfecting of our organisation, training, and equipping had been pursued with great earnestness on the part of all officers and men' during the months of optimism preceding the treaty agreement.[1] Disregarding the truce, the IRA became involved in attacks on the police and in the 'defence' of northern Catholics from September onwards. Since their main antagonists were not British oppressors but Irish Protestant vigilantes with Special Constabulary uniforms or arm-bands, the armed republicans were inexorably if reluctantly converted into Catholic vigilantes.

The riots, killings, burnings, and economic conflicts initiated in mid-1920 resumed with increased ferocity after the truce, leaving well over 100 dead in Belfast during 1921 compared with about 70 in 1920. Sectarian and political violence peaked in 1922, when nearly 300 murders were officially enumerated in Northern Ireland. The murder count exceeded 30 in each month between February and June, rising to 80 in May before subsiding to a trickle after September.[2] According to one of several conflicting estimates, over 550 murders occurred throughout the province during the two years ending in July 1922, including about 80 members of the crown forces, 300 Catholic civilians and rebels, and 170 Protestants. All but 100 of these murders were committed in Belfast. Despite the contending political rhetoric of 'loyalism' and 'anti-partitionism', the conflict had degenerated into a sectarian civil war prefiguring the still more horrific 'troubles' of our own times. The frequency of 'outrages' of all categories declined sharply after 1922, a year even more notable for political crime than the climactic period of Anglo-Irish conflict between October 1920 and July 1921. In 1923 and 1924, the number of reported outrages declined to about a third of the 1922 peak, the improvement being most evident in Belfast, which accounted for 57 per cent of outrages in 1922 but less than half in the two succeeding years. The incidence of malicious injury to property diminished still more rapidly, from over 1,500 cases in 1922 to less than 200 in the following year.[3] Despite its brevity and marked concentration in a single city, civil conflict in Northern Ireland had generated almost as much destruction and half as many killings as the Anglo-Irish war.

The reduction in disorder was largely accountable to systematic repression, spearheaded by the Special Constabulary. Notwithstanding its strong predilection for pursuing Catholic rather than Protestant miscreants, and the unmistakable involvement of errant members and units in illegal 'reprisals', the force played a critical part in suppressing sectarian violence and subduing the northern divisions of the IRA. Once remobilized in late September 1921, the 'Specials' became the most active security force on the streets of Belfast and, by degrees, throughout the province. By mid-1922, their strength had reached 32,000, though enlistment was sluggish for the new Royal Ulster Constabulary which replaced the disbanded RIC on 31 May. The most draconian instrument of coercion was the

Civil Authorities (Special Powers) act of 7 April 1922 (activated on 22 May), which in some respects outdid the punitive provisions of the Restoration of Order in Ireland act. Initially for one year, but eventually for half a century, the minister of home affairs was enabled 'to take all such steps and issue all such orders as may be necessary for preserving the peace', and to delegate his boundless authority to any police officer.

Though excluding trial of civilians by courts martial or other special tribunals, the application of the act involved the familiar apparatus of internment, prohibition of meetings and organizations, exclusion from designated areas, raids on houses, and imposition of curfews (applied to the entire province in June 1922 and maintained throughout 1923). The provisions for execution remained dormant, but numerous (mainly Catholic) offenders were flogged. By the end of 1924, over 700 internees had spent time aboard the *Argenta* on Belfast Lough. The principal target of repression was the IRA, but loyalist bands such as the unusually vicious Ulster Protestant Association (founded in East Belfast in autumn 1920) were also eventually suppressed. While breaches of public order under more conventional legislation diminished, the number of convictions under the Special Powers legislation remained roughly stable (exceeding 3,000 annually) between 1922 and 1924. Though eventually effective in subduing 'outrage' and terrorism, the systematic application of discriminatory coercion further estranged Catholic nationalists from the northern government and state.

The state's survival had been critically threatened by the hostility and recurrent irredentism of the provisional government as well as its republican opponents. Both contending parties in the south aimed to destabilize Craig's administration, in order to accelerate the unification of Ireland. Partly in the hope of retrieving support from militant republicans, Collins adopted a double-edged and devious northern policy which generated enduring mistrust among loyalists. As he wrote to an adviser in Co. Londonderry in February 1922: 'We must have a policy of peace and a policy of war for the North-East. The accepted policy for the moment is peace, and we must give peace a chance.'[4] In practice, Collins tried to apply both policies in tandem. The 'policy of peace' was incorporated in two agreements with Craig's government, brokered by Churchill and signed on 21 January and 30 March 1922. The first 'pact' required termination of the southern boycott of Belfast products in exchange for the restoration of expelled Catholic workers and the removal of religious and political tests by northern employers. Following the failure of both governments to secure these objectives, the second pact specified a more elaborate but equally ineffectual programme for ending republican violence, sectarian policing, and discriminatory employment.

The 'policy of war' was never overtly implemented, but had enduring allure for many supporters as well as opponents of the treaty. During the truce in August 1921, Mulcahy's deputy Eoin O'Duffy had told the Dáil in private session that 'as far as they in Ulster were concerned they thought force should be used in Ulster. There were sufficient Volunteers in Belfast to hold it for Ireland.' In Armagh, he had further assured a Sinn Féin rally that if Unionists persisted in being 'against Ireland', the army 'would have to tighten that screw [the boycott] and, if necessary, they would have to use the lead against them'. These threats lend a certain disingenuousness to O'Duffy's affirmation in public session, on 4 January 1922, that 'no one in this House, I think, suggests now, or ever suggested, that Ulster should be coerced.'[5] After the split, the provisional government made little effort to prevent either faction of the IRA from carrying out raids and terrorist attacks against northern targets. These incidents included the kidnap of forty mid-Ulster Orangemen and Unionists a week after the first pact; attacks causing twenty-seven deaths in Belfast in mid-February; and the IRA's attempt in late March to reimpose and 'drastically enforce' the Belfast boycott. Loyalist indignation was deepened by the murder of over a dozen Protestants in west Cork, and by a multitude of assaults, house-burnings, and other outrages against southern Protestants of all classes. The justified suspicion that Collins had limited power to control either the IRA command or its northern units only reinforced northern alienation: either his government was impotent, and therefore worthless as a negotiating partner; or else deceitful, and therefore unworthy.

The second interpretation gained force on 17 May, when the IRA initiated a military campaign against the six counties with the clandestine but explicit connivance of the national army. Most activists in the key northern divisions had accepted the treaty and the authority of Mulcahy and O'Duffy, who had managed to replace two dissident commanders without causing massive defection. Collins had already agreed to supply Liam Lynch, chief of staff for the dissident IRA, with arms to replace those sent to the northern divisions; when northern incapacity to use these weapons became evident, training was provided at the Curragh. The campaign entailed attacks on police barracks, the burning of several great and numerous smaller houses, and murders such as that of the Unionist member for West Belfast (the draper William John Twaddell). The most menacing action was the brief occupation by national forces of the Catholic village of Belleek, Co. Fermanagh, which resulted in a confrontation with British troops sent to Protestant Pettigo, just across the border in Donegal. A force of Fermanagh Special Constables under Sir Basil Brooke of Colebrooke (a former hussar and future prime minister) had failed to secure a defensive position after attacks by Irregular troops occupying the 'triangle' of northern territory north-west of the Erne. This 'invasion', less risible than generally believed, had caused the death of three Specials and seven IRA men, as well as prompting British occupation of a scrap of the Free State until August 1924.[6]

On 3 June, the provisional government resolved to discountenance and even try to prevent future invasions, instead adopting an almost equally threatening policy of 'peaceful obstruction'.[7] The proposed abandonment of the 'policy of war' was ineffectual, as shown by outrages such as the killing of six loyalists in Altnaveigh, Co. Armagh, by a group of southern terrorists in police uniforms (17 June). Pondering a raider's claim that this was 'done for the Roman Catholics of Belfast', one of the victims reportedly gasped out to his sister: 'Don't call them brutes; perhaps they had to do it. Don't send the Specials after them. I forgive them, and I hope God will forgive them, too. I am going to Jesus.'[8] Suspicions of the southern government's complicity in terrorism were revived five days later by the murder in Belgravia of Sir Henry Wilson, then military adviser to the northern cabinet.

The subsequent reduction in border conflict was partly attributable to the outbreak of civil war in the south, which encouraged redeployment of all available nationalist forces in mutual destruction rather than collaborative excursions. After their disbandment, most of the 'Ulster Exiles' who had been in training at the Curragh never returned to face arrest in Northern Ireland, instead enrolling in the national army to fight the Irregulars (or in some cases the reverse). Yet even before the civil war, the punitive response of the Specials and irregular paramilitary squads had evidently demoralized the northern divisions and so undermined the basis of military intervention. The formal decision to abandon the faltering offensive was taken by northern divisional officers and GHQ on 9 July 1922, after just over a week of southern civil war.[9] Northern fear of renewed military aggression was slow to disappear, being fostered by the formal survival of two northern divisions under Mulcahy's control until March 1923, and by the interception in Fermanagh, five months earlier, of a national army captain already implicated in ambushes. Long after Captain Thomas Heuston's release from prison in January 1926, the sour after-taste lingered of Collins's high-spirited dabbling in the 'policy of war'. Not without justification, Ulster Unionists were confirmed in their hitherto perhaps exaggerated belief that southern politicians should not be trusted.

The degeneration of political division over the treaty into armed conflict between the provisional government and its 'Irregular' opponents was predictable, but not inevitable. In retrospect, it is tempting to reflect (like Ernest Blythe) that civil war is an unavoidable by-product of any state's evolution, a maxim that exonerates all parties from culpability.[10] It is obvious that the imposition of a compromise tends to provoke the

reassertion of 'principles'; and that personal and factional conflicts often surface after the withdrawal of a common antagonist.
Yet, in contrast with the aftermath of the French or Russian
revolutions, disagreement in principle was relatively unimpor-
tant in generating renewed conflict in Ireland. Almost all leading
republicans had long since compromised their demand, whether
in pursuit of nationalist solidarity or of a negotiated settlement.
In any case, the ideology of Irish republicanism had never been
much contested or even debated by its proponents, whose political culture was innocent of the virulent intellectual battles associated with Marxism or the European Enlightenment. Among
opponents of the treaty until mid-1922, the defence of principle
against 'betrayal' was more often a rhetorical device than a
motive for rebellion. It was the subsequent experience of rebellion and defeat that created a powerful retrospective need for
such a justifying creed. Even so, the likelihood that the process
of polarization would eventually lead to armed conflict was
already apparent to de Valera on 18 March 1922. With characteristic indirectness, he explained in Killarney, Co. Kerry, that if
the treaty were accepted by the electorate and if the Volunteers
(as he hoped) were to 'continue until the goal is reached', then
it would regrettably be necessary for them 'to march over the
blood of their own brothers. They will have to wade through
Irish blood.'[11] For de Valera, this was a syllogism; for his opponents, a threat; for his supporters, an incitement.

Personal and factional divisions were a more significant
element in shaping Ireland's post-revolutionary line-up. Such
divisions were an unavoidable by-product of the revolutionary
struggle, as would-be heroes and contending families or factions
jostled for status. Once the imperative for public solidarity had
been removed, these rivalries tended to assume overt political
or military form. The most conspicuous case was the bitter antagonism between Collins and the former minister for defence,
Cathal Brugha. At local level, the alignments of 1922 reflected
alliances and antagonisms already well established before the
truce. This was exemplified in Co. Clare by the long-standing
animosity between the Barrett family (who led the Mid Clare

brigade against the treaty) and the Brennans (who eventually provided Collins with crucial support from the East Clare brigade). The existence of rival commands enabled Frank Barrett as well as Michael Brennan to be described as commandant of the 1st western division in 1922.[12]

Yet, as already suggested, the violent expression of factional rivalries and political disagreements might have been curtailed by more systematic repression, or defused by more effective conciliation. During the six months following the treaty, Collins and his colleagues struggled desperately to construct an executive capable of restoring order, and to conciliate their disaffected brethren. Both attempts very nearly succeeded, as protracted negotiations seeking restoration of nationalist unity kept pace with the development of new military and police forces. Eventually, Collins's ingenuity in combining conciliation with power-building proved self-defeating, as British suspicions of the provisional government's double-dealing forced an end to negotiation and thence the eruption of civil war. In any case, the effect of prevarication was cumulatively crippling, as noted by Kevin O'Higgins, the minister for home affairs, on the eve of hostilities. Observing that 'the internal morale of the country and its prestige abroad are very low indeed', O'Higgins lamented that the economy was stagnant for want of security and credit, unemployment rising, the judiciary ignored, and the North 'drifting from bad to worse'. 'What lies ahead? Civil War? A social revolution? Reoccupation by the British with the goodwill of the world, and a "moral mandate" such as they never had before with regard to Ireland?'[13] Had Collins succeeded in postponing conflict for another month or so, the state might nevertheless have acquired sufficient firepower and discipline to stifle its opponents without substantial bloodshed. As it was, the embryonic Free State was plunged into a conflict hardly less bloody and probably more destructive than the Anglo-Irish war.

Several factors encouraged opponents as well as supporters of the treaty to avoid violent expression of their political differences. The revolutionary experience had forged not only factional divisions but also strong fraternal links among those who had conspired, fought, gone on the run, and endured prison together, in a common cause. During and after 'the war of friends', otherwise 'brothers', the collapse of fraternal solidarity created a sense of loss and regret almost unvoiced in the Anglo-Irish conflict, when it had proved all too easy to visualize the soldier, policeman, or Protestant as an alien, evil, and scarcely human antagonist. The fraternal sentiment was manifest in the reiterated negotiations between army factions preceding and following the creation of a rebel army council at a convention in late March 1922. Confirming a resolution by senior dissident officers on 11 January, the convention insisted that the IRA should remain 'the Army of the Irish Republic' without regard for the authority of the provisional government, the Dáil, or Mulcahy's headquarters staff. The dissidents were termed 'Irregulars' by those loyal to the 'national' forces. On 14 April, the judicial process was interrupted by the new council's occupation of Dublin's Four Courts. The garrison was commanded by Rory O'Connor (known to Sir Henry Wilson as 'O'Rory O'Gory'), a Dublin engineer who had graduated from UCD before practising his skills on the Canadian railways.[14] Despite this provocation, Collins, Mulcahy, O'Duffy, and MacEoin were involved between January and June in numerous meetings with dissident leaders. Apart from O'Connor, these included Liam Lynch (the Irregular chief of staff), Liam Mellows (a soldier's son born in Manchester and reared in Wexford) and Ernie O'Malley (Mayo-born author of a brilliant memoir of the fight for independence, who had dropped out of medical studies at UCD in 1916). At least three conferences were arranged through the IRB, the most fraternal of all republican organizations.

The impulse towards reunification was not, however, purely sentimental. All military factions were conscious of the increasing risk of renewed British intervention as public disorder worsened and deaths from violence multiplied, in which case the division over the treaty would become superfluous. Furthermore, both sides hoped that the most contentious elements of the settlement could be ameliorated or even discarded through tinkering with the Free State's draft constitution. The abortive electoral pact of 20 May, which relied on this dubious strategy, very nearly resulted in the parallel creation of an army coalition council under O'Duffy as chief of staff. Procrastination was encouraged by the poor armament and organization of both protagonists, who were energetically preparing for possible conflict even as they bartered for peace. Until the collapse of the electoral pact after the British cabinet's rejection of the agreed draft constitution, both Irish armies therefore held back from irrevocable violent collision.

During the half-year of phoney peace, the provisional government rapidly assembled a surprisingly formidable array of security forces. In February 1922, three months before the postponed disbandment of the RIC, recruitment had begun for a new police force. The Civic Guard was initially an armed paramilitary force in the tradition of Irish policing, composed almost entirely of former Volunteers, about a third of whom had served in flying columns. After a serious mutiny in mid-May arising from the alleged influence of former members of the RIC at headquarters and in the officer corps, arms training was reduced and the recruits were removed from the Curragh to the former RIC depot at the Phoenix Park. During the civil war the police were virtually exempted from killing by the Irregulars in response to the prudent decision to disarm the uniformed force, which continued until recently to rely on truncheons, muscles, and ingenuity. Eoin O'Duffy had become chief commissioner in August 1922, displaying considerable flair in gaining communal acceptance of a new type of police force. Candidates were not only required to stand 5 ft. 9 in. high and puff out their chests to 36 in., but also to 'write a short composition or letter on a simple subject'.[15] The Civic Guard was backed up by a medley of less savoury paramilitary forces, armed, undisciplined, and often outrageous in their methods of interrogation. These detective and intelligence units included the CID based at Oriel House, the Protective Officers' Corps, and the Citizens' Defence Force. Their combined membership reached about 400, including many veterans of the British army, the IRA, and eventually the national army.[16] It was the last-named body, however, that was mainly responsible for ensuring the delivery and survival of the Irish Free State.

The evolution of the national army was tortuous, since Mulcahy and his staff continued to claim allegiance from the IRA and assert their continuity with the Volunteers, whose Irish title (Óglaigh na hÉireann) was retained by both aspirant armies. Most staff officers supported the provisional government, but the majority of divisional and brigade commands adhered to the dissident army council. The Irregular commands were clustered in the north-east, Connaught, and the south, these three regions being crucially separated by divisions loyal to Mulcahy. His supporters controlled units from Clare eastwards to Wicklow, with a further band of support in the midlands stretching north-westwards to Donegal. Irregular power was centred in Munster, the 1st and 2nd southern divisions having been the best armed and most violent elements in the Anglo-Irish war. This was however counterbalanced by active support for the provisional government in Clare and Longford, where the Brennans and Seán MacEoin, respectively, had organized highly efficient if somewhat less murderous guerrilla campaigns. The extent to which local units and individual Volunteers deviated from their brigade alignments is unknown, although most districts with pro-treaty commands faced some disruption from disaffected guerrillas, while the national army drew ex-Volunteer recruits from all counties. In Ulster, the bulk of the 2nd and 3rd northern divisions accepted O'Duffy's prompt dismissal of the Irregular commandants, whereas the initially neutral 4th northern division eventually repudiated the provisional government. The most common expression of dissent was undoubtedly abstention from both contending forces.

The supply of former Volunteers was quite inadequate to sustain an army which, by March 1923, employed 3,600 officers and nearly 45,000 men. Enlistment was conducted through a new Volunteer organization, recruits being encouraged after the outbreak of civil war to undertake active service for a six-month period. Many of these Volunteers were ex-servicemen from the British army, often thankful to escape unemployment and local unpopularity by offering their military skills to a new master and so rediscovering the solace of soldierly camaraderie. In addition, several hundred former officers and sergeants with war experience in British or foreign forces secured commissions in the national army, although most senior officers outside the technical services had served with the 'Old IRA'. As in the Civic Guard, the combination of veterans from the republican and the crown forces generated sharp resentments, which were to surface in the 'army mutiny' of March 1924.

On 27 June 1922, the provisional government approved a statement drafted by Arthur Griffith, announcing armed attacks on the Four Courts and occupied buildings 'in all parts of the country, where the Government of the Irish people is defied'.[17] The first Dublin attacks took place on the following morning, the Irregular forces having failed to act on an ultimatum to evacuate the Four Courts and also Fowler Hall in Parnell (Rutland) Square (headquarters of the Grand Orange Lodge of Ireland until its evacuation to Belfast on 1 January 1922). The immediate stimulus to action was Ernie O'Malley's abduction of O'Duffy's successor as deputy chief of staff, the former American National Guard J. J. (otherwise 'Ginger') O'Connell. Five days earlier, however, the murder of Sir Henry Wilson by two British army veterans in the London IRA had caused Lloyd George to demand prompt action against O'Connor's garrison. An alternative proposal for seizure of the Four Courts by the British army had been withdrawn when Macready protested that this would reunite all factions against the common enemy. Instead, Macready provided the ill-equipped and undeveloped national forces with sufficient Howitzers and shells to blast the Irregulars out of the Four Courts. The worst destruction was from a bomb deposited by the surrendering idealists, which simplified the historian's task by eliminating most of Ireland's public records.

Churchill, the colonial secretary, overcame predictable opposition from the war office, the admiralty, and the treasury to secure massive provision of arms, heavy artillery, armoured cars, and even tanks for the national army.[18] The tanks were never mobilized, for lack of qualified Irish tank-drivers; but aeroplanes and boats were subsequently supplied. Even before the civil war, the supply of British arms had vastly exceeded the stock remaining from the Anglo-Irish war. The latter amounted to only 1,700 rifles, 3,500 revolvers, and 35 machine guns (about half of the IRA's arsenal before the treaty); whereas about 11,900 rifles, 4,200 revolvers, and 80 Lewis guns were received from the British before 26 June 1922. By 30 July, additional British deliveries had provided 11,000 rifles, 1,000 revolvers, and another 80 machine guns. The British army also supplied four and a half million rounds of ammunition, eight 18-pounders, a dozen armoured cars, and hundreds of vehicles including nearly 150 quaintly rechristened Crossley tenders.[19] Despite the provisional government's failure to apprehend those responsible for the murder of several British serviceman during 1922, the supply of munitions continued thereafter on unlimited credit, 'the question of payment being left over to the general financial settlement'.[20] Macready could not however contemplate joint actions involving his own depleted garrison and the national forces, which he considered 'practically impotent to restore order' and of unreliable loyalty.[21] Even so, British support for the national forces was crucial to their eventual success, a fact tirelessly exploited by republicans ever since. The provisional government, and thence 'Staters' in general, were calumniated as the treacherous agents of British colonialism, their fingers having squeezed the Sassenach trigger.

The campaign against the Irregulars was directed by a 'war council' (renamed the 'army council' in reclamation of the title chosen by the Irregulars in January), to which the provisional government surrendered many of its functions after 12 July 1922. Its original members were Mulcahy, O'Duffy, and Collins (as commander in chief). By early August, a series of bloody encounters had resulted in the removal of Irregular garrisons from all of their urban bases, culminating on 10 August in the occupation of Cork city by national forces shipped into nearby Passage West and other harbours. This daring campaign was led by Emmet Dalton, the director of military operations, former lieutenant in the Royal Dublin Fusiliers, and future film producer. The vital stronghold of Limerick had already been secured artfully and bloodlessly by Michael Brennan in April, and the feeble republican units in Connaught were speedily ejected from the towns. On 5 August, Collins reported that the army's divisional strength had reached almost 13,000, the 'definite military problem' being restricted to parts of Munster. Only 59 national troops had so far been killed, though heavier losses soon followed with the reoccupation of the south; about 2,000 prisoners were known to be in custody.[22] In open conflict involving substantial forces, the national army had clearly outscored its Irregular antagonist.

The first six weeks of the civil war had been a bloody scramble for military living space, during which the national army secured possession of most of the scattered police barracks and other buildings occupied by Irregular forces from January 1922 onwards. By mid-August, the army had therefore accomplished the programme set out by the provisional government on 27 June. Having failed to hold their ground, the republican leaders might rationally have decided to cut their losses by seeking face-saving terms of surrender. In practice, however, rational calculation tends to be more effective in initiating wars than in bringing them to an end, a process complicated by the understandable reluctance of the losers to abandon their pride, honour, and ideals along with their weapons. As de Valera ruminated in September 1922, the choice for republicans was 'between a heartbreaking surrender of what they have repeatedly proved was dearer to them than life and the repudiation of what they recognise to be the basis of all order in government and the keystone of democracy—majority rule. Is it any wonder that there is, so to speak, a civil war going in the minds of most of us . . . ?'[23] For some months longer, the appeal to pride and honour remained paramount among the fighters. The Irregulars, bereft of barracks and 'on the run', rapidly reverted to the guerrilla tactics which had evolved in similar circumstances after 1918. As before, the rationale of resistance was to evade arrest, defend one's weapons, create military and social havoc, provoke counter-productive coercion, arouse popular indignation, and thereby destabilize the state to the point of collapse.

In reviving the strategy which had played so important a part in generating the truce and the Anglo-Irish settlement, the Irregulars were deluded by their own previous success. Admittedly, their destructive capacity greatly exceeded that of the Volunteers of 1919, despite the much smaller cadre of available activists. The practice of terrorism in the civil war was even more vicious and ruthless than in the Anglo-Irish conflict, during which many of the future participants had been coarsened and brutalized as well as receiving invaluable military training in the field and behind the hedge-row. Kevin O'Higgins had justifiably trembled at the prospect of hardened terrorists redirecting their skills towards former colleagues: 'In our struggle with the British we developed a type of war by which a comparatively small number of men can harass and hamper a government and finally reduce it to impotence and futility.'[24] Yet this advantage was negated by the matching ferocity of the national forces, confident in their widespread public support and therefore unrestrained by the need for moderation and conciliation. Despite the eloquence of de Valera, Childers, and their fellow-republican propagandists, the Irregulars were unable to persuade most Irish nationalists that a government inaugurated by Griffith and Collins was illegitimate and alien. Whereas the guerrilla fighters of 1919–21 had been sustained by popular sympathy, limitless provision of 'safe houses' and intricate networks of intelligence, their Irregular successors were forced to rely primarily on intimidation. Outside certain disaffected pockets, mainly in Munster, the guardians of the republic were more likely to encounter fear and resentment than griddle cakes and adoring glances. Unable to comprehend their change in status from hero to pariah, the Irregulars retreated into self-justifying reveries of the ideal republic, maintained their futile campaign of destruction, and waited in vain for the people to awaken from their slumber.

The guerrilla campaign involved the familiar elements: flying columns, raids, ambushes, slaughter of 'informers', cutting of communications, destruction of property, looting ('requisition-ing'), and bullying of opponents. The most widely lamented victim of an ambush was Michael Collins, shot down shortly after his prime at Béal na mBláth, near his homeland in west Cork, during a tour of inspection on 22 August. So prudent and elusive in the Anglo-Irish war, Collins revealed his inexperience of shoot-outs by recklessly exposing himself in order to fire at his assailants. The fortuitous proximity of de Valera, meeting fellow-fugitives a few miles away, made the ambush a sombre if mis-leading symbol for the entire conflict. The loss of Collins, compounded by Griffith's natural demise ten days earlier, did not foster a conciliatory spirit among their successors. While William Thomas Cosgrave presided calmly over a provisional government dominated by the increasingly grim Kevin O'Higgins, Mulcahy took effective charge of military operations as head of the army council. Their response to the guerrilla cam-paign was to secure the Dáil's approval on 28 September for the creation of military courts and committees, with powers exceed-ing the most egregious instruments created by the British or northern governments. Subsequent proclamations empowered these special tribunals to punish offences ranging from unlawful possession of property to attacks on the national forces with fines, internment, deportation, imprisonment, penal servitude, or (with the concurrence of two members of the army council) exe-cution. When the Labour leader, Thomas Johnson, moved unsuc-cessfully for the inclusion of a lawyer in each court, Seán MacEoin roared that he had 'no respect whatever for any legal adviser', confirming that he himself would be happy to sum-marily shoot any man whom he knew to be 'guilty of a particu-lar act'.[25] These measures were subsequently backed up by the revival of the once reviled Restoration of Order in Ireland act, under which republican suspects in Britain were arrested and shipped to the Free State for internment.

Far from becoming a dead letter, the special emergency powers were used to devastating effect after coming into force on 15 October, seventy-seven offenders being executed in the half-year from 17 November 1922. These included many celebrated revolutionaries, including Erskine Childers, who was found in possession of a revolver presented him by Collins. The executions were accompanied by numerous killings of prisoners and of republicans resisting arrest (including Harry Boland, gunned down in a Skerries hotel, and Cathal Brugha as he gamely if lamely blazed forth from the Four Courts). In several cases in Munster, most notoriously at Ballyseedy Cross, Co. Kerry, parties of prisoners were blown up when compelled to touch or remove barricades connected with mines laid by their colleagues. The killings in Kerry were in retaliation for the carnage of fourteen national soldiers by another landmine.[26]

The predictable response of the Irregulars was to initiate counter-reprisals, in accordance with a statement signed by the chief of staff (Liam Lynch) for the 'army council' on 27 November, threatening 'very drastic measures to protect our forces'. These reprisals included attacks on senators and deputies, the destruction of their homes, and the murder of Seán Hales, TD (whose brother Tom was a prominent Irregular officer in Cork). The destruction of houses belonging to parliamentarians provoked the government to order that, for each dwelling so destroyed, several houses of 'prominent Irregular leaders or supporters' should be closed by military order.[27] The killing of Hales prompted army headquarters to execute Rory O'Connor, Liam Mellows, and two other staff officers, 'as a reprisal for the assassination . . . and as a solemn warning to those associated with them who are engaged in a conspiracy of assassination against the representatives of the Irish people'.[28] For all the horrors of the Anglo-Irish war, neither protagonist had used assassination and statutory killing so systematically or so callously as their counterparts in the civil war. The intensity of the conflict was evident in the comparably severe loss of life over a shorter period, involving over 800 national servicemen, about 300 republicans (in addition to those executed), and unnumbered civilians.[29] Like a feuding family in pursuit of a contested inheritance, the survivors of the fight for freedom tore each other and their legacy asunder.

The manifest futility and degrading influence of the civil war led to numerous attempts at intercession by priests, ex-Unionists, and Labour leaders, as well as military conciliators who continued to exploit the vestigial fraternal networks of the IRB. As in the prelude to the truce of July 1921, the search for a ceasefire was impeded by the indiscipline and weakness of authority in the republican forces. Despite the impressive titles assumed by the Irregular hierarchy, with their army council, divisions, brigades, and battalions, central control and communications between units failed to match even the mediocre standard achieved before the truce. Most leading republicans were constantly on the run, while the few organizers manning headquarters in Dublin were derided for 'doing nothing' by provincial brigade and battalion officers, from whom they vainly sought information about casualties and engagements.[30] In mid-October, the Irregular commanders called upon de Valera to establish a provisional government, which would act as the 'supreme executive of the republic' until a free parliament could be re-established. Though pledged to give allegiance to this executive, the IRA paid only sporadic attention to the advice of de Valera, who had so far played an inglorious role in the civil war as a 'private' soldier and peripatetic propagandist.

When de Valera proposed negotiation in late March 1923, the army executive followed Liam Lynch's advice by denying defeat and resolving to fight on. After Lynch's killing in Tipperary a fortnight later, his surviving colleagues agreed to seek a settlement. Despite mediation from Labour and two 'Independent' senators (formerly Unionists), the protagonists failed to agree upon terms for the release of incarcerated republicans in exchange for the surrender of arms. Even so, de Valera instructed all units to 'suspend aggressive action' as from 30 April, his appeal being supported by an order from Frank Aiken (an Armagh Catholic who had commanded the 4th northern division and supported the Irregulars after initial neutrality, eventually succeeding Lynch as chief of staff). The Irregulars were also ordered to 'take adequate measures to protect themselves and their munitions'. On 24 May, following the failure of renewed attempts at conciliation, de Valera called upon the

'Legion of the Rearguard' to cease hostilities: 'Military victory must be allowed to rest for the moment with those who have destroyed the Republic. Other means must be sought to safeguard the nation's right.' The Irregulars were instructed to hide their weapons rather than surrender them, so enriching the secret landscape dotted with caches of rusting guns and damp ammunition dumped by their revolutionary predecessors of 1798 and 1867.[31]

The threat of renewed violence in future remained, and the illegitimacy of the Free State was continually reaffirmed by shadowy armies, political parties, parliaments, and governments purporting to represent the republic. Sporadic outrages continued for several years, but systematic terrorism was abandoned. The government granted amnesty only to those undertaking to repudiate the republic, and responded to the ceasefire by rounding up all suspected Irregulars. Though executions ceased, the number of prisoners and internees rose above 11,000, most of whom were released during the following year. This was fifteen times the number incarcerated in Northern Ireland. The civil war thus expired without either compromise or surrender, leaving no obvious path towards reconciliation or political coexistence. As in the case of northern nationalists, the militant opponents of the treaty had been cowed by state repression, at the cost of their further alienation from the political process. In 1923, there seemed little prospect that either minority would reconcile itself to the benign condition of a loyal opposition. The legitimacy of both states remained dangerously contested.

Partition and Power

Partition

The effect of civil conflict in both Irish states was to enhance mutual suspicion and consolidate partition. Ulster loyalists were more than ever inclined to regard their Catholic neighbours as treacherous Fenians, sustained and aided by the government and people of the Free State. The victors in the southern civil war, having barely withstood the armed republican challenge, had no stomach for a renewed border campaign or even a constitutional crusade for unification. The Council of Ireland, through which cross-border cooperation was to have been initiated under the Government of Ireland act and the treaty, was never convened. Neither the national army nor the Irregular IRA intervened in Northern Ireland after 1922. Other strategies of destabilization were also set aside, after some bizarre experiments by the provisional government. The construction of the northern civil service had been temporarily sabotaged by impeding the transfer of civil servants and departmental records. In February 1922, moreover, the provisional government had encouraged teachers in northern Catholic schools to withhold recognition and refuse salaries from Belfast authorities. The boycott eventually involved 700 teachers in over a third of the northern national schools under Catholic management. An amicable settlement was eventually reached in November 1922, so releasing the hardpressed provisional government from the burden of paying salaries for extra-territorial services. Craig's administration failed to take up Cosgrave's pathetic suggestion that it 'reimburse his government the salaries which have been paid'.[1] In the following month, the northern parliament exercised its statutory right to opt out of the Free State. No further overt interference in the administration of the six counties was attempted.

The prospect of a boundary commission encouraged continuing attempts to discredit the legitimacy of the northern state through symbolic protests and propaganda. A week after the inauguration of the new state, the secretary to the executive council urged ministers to alter the seals used by the former provisional government, in which Ireland's provincial emblems were conventionally displayed with Ulster's Red Hand in the upper left quarter. 'The position of the arms of Ulster should of course be altered from its present place to the right hand top corner of the shield. If considered desirable to symbolise in the design the present partition of Ulster, this could be done by leaving the Arms of that province incomplete and broken at the corner.' Following Mulcahy's refusal to 'countenance the Ulster arms being disfigured in any way', the seals were redesigned with a harp.[2] A more concerted rejection of partition was expressed in the propaganda campaign co-ordinated from October 1922 by the North-Eastern Boundary Bureau. This was headed by Kevin O'Shiel from Omagh, Co. Tyrone, a Catholic barrister who had acted as 'land commissioner' in the Dáil's campaign against land seizures in 1920. The bureau solicited advice and information from northern nationalists and priests, distributing books and leaflets in both Irish states and in Britain. As in the revolutionary period, it became embroiled in a propagandist war with Ulster loyalists, who continued to lobby British sympathizers and politicians as they had done so effectively in 1912–14 and 1920. In November 1922, the provisional government enthusiastically endorsed a proposal from Bishop Joseph MacRory of Down and Connor (whose diocese embraced Belfast) to disseminate a clerical exposure of the Belfast 'pogrom', agreeing that 'something ought to be done to try to counteract the influence of the large deputation which has gone to England from the Six Counties'.[3] The bureau maintained its activity throughout the prolonged attempt to redraw the border through a boundary commission, being dissolved only in early 1926.

The commission as envisaged in the treaty was never convened, since Northern Ireland declined to appoint its representative. Eoin MacNeill (then minister for education) was nominated by the Free State in July 1923; the South African judge Richard Feetham was appointed chairman by the British government in June 1924; Joseph R. Fisher from Raffrey, Co. Down (a former editor of the Liberal Unionist newspaper, the *Northern Whig*), was imposed on Northern Ireland following special legislation in October 1924; and the commission eventually assembled in November 1924. Craig maintained discreet but highly effective contact with Fisher to ensure that no serious mutilation would be attempted. After a year's fatuous deliberation, the commission recommended minor adjustments of the border entailing losses as well as gains for the Free State. Four-fifths of the affected population were to be transferred to the southern jurisdiction (mainly from Fermanagh and Armagh, though not from Derry); but over 2,700 Catholics (mainly from east Donegal) would have found themselves reallocated to Northern Ireland. When this embarrassing bargain was leaked in the press, MacNeill resigned as a delegate and a minister, and the commission soon collapsed. Fisher, who was probably responsible for the leak, was singularly content with the outcome and the cordial unanimity of the commissioners, despite the 'hitch at the end'. The inhabitants of 'the frontier' were 'living together in friendly fashion, as good neighbours, & only anxious to be let alone. . . . For myself, I am now back to work on a section of Irish History to which I have devoted several years & on which my pilgrimage on the frontier, & my walks & talks with John MacNeill, have thrown fresh light.'[4] On 3 December 1925, the three governments agreed to maintain the current border, and to grant the northern parliament jurisdiction over the services due to be transferred from Westminster to the Council of Ireland by December 1927. Though the two Irish administrations proposed to meet 'when necessary' to discuss matters of 'common interest', no alternative arrangements for collaboration were made and no such meetings occurred. The permanence of partition seemed assured.

Economic partition had already been achieved on April Fool's

Day, 1923, when the Free State's executive council created a customs' barrier along the border (and across the Irish Sea) despite protests from southern producers. Though few tariffs were at first imposed and smuggling was unstoppable, this decision further threatened cross-border trade, already severely disrupted by the reiterated boycotts of 1920–2. Most northern producers and wholesalers happily redirected their southern exports to British and local markets, though major border towns such as Derry and Enniskillen continued to serve hinterlands beyond the border. Restraints on southern trade only became a major menace to the northern economy during the 'economic war' of 1932–8. This had far more severe effects in Northern Ireland than in either Britain or the Free State, mainly because the escalating application of tariffs sharply increased the cost of imported food. These economic losses were officially downplayed or ignored, the economic independence of Northern Ireland from the south having long since been incorporated in loyalist rhetoric as an essential axiom. Northern adherence to the principle of partition, once a matter of reluctant acquiescence, became as rigid and righteous as affirmation of the Union.

This was exemplified in the prime minister's response to reiterated proposals for cross-border co-operation in the burgeoning tourist industry. In August 1927, the committee of the Ulster Tourist Development Association were invited to visit Cork and Kerry as guests of the Irish Tourist Association, which hoped to make 'the tourist industry a bond of union between North and South'. Robert Baillie, secretary to the Ulster body, besought his 'Lordship's guidance' (Craig having become Viscount Craigavon of Stormont in January 1927), remarking that 'up till the settlement of the Boundary question we kept our friends in the Free State more or less at arm's length while at the same time we were as courteous as possible. Since then we have relaxed to some extent.' Alert to the insidious implications of the proposed 'bond of union', Baillie anticipated his leader's preference for 'a diplomatic refusal', musing that 'I could without announcing your opinion at the meeting tell Sir Frederick Cleaver[5] and one or two other of our old friends on whom we can count, and they and I could get the matter settled quietly'. Armed with a wire saying 'Decline', Baillie activated the fraternal networks of Belfast business and repulsed the obnoxious invitation. Gaelic guile was again outsmarted in April 1930, when the southern body asked its Ulster counterpart to intercede with the White-hall-funded Travel Association of Great Britain and Ireland, in order to increase publicity for 'Ireland as a whole'. This was interpreted as a dodge by the unsubsidized Irish Tourist Associ-ation to make improper use of the resources of the Union, in order to promote 'special appeals to American Catholics' by 'advertising in Irish-American and Catholic Periodicals'. Craigavon agreed, advising 'that they should keep themselves absolutely aloof from the Irish Free State'.[6] No heritage trail would yet be blazed from Killarney to the Giant's Causeway.

Throughout Cosgrave's decade as president of the executive council, the Free State was regarded in Northern Ireland as an alien but only intermittently menacing neighbour, best left on its own. During the civil war, the northern government had rejected the option of trying to bolster the supporters of the treaty through conciliatory gestures. As the cabinet secretary cynically remarked in January 1923, 'we should best serve the interests of Ireland as a whole by acting as a lifeboat rather than to tie our-selves to a sinking ship'.[7] When Cosgrave's survival in power was threatened by military mutiny in March 1924, Craig noted without obvious regret that several leading officers 'had come out openly in revolt and had taken to the hills', concluding that the resultant threat to northern security rendered disbandment or reduction of the Special Constabulary out of the question.[8] For a brief period after the tripartite agreement of December 1925, Craig markedly softened his rhetoric without initiating practical co-operation with Cosgrave's government. The main function of such conciliatory murmurs was to reassure British politicians that partition was an amicable and stable settlement, meriting recurrent political and financial investment.

The accession of de Valera to the presidency, in March 1932, revived northern fears of infiltration, betrayal, and invasion *via* Enniskillen. Recruitment of B Specials was resumed in July, in

response to the stoning of a band returning from Belfast's ceno-
taph. Dawson Bates, the minister of home affairs, expected
'similar "tip and run" raids by parties [from the south] similar to
that which occurred in the former troubles', noting that 'if large
bodies of men came across the border we have no means whatever of dealing with the situation except by means of troops'.[9]
Despite growing antipathy between the new southern government and the intermittently truculent IRA, northern loyalists
remained suspicious of de Valera. His return to the northern parliament as the abstentionist member for South Down, in November 1933, evoked uneasy recollections of earlier interventions in
1924 (capped by his solitary confinement for an uncomfortable
month in Belfast jail). Though de Valera refused to supply northern nationalist leaders with seats in the Dáil, his party remained
bitterly hostile to partition and to Craigavon's government.
Nationalists of all parties were perturbed by the advice of senior
northern ministers to give Protestants preference in employment, and by renewed evictions and expulsions of Belfast
Catholics in July 1935. Seán MacEntee, the Belfast Catholic who
had become de Valera's minister for finance, asked 'whether the
position is not so acute as to merit some attention on the part
of the Government'. The disturbances in Belfast left over a
dozen dead, and renewed civil war was only narrowly averted.
The southern government took no practical action; but a spate
of attacks on homes and shops belonging to southern Protestants, masonic halls, and Protestant churches, exacerbated
sectarian animosities and cross-border hostility.[10] Such after-
tremors of 1922 recurred with disturbing frequency and ferocity,
reminding both states of the fragility of Lloyd George's Irish
'settlement'.

The latent menace of southern irredentism became officially
explicit on 29 December 1937, when de Valera's new 'Constitution of Ireland' came into force. Its second article asserted that
'the national territory consists of the whole island of Ireland, its
islands and the territorial seas'. In words calculated to give perpetual offence to every northern loyalist, the following article
grudgingly allowed that 'pending the re-integration of the

national territory, and without prejudice to the right of the Parliament and Government established by this Constitution to exercise jurisdiction over the whole of that territory, the laws enacted by that Parliament shall have the like area and extent of application as the laws of Saorstát Éireann and the like extra-territorial effect'. This formulation followed the same rhetorical sequence as de Valera's ambiguous 'addendum' on 'north-east Ulster' in December 1921, which had asserted Irish sovereignty while granting 'privileges and safeguards' to the recalcitrant inhabitants, and was likewise designed to placate republican suspicions of compromise and betrayal. By contrast, the 'Constitution of the Irish Free State (Saorstát Éireann)' had left the national territory inexplicit, its extent being defined in the treaty and subsequent agreements. Though entirely devoid of immediate practical consequences, de Valera's assertion of Irish sovereignty in Northern Ireland made the prospect of agreed reunification still more remote. It required the further proclamation of an Irish Republic in 1949 to provoke an explicit guarantee against imposed integration: 'It is hereby declared that Northern Ireland remains part of His Majesty's dominions and of the United Kingdom and it is hereby affirmed that in no event will Northern Ireland or any part thereof cease to be part of His Majesty's dominions and of the United Kingdom without the consent of the Parliament of Northern Ireland.'[11] To this day, the Republic's dormant irredentist claim and Britain's purportedly irreversible guarantee endure as twin pillars of perpetual partition.

Government

Both Irish states were governed by bicameral parliaments whose procedures were loosely modelled on Westminster's. Unlike its eponym, the House of Commons in Northern Ireland was elected by proportional representation, until this safeguard for minor parties was abolished in 1929. In the same year, following the recent British example, the franchise was extended to all adult women. The Senate provided no useful check, since all but two of its members were elected by the lower house. Its limited ability to delay or amend legislation was never deployed to the point of deadlock with the Commons, so that the two houses never had to be convened in joint sitting. Parliament was responsible to the lord lieutenant (until his supercession in December 1922), and thereafter to a governor representing the monarch. The division of powers between Westminster and Stormont[12] was complex and ill-defined. Westminster's formal supremacy seemed to allow for interference in local legislation, should this be deemed to breach the rights of the Catholic minority as vaguely defended in the Government of Ireland act of 1920. The practical limits to intervention were established in September 1922, when the northern government succeeded in abolishing proportional representation for local elections. At the request of Collins, royal assent had been withheld for two months, until Craig's threat of resignation prevailed. Faced by the dismal alternative of resuming direct reponsibility for northern conflicts, with the certain consequence of inflaming loyalist as well as nationalist opposition, all British governments until 1972 preferred to preach rather than enforce equitable administration. No northern legislation was ever to be overturned by either the monarch or the 'imperial' parliament.

Despite its practical immunity from being overruled, the northern parliament might well have been rendered impotent by its lack of financial autonomy. Though it was responsible for spending over four-fifths of the province's revenue in 1933–4, only a fifth of that revenue was raised under its authority. Apart from a few imposts such as duty on motor vehicles and certain excise licences, the northern parliament had to accept its 'residuary share' of taxes and duties levied at rates determined by Westminster. That share depended on the amount of revenue actually raised in Northern Ireland's backward economy, not on its proportionate population. The marked deterioration after 1920 of the northern economy, relative to that of Britain, ensured that the financial provisions of the Better Government of Ireland act would prove inoperable. Since the combined receipts per capita of income tax, surtax, customs duties, and excise duties fell below half of the British level in 1929–30, the resultant allocation of revenue was pitifully inadequate.[13] Furthermore, Whitehall deducted an 'imperial contribution', which in 1923 actually exceeded total northern expenditure on transferred services. Despite the fantasy that thrifty Ulster could somehow 'pay her own way', as sometimes averred by Hugh McDowell Pollock (minister of finance from 1921 to 1937), the northern budget could only be balanced through massive subventions from the imperial exchequer.

After a series of ameliorations and hand-outs, Craig secured a 'most favourable' reassessment of the imperial contribution from Lord Colwyn's arbitration committee in a report presented at Westminster in March 1925.[14] The revised rubric ensured that the burden of supporting imperial services became negligible by the early 1930s, further relief being afforded by the cancellation in 1926 of Northern Ireland's contribution to the imperial war debt. Nevertheless, the definition of the 'residuary share' continued to generate a critical shortage of revenue. Even without the abnormal burden of its swollen apparatus of policing and repression, Northern Ireland should have gone rapidly and irretrievably bankrupt. This outcome had indeed long been predicted by opponents of partition, who looked forward to acting as benevolent liquidators for the depleted assets of their chastened former opponents. In fact, Northern Ireland's wily leaders and senior officials managed to subvert the underlying principle of provincial devolution, by progressively establishing the province's entitlement to services equivalent to those offered in Britain. Craig and Spender (head of the civil service from 1925 to 1944) retained valuable allies in the British civil service as well as the Conservative Party, though they also faced relentless criticism from mandarins such as Sir John Anderson and Sir Otto Niemeyer. Effective integration between the social services of Northern Ireland and Britain was not achieved until May 1938, when the chancellor of the exchequer (Sir John Simon) undertook to provide sufficient subsidies to maintain northern services at British levels. Twelve years earlier, however, the northern government had secured a form of parity between the

two unemployment insurance funds through British subventions, the calculation being amended to the province's
further advantage in 1929 and 1936. The principle of parity was
not only rhetorically appealing to Unionists, but also profitable.

British acquiescence in this basic revision of Home Rule was
partly motivated by the inconvenience of maintaining a backward province liable to flood the mainland with migrants greedy
for British benefits, an accusation more openly levelled against
emigrants from the Free State. This might explain British opposition in 1931 to a northern proposal for 'drastic retrenchment'
rather than imposition of additional local taxes or levies.[15] Yet
this argument alone could scarcely have outweighed treasury
outrage at northern profligacy, as expressed by Sir Richard
Hopkins in February 1939: 'Since 1931 Northern Ireland has
been in effect a depressed area. So far from receiving any large
Imperial Contribution we have invented a series of *dodges* and
devices to give them *gifts* and *subventions* within the ambit of
the Government of Ireland Act so as to save Northern Ireland
from coming openly on the dole as Newfoundland did.'[16] Such
largesse could only be justified by the belief that the social and
political costs of reintegration would far exceed the economic
costs of subsidizing the province.

Craig's ministry generally imitated English legislation after a
brief delay, in order to emphasize the province's full participation in the United Kingdom. This principle restricted the ideological independence of conservative-hearted ministers who
nevertheless felt bound to emulate British social reforms if subsidized by British taxpayers. State intervention in the northern
economy only occasionally anticipated British initiatives, the
licensing and marketing of farm products being a rare exception.
On occasion, the government's determination to keep in line
with Britain produced droll consequences. In July 1927, the
cabinet agreed to mimic British restrictions on trades unions in
response to the general strike, despite the admission by John
Andrews (the minister of labour) that there was 'no necessity
for the introduction of such a measure here', since 'the overwhelming majority of the industrial classes in Northern Ireland

remained at work'. The measure should be adopted (if at all) in its entirety, incorporating the British ban on unionization of established civil servants, even though northern bureaucrats showed no disposition to be unionized. To do otherwise, so Andrews wittily maintained, would be tantamount to 'introducing class legislation'.[17]

The constitution of the Irish Free State specified a variant form of parliamentary democracy, with some American touches. The lower house (named Dáil Éireann in order to claim apostolic succession from the republican assembly of 1919) was elected by proportional representation, with universal suffrage for men and women from 1923 onwards. Seanad Éireann (the Senate) was initially divided between thirty candidates elected by the Dáil and an equal number nominated by the president to represent minority interests. At triennial intervals, a quarter of Senate seats were to be filled through proportional representation, the constituency being the entire Free State. Though intended to favour eminent candidates with little local support but nationwide respect, the system in fact enabled parochial bosses to mobilize their associates in intense local campaigns, and so defeat non-campaigning celebrities such as Douglas Hyde (founder of the Gaelic League and future president of Ireland). In response to the fiasco of 1925, popular elections were replaced by joint votes in the two houses, so terminating the Senate's independent mandate (July 1928). The Senate was abolished by de Valera's government in 1936, after two years in adjournment following its suspension of several constitutional amendment bills including that for its own abolition. Though unable to reject legislation, or hold up money bills for more than twenty-one days, the upper house had proved tiresomely diligent in initiating, amending, and occasionally suspending legislation (for up to nine months, a period doubled in 1928). De Valera's substitute Seanad, as defined in the constitution of 1937, included representatives of the universities and five vocational panels in addition to some government nominees. In practice, the vocational panels were composed largely of aspirant or former members of the Dáil, and the Seanad (its power to suspend bills having been curtailed to a period of three months) meekly submitted to the government's will.

The powers of the governor-general, who had replaced the lord lieutenant in December 1922, were also drastically curtailed by Fianna Fáil. The first incumbent, the maverick anti-Parnellite Tim Healy, had mainly performed with uncharacteristic discretion in his ceremonial role as the monarch's representative. In 1928, Healy was succeeded by Eoin MacNeill's brother James, whose long experience in the Indian and colonial services led him to expect respect and deference from his ministers. De Valera humiliated and then dismissed McNeill in 1932, replacing him by Domhnall Ó Buachalla, a chirpy Maynooth shopkeeper whose subservience to the Chief induced him to surrender the viceregal lodge in Phoenix Park, commute to his office by bicycle, avoid all official functions, and adopt the demeaning title of An Seanascal (chief steward). In the new constitution of 1937, the governor-general was replaced as the formal executive authority by a popularly elected president. Though lacking most of the powers of his American counterpart, the Irish president could refer dubiously constitutional bills to the supreme court, and submit proposals of 'national importance' to referendum. He could also decide whether or not to dissolve the Oireachtas (parliament) should the government lose the confidence of the Dáil (art. 13.2.2°). By contrast, the constitution of 1922 had precluded the governor-general from dissolving parliament on the advice of such a government (art. 53). Seldom exercised, these presidential powers have occasionally permitted significant interference with arbitrary government. Another check was expected to be provided by the referendum, common in Europe and the dominions but then unknown in Britain. The provision that all amendments to the constitution after 1930 would require approval by referendum was never operative, following an amendment just before the deadline. This safeguard was finally incorporated in de Valera's constitution, resulting in the rejection of most amendments by a justifiably sceptical electorate. The constitution of the Free State also contained an elaborate but inoperative provision for the initiation of referenda by popular petition. This amenity was abruptly abolished when de Valera attempted to invoke it in 1928; once in power, Fianna Fáil made no attempt at resuscitation. The frills of participatory democracy did not survive their first challenge in a state baptized in blood and confirmed by coercion.

The constitution of 1922 specified a distinctive form of government, headed by the president of an executive council equivalent to a cabinet and bound by collective responsibility. The Dáil was charged with electing the president, approving his nominations for the executive council, and convening a committee to select any suitable 'extern ministers'. These were to be 'impartially representative of Dáil Éireann' without necessarily belonging to it (art. 55). President Cosgrave acted as *primus* and sometimes *ultimus inter pares*, conciliating between rival interest groups but bending with ever greater frequency to the authoritarian policies of his deputy and minister for home affairs (later justice), Kevin O'Higgins. Cosgrave's control was most secure during his first year of office, when he acted as minister for finance; though even then, his influence on policy was far feebler than that of Craig as prime minister of Northern Ireland. Cosgrave's authority was further weakened by the assassination of O'Higgins in July 1927. By contrast, de Valera used his supremacy as founder of Fianna Fáil to impose tight control over his cabinet. Though often deferring to ministers in matters outside his central preoccupations, such as industry and commerce (Seán Lemass) or finance (Seán MacEntee), de Valera had no hesitation in taking personal charge of any policy arousing his interest or touching his cherished principles. He also retained direct ministerial control over external affairs, including relations with Britain and Northern Ireland. De Valera's preference for strong leadership was expressed in the role of taoiseach (chief) as defined in the constitution of 1937. The taoiseach, unlike the president of the executive council, could instruct the president to dismiss any of his ministers, a function hitherto reserved for the Dáil. However, his powers fell far short of the dictatorship which many of de Valera's enemies, and some of his admirers, had anticipated. Irish democracy remained firmly derivative from its detested British prototype.

As Collins and O'Duffy had predicted, against de Valera's dire warnings to the contrary, the constitution incorporating the treaty proved to be a provisional and manipulable instrument. The rapidly changing character of the British commonwealth, as the empire was increasingly termed, offered Cosgrave and O'Higgins ample opportunity for advancing the Free State's autonomy through negotiation and active involvement in imperial conferences. The introduction of 'O'Higgins's comma' to the monarch's official title in 1926 provided symbolic confirmation of the Free State's integrity as a dominion. No longer 'of Great Britain and Ireland and of the British Dominions beyond the seas', the monarch was now 'of Great Britain, Ireland, and the British Dominions beyond the seas'. The same conference also pronounced that the dominions were 'autonomous Communities within the British Empire, equal in status'.[18] Of greater practical utility was the so-called Statute of Westminster of December 1931, which precluded imposition of any law on a dominion without the request and consent of the local parliament. This offered apparently limitless opportunity for constitutional innovation without fear of imperial interference. Eight years earlier, the flexibility of dominion status had been tested by the Free State's success in joining the League of Nations and registering the treaty as an international agreement, despite British objection to these assertions of individuality in foreign relations. The dominions later supported the Free State's entry to the council of the League in 1930, the Antrim-born Methodist Seán Lester acting as its permanent representative from 1929 to 1934 and as the League's last secretary-general (1940–6). Cosgrave's pursuit of further autonomy through negotiation rather than confrontation also secured vital financial benefits for the Free State, despite his secret undertaking in February 1923 to pay over land purchase annuities and other debts in return for various concessions. The tripartite settlement of December 1925, followed by the 'ultimate financial settlement' of March 1926, exempted the Free State from servicing its share of the United

Kingdom's public debt and contributing to war pensions, as required by the treaty (art. 5). Exploiting rather than challenging the British connection, the Irish Free State inched towards solvency and the practical autonomy of a post-war dominion.

The challenge was resumed, with spectacular effect, after Cosgrave's defeat in 1932. De Valera used his election in September 1932 to presidency of the League of Nations council to affirm the camaraderie of small countries in resisting the warlike designs of the greater powers. Applying confrontation to achieve what might otherwise have been painlessly negotiated, the new government renewed the spirit of revolution by goading the former enemy into surly if half-hearted reassertions of imperial authority. With surreal logic, de Valera refused to take rhetorical advantage of the abnegation of British authority in the Statute of Westminster, on the ground that it was a British statute and therefore without authority. Instead, he initiated a series of constitutional amendments and statutes to extinguish the symbols of dominion status and fidelity to the crown. His targets included the parliamentary oath of fidelity and allegiance (abolished in May 1933 after suspension of the amending act by the Seanad); the governor-general's formal control over the appropriation of money and his right to withhold assent from bills (November 1933); the right of appeal against Irish judgements to the privy council (November 1933); the Seanad (May 1936); and all constitutional references to the crown and governor-general (December 1936). The governor-general's remaining powers were transferred to the executive council in June 1937. No trace remained of the vesting of executive authority in the crown (art. 51), apart from the monarch's ceremonial function in accrediting diplomats and executing international agreements, confirmed in the External Relations act of December 1936.

Having dismantled the constitution of the Free State and effectively repudiated the commonwealth, de Valera nevertheless refrained from declaring Ireland a republic, in the absence of two-thirds of its fourth green field (north-east Ulster). Instead, he proposed a new 'Constitution of Ireland', the name of the state being atternatively 'Éire' or 'Ireland'. This document was approved by a substantial majority in a referendum, and brought into effect in December 1937. It embodied de Valera's favourite formula of popular sovereignty with a dash of external association, declaring that 'all powers of government, legislative, executive and judicial, derive, under God, from the people' (art. 6.1). Britain declined to resuscitate de Valera's republican support by seeking the expulsion of Éire from the commonwealth. Instead, the credit for severing formal links through declaration of the 'Republic of Ireland', inaugurated on Easter Monday 1949, went to a coalition of his opponents under John Aloysius Costello (Cosgrave's attorney-general from 1926 to 1932). With this rather limp gesture, the republican grievance was reduced to a single demand, the revendication of Northern Ireland.

The long march towards external association, though politically useful in sustaining the anachronistic image of Hibernia struggling to free herself from Britannia's clinch, brought no practical benefits. In June 1932, however, de Valera attempted to reduce the Free State's financial liabilities by retaining the annuities payable by purchasers of land who had received government loans under the Union. In Northern Ireland, these annuities were already retained under the Home Rule settlement. Though the annual liability of Irish farmers amounted to over £3 million, the retained revenue was greatly reduced by a long-standing campaign to dissuade farmers from paying their annuities in the first place. The retention of annuities, in combination with the abolition of the oath of fidelity, rapidly caused Anglo-Irish breakdown, followed by the imposition of punitive tariffs on most exports from the Free State to the United Kingdom. The resultant 'economic war' of mutual trade restrictions and retaliatory tariffs was not fully resolved until April 1938, when Neville Chamberlain extended his policy of appeasement to Éire. In return for a lump payment of £10 million, Britain waived its entitlement to Irish land annuities and tariff barriers were relaxed. Less predictably, Chamberlain rashly surrendered sovereignty over the ports and harbours that had been reserved to the admiralty under the treaty. Even de Valera's detractors were impressed by this coup, without which Éire could scarcely have maintained its status of friendly neutrality during the 'Emergency' which found Europe again in a state of war by September 1939. The Anglo-Irish agreement of 1938 belatedly demonstrated that the campaign for dismantling the treaty could be beneficial as well as exhilarating. Contrary to O'Duffy's dictum, there were indeed pleasures in freedom apart from fighting for it.

Administration

If both Irish states adopted and sustained parliamentary systems broadly based on Westminster, the associated structures of administration and justice were still less revolutionary in form. In Northern Ireland, the civil administration was transferred to local control with only minor structural adjustments, although southern interference with the transfer of staff and records complicated the always formidable problem of constructing a new state amidst chaos and destruction. The eventual triumph of bureaucratic values was largely attributable to the resourceful direction of Sir Ernest Clark, the English assistant undersecretary for Ulster who became first head of the northern civil service, before retiring in 1925 to assume multiple directorships and eventually the governance of Tasmania. He was succeeded by another punctilious Englishman (albeit a chief architect of the UVF and the Special Constabulary), Sir Wilfrid Spender. To a raw recruit in 1937, Spender seemed 'remote, kindly, lisping, out of touch, hospitable, croquet-playing, correct, wary of political interference in civil service affairs'. Although the highest officials were seldom Ulstermen, transfers from Dublin Castle provided only a small minority of junior members of the new establishment (less than a quarter of the ministry of home affairs in January 1924). The residue were mainly recruited locally, with an examination for clerks from 1926; although senior grades were selected through the imperial examination system after 1929. As in Britain, priority was given to ex-servicemen, with special preference for the disabled. Political patronage enabled the former gun-runner, Colonel Fred Crawford, to enter old age 'still harmlessly occupying a chair, unnoticed and undisturbed', in the ministry of labour.[19]

Conspicuous for their absence were Catholics, who comprised only a tenth of lower officials in 1934 and less than 6 per cent of the administrative grade in 1943. Even these proportions were considered excessive by many loyalists, who had constantly to be reassured of the ministry's determination to intensify discrimination against this potentially 'disloyal' element.[20] Northern Ireland's administrators were almost invariably Protestants with political views indistinguishable from those of their masters. A rare exception in religion alone was the Limerick-born great-grandnephew of Napoleon I and product of Downside, Andrew Nicholas Bonaparte-Wyse (permanent secretary of the ministry of education, 1927–39). Though seemingly partisan and sectarian in its composition, the northern civil service subscribed whole-heartedly to the conventional insistence upon impartial application of the prescribed procedures. It therefore acted as a brake upon the more daring experiments in discrimination perpetrated by parliamentarians and local politicians.

The judiciary, as in Britain, were selected according to their political soundness and legal expertise in unknown proportions. The appointment of the Catholic Unionist Sir Denis Stanislaus Henry, as the province's first lord chief justice, is invariably cited as proof of Craig's initially liberal inclinations. In fact, since the superior courts remained a reserved service, his elevation was nominally in the gift of the crown acting on the advice of the British cabinet.[21] Political control of the dispensation of justice was reinforced in July 1935, when local landlords and notables lost their judicial powers as unpaid justices of the peace. These powers were transferred to paid ('resident') magistrates, recalling the use of special courts comprising two resident magistrates during the Anglo-Irish war. As in the case of the civil service, political partiality among the judiciary was restrained by professional ethics rather than ecumenical procedures of selection.

The existing system of elected local authorities was retained, but the northern government ruthlessly curtailed the activity of nationalist councils (long after these had ceased to attest their allegiance to Dáil Éireann). This was achieved by the abolition of proportional representation and the imposition of a declaration of allegiance on paid officers (September 1922), accompanied by the dissolution of recalcitrant bodies such as the county councils of Fermanagh and Tyrone. The convenience of direct control through a commissioner was outweighed by the loss of a local forum for aspirant Unionist politicians. Through gerrymandering ward and divisional boundaries, strenuous efforts were made to secure Unionist majorities in areas where Protestants were only slightly outnumbered, so allowing the resumption of 'representative' local government. Aided by the refusal of most local nationalists to make submissions, the responsible boundary commission executed its task with such ingenuity that the substantial Catholic majorities in Fermanagh and Tyrone, and in many rural districts, no longer resulted in the election of nationalist councils in 1924 or thereafter. Further municipal tinkering secured the defeat of nationalists even in Enniskillen and Derry (where a supplementary gerrymander of staggering insouciance was accomplished in 1936), leaving only a handful of towns in 'disloyal' hands. The virtual restriction of local democracy to Protestants reinforced nationalist indifference, so that scarcely any contests occurred in subsequent rural or county elections.[22] Urban elections were more vigorously fought, nationalist control in Armagh being abruptly terminated by dissolution of the council (on grounds of corruption) in 1934.

Indifference was compounded by the progressive reduction of local autonomy, in a province where local taxation was already of negligible importance by British standards. Unable to extract substantial local support for either education or policing, the government had little reason to resist further centralization. Following the British example, agricultural rating was peremptorily abolished in 1929 (nearly half a century earlier than in the south), so rendering local bodies still more dependent on grants-in-aid from the exchequer. The central government thus exercised an ever tighter administrative and political control over all organs of the state, without fundamentally altering the inherited structures. So long as Unionist power could be maintained and asserted through the conventional mechanisms, there was no need to tamper with them. Suppression or modification were required only rarely, whenever rash attempts were made to activate the potentially subversive liberal principles of judicial, bureaucratic, or local independence from political dictation. In practice, that challenge was virtually restricted to local government and to the period of initial turmoil before the state took form.

The future administrative shape of the Free State was less predictable in 1922 than that of Northern Ireland. In each sphere of administration, the provisional government had the choice of taking over 'British' institutions, adapting the rival revolutionary bodies, or creating novel structures. The third option was virtually irrelevant, at least until the authority of the Free State had been established. The skeletal departments, commissions, and courts surviving from the revolutionary period were brilliant improvisations, typically unsuitable for bureacratic perpetuation in peacetime. Collins's back-of-the-envelope department of finance could scarcely be expected to administer the revenues and expenditures of a functioning state. Moreover, like all republican institutions, such bodies were riven by the political split and subject to manipulation by rival military factions. Although the courts and local councils continued to operate sporadically during 1922, the pressure to disband the existing structures became more acute as civil animosities intensified. In most administrative sectors, such as education, agriculture, fisheries, or the post office, there was in any case no substantial revolutionary body in existence. The new government therefore relied almost exclusively on the existing civil service. With the exception of a few senior officials and non-established posts, the new departments of state were manned by those members of the Irish civil service who chose not to retire on pension or move to Northern Ireland. Some 21,000 serving officials were so transferred, compared with only 131 officials of the revolutionary

Dáil and 88 former civil servants who had lost or resigned their posts on political grounds. Even among senior officers, Castle veterans still accounted for half of the élite after the first decade of independence.[23] Though greatly easing the administrative transition, this continuity virtually eliminated the chance of radical structural change.

The fiscal rectitude of the civil service was assured by the choice of permanent secretary for the department of finance, which handled monetary transactions for all departments. The first incumbent was Joseph Brennan, a Catholic from Bandon, Co. Cork, whose secret dealings with republicans had not prevented him from becoming a paragon of administrative prudence when a clerk in the chief secretary's office. His conservatism was equalled by that of his successor, J. J. McElligott, the versatile Kerryman, dismissed as a clerk in Dublin Castle after the 1916 Rising, who had edited the *Statist* before returning to Dublin. Civil service ethics were further implanted by Cornelius Joseph Gregg, a Kilkenny Catholic on loan from the Board of Inland Revenue who devised the Ministries and Secretaries act of 1924.[24] Before long, the inspirational methods and rapid decision-making of the revolutionary administrators had been supplanted by the conventional forms and procedures of the British civil service. Nevertheless, in its selection of additional staff the Free State paid scant attention to the meritocratic British model. Despite retention of the system of competitive examinations at higher levels, political factors were crucial from the outset. The introduction in January 1923 of Irish as a standard element for examination, even for the nascent diplomatic service, strongly favoured those brought up in 'Irish Ireland'. Furthermore, redundant veterans of the national army were given exclusive access to vacancies for messengers, postmen, and other subordinate positions, mirroring the less systematic preference for war veterans in Northern Ireland and Britain. Deserving former army officers were exempted from examination for administrative and clerical posts, further denting the principle of merit introduced in 1871.

The suspension of hundreds of Irregular supporters and

internees during and after the civil war, which particularly affected postal workers and primary teachers, created extensive opportunities for the temporary employment of attested supporters of the treaty. The new government treated its employees with greater severity than that shown by its predecessor, which had retained Richard Mulcahy's brother in the post office despite securing comprehensive information on his revolutionary activities.[25] Permanent posts also became available upon the dismissal of officials whose 'active association with the Irregulars' had been demonstrated to the definite satisfaction of an advisory committee. Appeals against harsh decisions continued to engross the executive council for several years, every case being determined individually. Little attention was paid to the conciliatory advice delivered in February 1925 by James J. Walsh, the Corkonian minister for posts and telegraphs. He declared that 'the time has come when, in the interests of the Nation, a good deal of allowance can be made for the actions of men at a time of doubt and agony, when the right path was by no means clear'. Walsh urged reinstatement of all those willing to sign the required declaration of loyalty to the elected government.[26] Despite a steady trickle of reinstatement, many republican victims remained to be belatedly vindicated by Fianna Fáil after 1932. Even those who had lost employment with local authorities 'for political reasons' were sometimes offered the solace of civil service posts, as in the case of fourteen men and two women who were invited by the executive council to become employment clerks in 1935.[27] The supremacy of political affiliation over merit, an unavoidable consequence of civil conflict, long remained characteristic of a civil service universally derided as a source of 'jobs for the boys'.

Patronage was also ubiquitous in judicial and local appointments, both before and after the creation of the Free State. The few barristers who had imperilled their careers by acting as republican justices were shamelessly favoured in the selection of judges, provided that they had not shown Irregular sympathies during the civil war. The decentralized structure of the revolutionary courts had rendered them uncontrollable after the split over the treaty, leading to the summary dissolution of those outside Dublin in July and October 1922. They were replaced by a reorganized system of district and circuit courts, the new 'district justices' being resident magistrates under a less tainted name. As a future district judge observed sardonically: 'If you are appointing professional minor Justices, don't call them "R.M.s" or you will damn the whole system. Call them "leis-breithimh" or something.' The revolutionary high court and supreme court in Dublin were temporarily retained, although subordinate after July 1923 to a 'judicial commission' established to complete the abandoned work of the Dáil judiciary. These revolutionary vestiges coexisted with the moribund but undisbanded judiciary left over from the Union, and an attempt was even made to resuscitate the criminal assizes in June 1922. The legal administration was therefore in chaos until April 1924, when the long-presaged Courts of Justice act was at last assented.[28] With district justices performing the functions once assigned to petty sessions, local influence over the administration of justice was terminated a decade earlier than in Northern Ireland. The recurrent use of special military tribunals, manned by army officers sometimes without legal qualifications as under British rule, further curtailed judicial independence.

Local government also became progressively subordinated to central control, even more rapidly than in Northern Ireland. In accordance with the welfare policy of Griffith's Sinn Féin, not to mention the pursuit of thrift, the elected boards of guardians were dissolved, the workhouses were closed or redeployed, and outdoor relief was renamed 'home assistance'. The new county boards of health were appointed by the county councils, so reducing local autonomy. Under the Local Government act of March 1925, these boards also took over local services such as sanitation, housing, drainage, and water from the disbanded rural district councils. After 1929, the city authorities were progressively placed under the supervision of salaried managers, central management being extended to the county councils in 1942. Local responsibility had already been crucially undermined by the enactment of a local appointments commission in

July 1926, which was intended to negate local patronage in senior administrative and professional posts by conducting competitive examinations. This led in December 1930 to the replacement of the Mayo county council by a commissioner, following its rejection of the appointment of a female Protestant as county librarian. As in most sectors of administration, the Free State's government proved more systematic than its predecessor in asserting central political control over local interests, whether for better or worse.

Security

The most overt assertion of central power was embodied in the police and security forces, and in the coercive legislation that supported them. Northern Ireland's Civil Authorities (Special Powers) act of April 1922, initially introduced for one year, was renewed repeatedly until its permanent enactment in 1933 (to be repealed only in 1972). Although the last internees were released in December 1924, and most convicted political prisoners just over a year later, the threat of massive re-incarceration of nationalists remained (being reactivated in December 1938 and especially during the Second World War). Just as Carson's Ulster Unionists had relied on the menace rather than the practice of violence to secure their own political freedom, so Craig normally found the menace of coercion sufficient to stifle the pursuit of political freedom by his opponents. That menace was incorporated in a formidable array of police and paramilitary forces, occasionally aided by Northern Ireland's small garrison of British soldiers.

The terms of Home Rule precluded formal establishment of a separate military force, though recurrent attempts were made to extend the territorial army to the province. Worried by the confusion of police and military functions in the Special Constabulary, the secretary of the ministry of finance protested thus in September 1922: 'If one wants a volunteer force to act in the place of the British troops withdrawn (the old bogey which is made more frightful from time to time) why should we not have a regular territorial force? . . . Ireland, or rather three-quarters of it, has an army of its own. Why should we be the only portion of the remainder of the United Kingdom which has no local military force? I think they have it even in the Channel Islands!'[29] Subsequent attempts to embody sections of the Special Constabulary as territorials failed, although the associated Local Defence Volunteers achieved military status as a home guard in 1940. The task of suppressing disorder and intimidating potential rebels therefore continued to fall to the police.

In May 1922, the RIC had been re-embodied in Northern Ireland as the Royal Ulster Constabulary. The declared intention that a third of the force should be Catholics, in proportion to the province's population, was never fulfilled. This was doubtless attributable to the scarcity of Catholic applicants, discouraged by the indelicate arrest of two Catholics on the police advisory committee established in May 1922 to promote the pluralist programme of the second pact between Craig and Collins.[30] In both 1925 and 1931, the Catholic proportion was just over a sixth, mostly drawn from the rather small and often elderly residue of the RIC whose commitment to policing had survived the Anglo-Irish conflict. By 1931, nearly half of the RUC were former Specials, whose sectarian reputation was unavoidably transferred to the regular force.[31] Nationalist confidence in the RUC was further reduced by the creation with ministerial blessing of a flourishing Orange police lodge (the Sir Robert Peel, LOL 1334), whose first worshipful master was dismissed from the police in 1924 for inciting Orangemen to defend the border against any British-sanctioned tampering. The disgraced inspector (John William Nixon) had previously been implicated in the murder of Belfast Catholics, such as the family of the Devlinite publican, Owen McMahon, in March 1922. After his belated dismissal, Nixon immediately became an Orange martyr, progressing to a parliamentary career of twenty-one years as an independent Unionist.[32]

Though formally under the command of Colonel Charles Wickham, inspector-general of the RUC, the various divisions of the Ulster Special Constabulary had their own practically autonomous hierarchies of officers. The B Specials, like the Orange lodges and Ulster Volunteers from which they had emerged, were revered in loyalist folklore as the protectors of Protestant liberty and paragons of selfless manhood serving the public good. Unlike other Special divisions, they were instructed to intercept incursors into predominantly Protestant districts rather than to impose discipline upon Catholic neighbourhoods. As a loyalist newspaper mused in August 1923, 'theirs is largely a labour of love. . . . But their sense of duty, always a strong point with Ulstermen, has carried them through every difficulty and trial.' The social origins of the B Specials testified to the populist appeal of loyalism: 'They are drawn from many classes and occupations, and professional and working men may be found side by side in the ranks. Farmers and farmers' sons, shopkeepers and shop assistants, and working men of various grades constitute a large proportion of the force.'[33] The appeal of this democratic idyll was not universal among loyalists, as exemplified by the force's organizer in Derry in November 1924. He bemoaned the resignation of businessmen and ex-army officers, noting 'a tendency for labour to increase their numbers among the commissioned ranks. You can understand what is likely to happen if labour gets control with possibly a socialistic element. This force could either make or mar a Government.' Chillingly, he added that it would be 'quite impossible' to disarm the B Specials, should they resist disbandment.[34] Protected 'during the course of the present Troubles' from both civil and criminal actions under the Indemnity act of May 1922, the force seemed perpetually in need of firmer discipline and restraint. Meanwhile, the northern government's citizen army remained free to intimidate nationalists and reassure Unionists with their night patrols, roadblocks, rough-and-ready interrogations, and 'fire-fighting' sorties in pursuit of rioters.

Despite the sharp reduction in unrest after 1922, the Special Constabulary stubbornly resisted proposals for its abolition or reform. In January 1923, the C1 division in Belfast had been reorganized in military fashion, 'groups' and 'districts' being replaced by 'brigades' and 'battalions' (twenty in number, each with sixteen Lewis guns). In September 1924 the boundary commission received a deafening signal when the USC was allocated a further 150 Lewis guns and 5 million rounds of ammunition. The full-time A Specials were nevertheless disbanded in December 1925, having secured acceptable terms after seizing barracks, arresting their officers, issuing an ultimatum to the government, and then respectfully withdrawing it. Recruiting for the C1 division ceased in February 1926, so heralding the end of a formidable urban army in which over 150 men had been trained as Lewis gunners up to July 1923. The reductions were forced upon Craig by the British government, which had already been obliged to donate almost the entire cost of this 'transferred service' in dollops amounting to £6.8 million. A more modest force, eventually reduced to about 12,000 B Specials, was retained. The continued employment of Ulster's part-time heroes was imperilled by their own previous success, their only duties in 1928 being to attend the Ulster Tourist Trophy Race and to safeguard Princess Royal.[35] In August 1929, further cuts were averted after fervent reference by Sir Dawson Bates to 'this loyal and disinterested body of men' acting 'in the interests of the community'. Bates added the surprising claim 'that from observation and conversations, I find the Special Constabulary are very popular with their Nationalist neighbours'.[36]

The preservation of the force was assured by its role in the Belfast riots of summer 1935, after a decade of relative quiescence. Since 1922, only two sectarian killings had occurred in the city, in November 1933 and November 1934. Following the murder of a Catholic publican in April 1935, and subsequent riots during the silver jubilee celebrations for George V, the government had imposed a curfew and prohibited all parades. After a sharp reminder from the grand master of the Orange Institution that 'no government would prevent Orangemen from marching' on the Twelfth, and under pressure from Craigavon, Bates prudently rescinded the ban. The march generated further riots resulting in the deaths of eight Catholics and five Protestants, together with the eviction of families from 430 Catholic and

64 Protestant houses. The wildest Protestant provocations came from the 'Billy Boys', a band from Glasgow inflamed to distraction by the tune of 'Onward Christian Soldiers'. Though the main burden of policing lay with the RUC, the B Specials were assigned the novel function of arresting Protestant looters in Catholic precincts. Three-quarters of those arrested were Protestants, a remarkable deviation from the pattern of 1922.[37] Despite a subsequent boycott of Catholic pubs and lingering disputes over rehousing those evicted, sectarian civil war did not ensue. The next major mobilization of the Specials followed the outbreak of war, which prompted the resumption of general active patrolling. Despite marked improvements in discipline and even-handedness, the retention of a substantial force of Protestant vigilantes, armed by the state, still provided northern Catholics with the most explicit and triumphal symbol of their subordination.

In the Free State as in Northern Ireland, the end of murderous civil conflict failed to prompt the abandonment of emergency legislation and repression of dissidence. Admittedly, the dumping of republican arms in May 1923 did not signal an end to widespread violence, property offences, public disorder, and social conflicts. The persistence of social and political outrages justified O'Higgins in promulgating a series of emergency measures further suspending civil rights. The first of several Public Safety acts was passed in August 1923, allowing for the continuation of internment without trial. A consequent act of November 1926 allowed the government to declare a state of national emergency, and suspension of habeas corpus; nine months later, the vicious murder of O'Higgins (by three IRA men on their way to a Gaelic football match) prompted further legislation to proscribe associations, suppress periodicals, and establish special military courts. Although this measure was repealed in December 1928, another military tribunal was established through amendment of the constitution in October 1931, in order to suppress no less than twelve republican associations. Though Sinn Féin was exempted, the 'unlawful associations' included not only the IRA, Cumann na mBan, and Fianna Éireann, but also Saor

Éire (Free Ireland), the political front of the IRA, and several tiny socialist organizations such as the Friends of Soviet Russia. Though terrible in the seditiousness of their utterance, these bodies were far smaller, more disorganized and less destructive than their predecessors of the civil war period. The ruthlessness of their suppression demonstrated the continued will of the founders of the Free State to consolidate their power and silence those who renounced the government's legitimacy.

The electoral success of de Valera's Fianna Fáil, which had received enthusiastic if not always welcome support from republican vigilantes, was predictably followed by the release of political prisoners, the suspension (but not repeal) of the constitutional amendment act of 1931, and the abolition of the military tribunal. Yet, when challenged by the mass mobilization and sporadic violence of the National Guard and the Blueshirts (discussed in the next section), de Valera's government soon imitated the coercive measures of its execrated predecessor. In August 1933, O'Duffy's National Guard was proclaimed, and the Special Powers tribunal revived in the form of five senior army officers. By now, the growing alienation of Fianna Fáil from diehard republicanism made it expedient to sentence not only Blueshirts but republicans, thirty-four members of the IRA being imprisoned by the tribunal during 1933. Those sentenced included Tom Barry, the maturing hero of Kilmichael Cross, who was convicted for possession of arms and ammunition and went through the nostalgic routine of declining to recognize the court. During the following year, about 100 republicans and 350 Blueshirts were convicted. The wearing of uniforms by civilians was prohibited in March 1934, but this act was suspended for eighteen months in the Seanad's final burst of defiance.[38]

By June 1936, the IRA was once more an unlawful association, as a result of its proposed national mobilization at Sallins and Bodenstown, Co. Kildare, scheduled for 21 June. The executive council resolved, rather long-windedly, that 'the methods and activities of the organisation styling itself the Irish Republican Army and the commission of crimes of violence obviously organised make it necessary that it should be made clear that the continuance of this unlawful organisation will not be permitted'.[39] In June 1939, the IRA was yet again suppressed under the Offences against the State act, which also enabled de Valera to revive the military tribunal with expanded powers as the special military court (August 1939). The government was therefore well prepared for the wartime 'Emergency', during which a host of coercive measures were summarily imposed through executive order rather than specific legislation. Internment was applied on a massive scale, several republicans were executed, and others (after initial appeasement) were left to die on hunger strike. The Offences against the State act proved so convenient that it has never been repealed; while the state of 'national emergency' declared in September 1939 remained in force until 1976. Ireland's revolutionaries had learned their British lessons in coercion only too well.

The reiterated resort to repression and suspension of legal rights betokened feebleness rather than strength in the rule of law. The civil chaos of 1922 had left the Free State without an efficient police force: the RIC had been disbanded, the G division of political detectives in the Dublin Metropolitan Police mainly murdered, the republican police repudiated by the provisional government, and the new Civic Guard disarmed. Following British precedent, the reorganization of policing was placed in military hands. In August 1922, Eoin O'Duffy relinquished control of the key south-western command to become chief commissioner of the Civic Guard; and eight months later, the Dublin Metropolitan Police was assigned to his deputy and successor in Kerry, William Richard English Murphy. Major-General Murphy's preference for massive cross-country sweeps, like his subsequent record as director of army training, was doubtless conditioned by his experience of trench warfare as 2nd Lieutenant (later acting Lieutenant-Colonel) English-Murphy of the South Staffordshire regiment of territorials. His organizational skills were again demonstrated in 1940, when he raised a Local Security Force of 25,000 men for service during the Emergency. The integration of the Civic Guard (now Garda Síochána) and the Dublin Metropolitan Police was accomplished in April 1925, Murphy resuming his familiar role as O'Duffy's deputy. A year later, the consolidated force numbered 6,000, nearly 2,000 below the strength of the RIC in the same counties in 1914.[40]

Under O'Duffy's inspirational command, the Garda acquired an impressive *esprit de corps*, pugnaciously affirmed in repeated boxing matches against British and foreign police forces. Competitive fraternization transcended politics, as shown by the attendance of gardaí (guards) at the RUC sports in Derry and Dungannon, Co. Tyrone, in July 1925, and the annual dance of the RUC at Armagh in February 1926.[41] O'Duffy encouraged not only manly relaxation through sport and martial music, but also self-improvement through cultivation of the Irish language and especially the soul. In September 1928 he led a pilgrimage of 250 gardaí to Rome, featuring a choral performance for the ear of Pius XI which would surely have chilled the heart of any Orangeman straying into St Peter's Square:

> A Song for the Pope, for the royal Pope
> Who rules from sea to sea,
> Whose kingdom or sceptre can never fail
> What a grand old king is he.

As with the Ulster Special Constabulary, there was no snug niche in O'Duffy's force for religious minorities. The pilgrimage culminated in an audience with Mussolini, 'Il Duce', by whom O'Duffy was 'very warmly received in typical Fascist fashion'. He 'expressed his great interest and affection for the Irish people and appeared to understand the history and evolution of the Saorstát in a marked degree'.[42] O'Duffy's Garda was the quintessence of nationalist political culture, embodying the martial spirit of Fianna Éireann and the Irish Volunteers, sugared with the pietism of the Ancient Order of Hibernians.

Muscular Christianity was not, however, a fully effective substitute for firepower in winning public respect in a trigger-happy society. The unarmed uniformed gardaí had mostly evaded assassination during and after the civil war by steering clear of political offenders and organized criminals, though ten members of the force (including an armed detective) were gunned down between 1922 and 1931. No further killings occurred until 1940. The price of their survival was chronic inability to subdue paramilitary bandits. The IRA and gangs of armed criminals carried out bank-raids and robberies with impunity, beating, humiliating and kidnapping policemen, and burning, raiding, and looting their barracks, in order to mock the impotence of the state. During the year ending in September 1923, when only one garda was killed, about 200 stations were attacked and 60 destroyed, while 400 gardaí were assaulted, stripped, or robbed. The campaign continued long after the republican ceasefire, most notably in perennially 'disturbed' counties such as Clare and Leitrim. It is noteworthy that the same counties had exceptionally high rates of enlistment to the Garda, suggesting strong local polarization over the issue of social control.[43] A simultaneous assault on twelve Garda barracks in November 1926 led to the arrest of almost the entire headquarters staff of the IRA, yet republican violence soon resumed. In January 1927, the executive council considered, but rejected, a proposal to resurrect the 'Peelers' by arming the entire Garda.[44] Throughout the inter-emergency period, the maintenance of public order proved beyond the power of the regular police, who commanded even less popular respect than the pre-war RIC.

Police impotence encouraged successive governments to counteract unrest and subversion through a bewildering array of irregular armed gangs, just as Lloyd George had resorted to the Black and Tans and the Auxiliaries in 1920. These units acted as bodyguards, intelligence agents, detectives, armed raiders, and interrogators. The nucleus of the country-wide special branch, attached to the Garda in 1925, was the informal network of spies, informers, and thugs who had swarmed about Michael Collins during the Anglo-Irish conflict. His two key informers in the G division of the Dublin Metropolitan Police, David Neligan and Eamon Broy, remoulded the detective system after the civil war, in which both participated (Broy heading the fledgeling airforce, while Neligan became chief of army intelligence). The special units at their disposal were uncoordinated, undisciplined, and often outrageous. In May 1923, O'Higgins informed the executive council that over a third of the CID (founded by Collins in August 1921 and based at Oriel House in Westland Row, Dublin) 'were "hopeless" and would have to be got rid of'. A later report indicated that only 30 of the 350 personnel of the various special forces were 'Efficient Detective Officers', the remainder being a medley of street patrollers, 'Touts' and secret agents, 'Women Observers', part-time 'Volunteers', and support staff. In pursuing Irregulars, the CID employed 'Mouse Trap Raids' in 'well known haunts', resulting in the incarceration of all those present, who were thereupon submitted to methods of interrogation 'at least as humane as that form at present extensively used in America and known as the Third Degree'.[45] After an extensive purge, Neligan transferred the less uncontrollable special men to the new Dublin detective branch, incorporating the residue of the old G division. Following a further tussle with the army, which had been primarily responsible for the collection of political intelligence (through its 'Second Bureau') and the suppression of social unrest (through the Special Infantry Corps), Neligan was given command of a unified special branch of the Garda.[46] It was this unit, not the uniformed police, which turned the techniques of the terrorists against themselves.

The response of the special branch to social and political disorder was to send in flying columns armed with rifles and revolvers, employed with the same ruthlessness and indifference to legality as their opponents.[47] Though often locally effective in rounding up suspects and suppressing outrages, reliance on coercion by plain-clothed gunmen reinforced the impression that the Free State was ruled through force rather than justice. Moreover the special branch, like the Garda in general, was a partisan instrument, composed mainly of national ex-servicemen discharged after the civil war. From August 1922 to December 1923, enlistment to the police had been restricted to veterans of other national forces, who could scarcely be expected to treat their former Irregular opponents impartially.[48] The Garda's revulsion for republicans, even in the non-violent embodiment of Fianna Fáil, was made manifest in 1932, when O'Duffy vainly attempted to persuade Neligan and Michael Brennan (the army chief of staff) to collaborate in a *coup d'état* installing himself as the Free State's Mussolini.

When rebuffed, O'Duffy resumed his police duties under the new government with surprising composure and the appearance of co-operation. Despite reiterated demands from Fianna Fáil cumainn (clubs) for the disbandment of the special branch, the government evidently accepted O'Duffy's warning that this would undoubtedly cause the 'conditions presently existing in Clare and Leitrim' to 'spread over the State'. Nevertheless, de Valera eventually removed Neligan, O'Duffy, and other key police officers, his choice of chief commissioner being Neligan's fellow-informer Eamon Broy.[49] Though Broy was a long-serving police administrator in Dublin, he proved admirably loyal to his new masters. In August 1933, the Garda was flooded with several thousand untrained former Irregulars, armed with rifles, and known as the Special Protective Unit or 'Broy Harriers' (the second Irish police force to be named after a pack of hounds, this time in Bray, Co. Wicklow). The force was raised by Oscar Traynor, the Dublin bookseller's son who had demonstrated his regard for procedural niceties when destroying the Custom House in 1921 and blowing up the Four Courts in 1922, together with their archival contents. The Broy Harriers soon absorbed the special branch, excelling even their predecessors in lawlessness, brutality, and partisan pursuit of political opponents. For a few months, both the special branch and the uniformed Garda were dangerously divided between supporters of the current and previous governments, open conflict being averted by de Valera's redirection of police persecution towards his former supporters in the IRA. Nevertheless, the Free State's policemen remained all too obviously the tools of political parties. De Valera's innovation was to create a polarized force, in which both major parties could influence the police to abuse their powers at the expense of different sections of the community. Such was the rough justice administered in de Valera's Ireland.

If democracy was curtailed by persistent subversion, recurrent coercion, and partisan policing, its very survival depended on the subordination of the army to parliament. During and even after the civil war, Cosgrave's ministers and the Dáil had delegated executive authority to the army council, retrospectively rubber-stamping its sometimes horrifying edicts. The Dáil itself had the atmosphere of a parade-ground, as Cosgrave recalled in June 1924: 'We had a political army in this country until the last election in August, 1923. Men came in here in uniform day after day to vote up to the time of the last election.'[50] Civil authority over the army, and its own internal discipline, were tested and found wanting in March 1924, when two disaffected officers presented the executive council with an 'ultimatum'. This demanded disbandment of the army council, suspension of demobilization, and a conference with the government to discuss reinterpretation of the Anglo-Irish treaty. The signatories were Major-General Liam Tobin and Colonel Charles Dalton, close associates of Collins and veterans of his notoriously ungovernable 'Squad', who maintained that 'the late Commander-in-Chief' would, like themselves, have regarded the imposition of the treaty as 'a successful ambush by the enemy' rather than a final settlement.

In the absence of the dead Collins and the diplomatically ill Cosgrave, O'Higgins induced the executive council to order their arrest, so provoking the resignation of Joseph McGrath (minister for industry and commerce, former 'Squad' man, and chief political ally of the refractory officers) and of about fifty officers, while an equal number absconded with their arms. This seemingly firm response was soon undermined by an informal deal forgiving the mutineers for their lapse, and the temporary appointment of the conciliatory O'Duffy in command of all defence forces. Thereupon Mulcahy as minister for defence, without authorization from O'Duffy or the executive council, approved the arrest of several mutineers celebrating their presumed exoneration in a Dublin pub. The outcome of this bizarre sequence was the enforced resignation of Seán MacMahon (chief of staff) and Mulcahy, who was replaced by a minister innocent of military rivalries (Peter Hughes, a taciturn grocer from Dundalk, Co. Louth).[51] The authority of both the executive council and the army command was left temporarily in tatters.

The 'army mutiny' exposed several deep fissures within the forces upholding the Free State. Tobin and Dalton represented an army faction known as the 'Old IRA' or the 'IRA Organization', a fraternity in competition with the dominant IRB. The latter had been reorganized in late 1922 under the presidency of Seán MacMahon, with support from Mulcahy and several staff officers, in order to tighten central control over the officer corps in the manner practised so effectively by Collins in the war of independence. Though apparently 'in existence at least in embryo' before the civil war, formal organization of the 'Old IRA' was prompted by the re-emergence of the Brotherhood.[52] The mutiny was thus in part the outcome of a struggle between two fraternal élites, attempting to protect their corporate interests in a period of rapid demobilization following the civil war. The mutineers preferred, however, to direct their rhetorical indignation against the favouritism allegedly shown to a third fraternity, that of former members of the British forces. This crowd-pleasing accusation was baseless, since only perhaps a third of the officers with previous service in other armies had been retained under the reorganization scheme to which Tobin and Dalton objected.[53] Yet the anti-British rhetoric of the mutineers manifested a genuine cleavage between proponents of the Free State who viewed partition and dominion status as an acceptable *fait accompli*, and those who looked forward to non-violent progression towards the promised republic. The latter strategy virtually ceased to influence Cosgrave's executive council after the resignation of McGrath, re-emerging in the pseudo-constitutional republicanism of de Valera's Fianna Fáil.

The eventual outcome of the mutiny was a substantial purge of the army, curtailment of its intelligence functions, reinforcement of its internal discipline, and reduction of its political influence. The strength of the army was progressively reduced from 48,200 in March 1923 to 16,400 after the mutiny, falling to 11,600 by 1927. The permanent establishment was further cut after the introduction of reserves from 1927 onwards: by 1932, there were

8,800 reservists but less than 5,800 regulars in the army.[54] Though the vast majority of those retrenched had no connection with the mutineers, Tobin's associates were ruthlessly hunted down, leading to the dismissal not only of the mutinous officers, but also of 'a selection of N.C.O.'s and men believed to be in association with the conspiracy of the ex-officers'.[55] Active resistance against retrenchment was undermined by the continued preferential access of ex-servicemen to posts in the civil service and the police. Yet resentment was fuelled by reiterated further cuts in military spending and personnel, which were strongly resisted by senior officers as well as humble victims.

In August 1929, military discontent was embodied in the National Defence Association, which soon claimed the membership of nine-tenths of serving regular officers and four-fifths of retired officers. Among its prominent members were O'Duffy and Seán MacEoin, whose lack of deference towards his political masters had led to his removal as chief of staff in May 1929, after only eleven weeks in office. Despite initial toleration from the general staff and the executive council, serving officers were subsequently ordered to leave the association. In November 1930, a forceful manifesto was signed by its acting president, MacEoin, who had recently entered the Dáil and was about to resign from the reserve of officers. The army was so poorly organized that it might well not prove 'capable of acting in any circumstances as a useful instrument of national defence'; its conditions of service were 'calculated to promote serious discontent and demoralisation'; and officers had been victimized and subjected to illegal interference when conducting courts martial.[56] Though the association was dissolved after uttering this protest, many of its members and grievances were to reappear in February 1932, with the creation of the proto-Fascist Army Comrades' Association.

The uncertain loyalties of the officer corps in 1923–4 had contributed to the belated transfer of political intelligence from the army to the police. In April 1923, the army's director of intelligence had justified the wide-ranging political functions of his department by remarking that 'the circumstances of the time and the absence of a normal police system rendered it necessary'. He admitted that his personnel had been 'hastily recruited', that 'the discipline existing was lax in the extreme', and that some intelligence officers had come 'to regard themselves as independent of control'.[57] Since the same applied to its civilian counterparts, the ramshackle military intelligence service was retained and its index of criminals, ex-prisoners, and 'hostile persons' augmented until 33,000 names were registered. On O'Duffy's recommendation in May 1924, its functions of surveillance were reduced, though still encompassing subversive organizations and also 'the activities of "cliques" principally to be found in the Officer personnel of the Army'.[58] By the following year, however, external surveillance had been formally transferred to the special branch of the Garda, so remaining under the control of O'Duffy after his withdrawal from military command.

The restriction of military intelligence to internal problems facilitated the gradual development of a competent professional army under increasingly effective discipline. In the immediate aftermath of the civil war, members of the national forces had been one of the most lawless elements in the Free State: in the second half of 1923, they were believed to have committed 19 of the 40 reported murders and manslaughters, 6 of the 29 attempted murders, 110 of the 516 armed raids and robberies, and 13 of the 42 sexual attacks.[59] By October 1926, however, the army was sufficiently well disciplined and presentable to provoke a remarkably favourable appraisal by the leader of a British army boxing team, whose unprecedented exchange of fraternal blows with the flower of Ireland's manhood symbolized the contemporary spirit of Anglo-Irish reconciliation. Captain Noel Joseph Chamberlain ('Tank'), a Liverpool Catholic without known Irish connections, was impressed by the courtesy of orderlies and the efficiency of senior officers. His least favourable comments were reserved for junior officers and turncoats from his own army. Chamberlain's report evokes an Irish military élite already well steeped in the fraternal culture of a conventional officers' mess, cementing informal links through golf or bridge, lamenting the pettiness of politicians, and proclaiming the solidarity of soldiers everywhere.[60]

The national army, like the Garda, was by no means a British replica: its founders had made elaborate efforts to apply French or American rather than British models, and had sent their most promising officers for training to West Point. The British military influence was enhanced in 1926, when it seemed likely that the Irish army would become involved with Britain in coastal defence, upon the expected renegotiation of article 6 of the Anglo-Irish treaty. The creation of an Imperial Defence College to train officers from the dominions in British military methods and mentality also beckoned Irish participation. These half-promises came to nothing, since the war office and the committee of imperial defence obdurately resisted Irish involvement in either enterprise. As the chiefs of staff informally agreed in October 1929, the Irish were not competent to benefit from British instruction: 'The education of officers of the Irish Free State Forces is of too low a standard to admit of their deriving any value from a course at the Imperial Defence College; and their presence would lower the whole standard of instruction.'[61] Despite this patronizing evaluation, numerous Irish officers received training in other British military colleges, an experience which doubtless facilitated the surprisingly smooth co-operation between the two forces during the 'Emergency' of 1939–45. The professionalization of the reduced national army was completed during the prolonged tenure of Michael Brennan, Chamberlain's 'iron disciplinarian', as chief of staff between 1931 and 1940.

Brennan was also a key figure in proclaiming the army's independence from partisan interests, notably when he rejected O'Duffy's suggestion for a *coup d'état* in the event of electoral victory by Fianna Fáil in February 1932. The possibility of a military putsch, supported by prominent members of Cosgrave's administration, was no mere policeman's fantasy. In March 1930, an article in Irish attributed to Ernest Blythe, then minister for finance, had pondered the possibility of Fianna Fáil's 'changing the Constitution against the will of the people or destroying it with the object of putting aside the supreme power of the people'. If such a 'tyranny' were attempted, 'it would be right that the Army should undertake the work first, since they possess the instruments best fitted for it'.[62] Brennan's rejection of military action in 1932 encouraged de Valera to avoid tampering with the army command, so averting the political polarization and loss of morale which so damaged the Garda. No extensive commissioning of republicans was attempted, and even the special military tribunals involved long-serving officers who had fought the Irregulars. The strength of the regular army remained almost static at about 5,000 until extensive wartime mobilization in 1940; but a part-time Volunteer force of about 10,000 men was inaugurated in March 1934.[63] De Valera's government was justifiably apprehensive of the continued influence of fraternal networks, and resolved in April 1935 that every officer, soldier, and Volunteer should undertake to 'obey all orders issued to me by my superior officers appointed by the Executive Council [and] that I will not join, or be a member of, or subscribe to, any Secret Society whatsoever. So help me God.'[64] True to his assumption in 1920 that Ireland, like Cuba, could not escape strategic dependence on its more powerful neighbour, de Valera supported and reinforced the army in its preparations to co-operate with Britain in the case of European war or invasion.[65] The national army had become not only a loyal instrument of government, but a potential military partner for the former British antagonist.

Political Organization

By 1922, Ireland had become a land of politicians. This was temporarily obscured by the obvious militarization of political life in both states, as armed bands of former freedom fighters or veterans of the Great War contributed their destructive skills to every political interest. Yet the most pervasive revolutionary bequest was expertise in political organization rather than the use of arms. Sinn Féiners, like Orangemen, had perfected the techniques of mass mobilization, collective protest, co-ordinated propaganda, passive resistance, and discreet lobbying of potential British or foreign allies. The vast membership of the major political bodies meant that many thousands of Irish men and some women knew how to organize a public meeting, elect a committee, canvass for support, design a procession or a funeral cavalcade, make an appropriate speech or interjection, compose a possibly fictitious report for the press, devise a petition or pledge, and intimidate an obstinate opponent. These skills had been applied to extraordinary effect in the defensive or obstructive campaigns of both loyalists and nationalists up to 1922. Partition left ample opportunity for mobilizing political dissent in both states, reapplying the techniques of the revolutionary period. Less obvious was the model of political organization likely to be adopted by the new rulers, now committed to the preservation rather than obstruction of the state and its institutions.

For almost half a century after partition, the Ulster Unionist Party governed Northern Ireland with a substantial parliamentary majority. Its failure to fragment after securing provincial autonomy is one of the puzzles of Irish political history. Even though northern Protestants were not riven by any counterpart to the southern civil war, the furious social conflicts which made the Labour Party a major force in Britain also affected the province. The existence of a large proletariat in Derry, Belfast, and other industrial towns provided northern Labour (unlike its southern counterpart) with a large and restive constituency. Within the Protestant middle classes who dominated Unionism, there was further potential for factional division in pursuit of the spoils of power. The maintenance of a virtually united Unionist front must be attributed to lingering fear of a Catholic uprising, originating in the desperate sectarian conflicts of 1920–2. Unionists and Orangemen remained perpetually on guard against renewed subversion, which eventually erupted only after the fragmentation of Unionism in the later 1960s.

Northern party politics had a dual focus, with representation in the House of Commons at Westminster as well as Stormont. The retention of northern representatives in the imperial parliament provided the handful of Ulster Unionists, and the odd nationalist, with invaluable opportunities for propaganda and press coverage. Vastly outnumbered, the northern members had far less influence on relevant legislation than the government in Belfast, which proved quite adept at manipulating fraternal networks in Westminster and Whitehall. The democratic interplay of political parties would therefore occur, if at all, at Stormont. The general election of April 1925, conducted through proportional representation, suggested that Protestant solidarity was indeed crumbling as social issues complicated the basic division over nationality. Although thirty-two of the fifty-two successful candidates were official Unionists, eight other Protestants secured election on behalf of tenant farmers (one), Labour (three), and independent Unionism (four). Official membership returns for the Orange Institution suggest a gradual decline in membership after the enthusiasm of the revolutionary period. In Tyrone, membership fell by a sixth between 1918 and 1929; in Belfast, it declined by two-fifths between 1920 and 1932. Even the Sandy Row True Blues, LOL 1064, shrivelled from their peak of 117 in 1922 to only 48 a decade later, before a marked revival in the riotous conditions of 1935. Alert to such signs of dissent or indifference, Craigavon and the Ulster Unionist Council prudently decided to abolish proportional representation in order to disfranchise Protestant (more than Catholic) minority interests. As Craigavon explained to an Orange gathering on 12 July 1927, 'in the interests of Northern Ireland it was desirable to eliminate from parliament all minorities except that represented by the Nationalist Party'.[66] If disunity could not be eradicated, it might at least be concealed from southern and British eyes.

This measure clearly reinforced Unionist predominance during the turbulent period of heavy unemployment and urban unrest after 1929. Craigavon's party secured 37 seats in 1929, 36 in 1933, and 39 in 1938, though the success of several minor parties in 1945 would again rock Unionist complacency by reducing its representation to 33 members. Labour retained a tenuous parliamentary foothold and independent Unionism was never eliminated, three dissentients being elected at each poll between 1929 and 1938. Most of these were diehards in the mould of ex-inspector Nixon, whereas all twelve candidates of W. J. Stewart's relatively radical Progressive Unionist Party were outvoted in 1938. With almost a third of the poll in those twelve constituencies, the Progressives would clearly have achieved representation under the proportional system. The ubiquity of Unionist supremacy, outside the few strongly Catholic localities, provided little incentive for electoral challenge. Over two-thirds of those returned in 1933 were unopposed, the figure exceeding two-fifths in both 1929 and 1938. Well over nine-tenths of the county and rural councillors elected triennially between 1924 and 1939 had no opponents; and even in urban council elections, where conflicts over labour and capital were more acute, the majority of places were uncontested at every election between 1923 and 1939. The nadir for northern local democracy occurred in 1932, when less than a fifth of urban councillors obtained an electoral mandate.[67]

For most Unionist politicians, that mandate was secured through service to the Orange Institution, whose members dominated the Ulster Unionist Council, local electoral conventions, and therefore the choice of official candidates. Though delegates accredited to the Institution formed only a small fraction of the cumbersome council, and lodge officers were no longer ex-officio members of most constituency associations, the delegates of other Unionist bodies were almost invariably Orangemen. The mechanism of the Institution's influence over the party and government remains obscure, although it was clearly less regimented and homogeneous than that of the Communist Party within conventional front organizations. Yet every Unionist parliamentarian between 1921 and the late 1960s was an Orangeman when first elected, with the exception of three ministers, one male backbencher, and seven women.[68] Popular participation in Unionism was somewhat broadened by the sporadic encouragement of auxiliary bodies such as the Ulster Women's Unionist Council, the Junior Imperial and Constitutional League (extended to the province in 1924), and other decreasingly youthful 'junior' associations. Yet the seeming permanence of the ruling party's predominance bred smugness and lethargy among organizers and propagandists, whose once thrilling denunciations of republican and socialist subversion gradually lost their edge.

Under Craigavon's formidable if often distant shadow, the 'executive committee of the privy council' (cabinet) provided strikingly stable leadership until the 1940s. The six (later seven) ministries had only twelve incumbents between 1921 and 1939, and four of the original ministers were still officiating in 1937. Both Archdale (a Fermanagh landlord) in agriculture and Pollock in finance served into their eighties, and even in 1921 the median age of ministers was 50.[69] Whereas the early rulers of the Free State were remarkably young for politicians, ensuring many decades of dominance by the revolutionary élite that had reached maturity around 1916, Craig and his ministers had mostly established their loyal credentials well before the Great War. Most were prominent businessmen or manufacturers, and the first and third ministers for finance (Hugh McDowell Pollock and John Milne Barbour) gained appointment without belonging to the Orange Institution. Both were former presidents of the Belfast chamber of commerce, and have been identified along with Spender as 'anti-populists' of fiscally orthodox but relatively liberal inclinations.[70] Barbour's fraternalism was exhibited in the plusher world of esoteric freemasonry, wherein he became High King of the Supreme Grand Royal Arch Chapter of Ireland and a member of the Supreme Council of the 33rd Degree. A still loftier glow of liberalism softened the rhetoric of the first two ministers of education, the 7th marquess of Londonderry and the 8th Viscount Charlemont (who presided over a staff of great-hearted retired generals in seeking conciliation with southerners through the Irish Association, founded in December 1938).[71] Yet the dominant strand of Unionist fraternalism was epitomized by Craigavon's folksy forays among Protestant petitioners and brethren of all classes, who came to rely on his spontaneous showers of largesse and half-promises of largesse. As the leader told an acrimonious conference of farmers and retailers, locked in combat over the price of milk in 1931: 'In such a small area as ours it is a much happier position of affairs if we are able to arrange our differences ourselves. . . . Lady Craigavon is anxious that we should go for tea and I think we will adjourn for that purpose.'[72] At its merriest, life in Craigavon's Ulster was a bowler-hatter's tea-party.

The political organization of Labour in Northern Ireland, always bedevilled by animosities between Catholic and Protestant workers, was also complicated by competing bonds with Labour bodies in the Free State and in Britain. Though most northern trades unions were affiliated to British conglomerates, many had continued to send delegates to the Irish Trades Union Congress even during the revolutionary years. In March 1924, however, the sharpening southern focus of Johnson's Labour Party and TUC encouraged formation of the Labour Party (Northern Ireland). Though not yet formally linked to the British Labour Party (whose leader James Ramsay MacDonald had become prime minister two months earlier), the new organization was influenced by the long-standing involvement of the Independent Labour Party in Belfast. The dual tug was exhibited in the party's reaffiliation with the Irish TUC in 1927; its separation from that body in 1930 (when the Irish Labour Party also drifted away); its objection to the southern party's denunciation of partition in 1936; its ever closer liaison with the British Labour Party; and the consequent refusal of the Irish Labour Party to send a fraternal delegate to the northern conference in 1938. By 1935, seven out of every eight trades unionists in Northern Ireland belonged to bodies with headquarters in Britain, though only just over a third of the northern insured workforce was unionized.[73] In its industrial and political organization alike, northern Labour was emphatically British rather than Irish.

The northern Labour Party had secured three seats in 1925, defeating candidates representing the Ulster Unionist Labour Association and so hastening the decline of Carson's conduit for the harmless expression of proletarian grievances. The UULA was in any case showing dangerous signs of independence, and one of its remaining representatives (the shipwright William Grant) opposed the government in twenty-six parliamentary divisions during 1925.[74] Devlin's nationalists retained the support of most Catholic workers, particularly in proletarian West Belfast where Devlin presided like a benevolent and mysteriously incorruptible *mafioso*. The Labour Party's parliamentary representation was reduced to one in 1929, two in 1933, and one in 1938 (along with an independent Labour member). As before 1921, northern workers had no practical alternative to seeking a hearing within the dominant organizations of loyalism and nationalism.

Labour's quandaries were reflected in the zig-zag career of Harry Midgley, a Presbyterian joiner from North Belfast who had joined the Independent Labour Party under the influence of the socialist opponent of Home Rule, William Walker. Having shifted allegiance to Connolly, served with the Ulster Division, and then bottomed the poll as an anti-partitionist candidate in East Belfast in May 1921, he eventually secured Belfast's Dock ward for Labour between 1933 and 1938. After returning to Stormont in 1941, Midgley was expelled from the Northern Ireland Labour Party, thereupon founding his own short-lived Commonwealth Labour Party. In 1943, he was surprisingly chosen as wartime minister of public security by the new prime minister (Sir Basil Brooke). He eventually resolved the problem of multiple allegiance by joining the Ulster Unionist Party, the Orange Institution, and post-war Unionist cabinets.[75] Prior political loyalties, internal divisions, and conflicting external associations prevented the northern Labour Party from becoming a significant political force.

So long as the political polarization of Protestants and Catholics endured, northern nationalists could not hope to secure more than a third of the parliamentary vote or to participate in the provincial government. For Joseph Devlin and his still active Ancient Order of Hibernians, the prospect of permanent opposition merely recalled the constitutionalists' role at Westminster under the Union. Just as Irish nationalists had almost succeeded in wresting Home Rule from an initially hostile British parliament, so unremitting propaganda and collective protest from northern nationalists might conceivably extort loyalist acceptance of some form of Irish union, or at least an acknowledgement of Catholic civil rights. Devlin's attempt to reapply the strategy of Parnell and Redmond was postponed until 1925, once the reduction of sectarian conflict had made it feasible for a Catholic politician to attempt dialogue with his Protestant adversaries.

Though continuing to represent West Belfast at Westminster, Devlin (like his five nationalist colleagues) had not taken his seat in the northern parliament elected in May 1921. Furthermore, he had followed de Valera's urging by arranging an electoral pact with Sinn Féin, whereby both parties fielded candidates but advised their supporters to exchange preferences. Though Sinn Féin secured a fifth of votes cast, compared with less than an eighth for the smaller group of nationalist candidates, each party achieved equal representation. The drift from Hibernianism to republicanism, rapid during the truce, was reversed after the fracturing of Sinn Féin and the collapse of the IRA in Northern Ireland. Most remaining northern Sinn Féiners supported the treaty, as in the case of Cahir Healy from Enniskillen (twice elected to Westminster during his internment between 1922 and 1924). The republican rump of Sinn Féin never abandoned its policy of abstention. It secured only two seats in the election of 1925 and one in 1933, having not a single representative to make the ritual declaration of dissent in either 1929 or 1938. Even seeking election as an abstentionist involved a disturbing exercise in mental reservation after 1934, when all candidates were required to declare their intention to take their seats if elected. This imposition was largely superfluous, since neither republican Sinn Féin nor the associated IRA had commanded significant overt support among northern Catholics since the triumph of coercion in 1922.

Despite the decline of republicanism after mid-1922, neither Devlin nor the Catholic hierarchy managed to devise a credible strategy of non-violent opposition. The northern bishops were embarrassingly divided: Cardinal Michael Logue (Armagh) and Devlin's confidant Patrick O'Donnell (Raphoe) had little to say, while Joseph MacRory (Down and Connor) veered between pragmatism and intransigence. Having cautiously proposed recognition of the new state in January and April 1922, MacRory responded to the subsequent coercion by insisting that 'until the Northern Parliament is ready to go whole-heartedly into an all-Ireland Parliament, they should not be recognised, and though this must inevitably mean many years of unrest and suffering and even bloodshed, his lordship is prepared to face it'.[76]

So long as the abolition or amendment of partition seemed even faintly possible, northern nationalists dared not deviate from the southern insistence upon 'non-recognition' of Northern Ireland and its institutions. Until the collapse of the boundary commission, Cosgrave's government continued to resist nationalist participation in Stormont, so generating frustration and resentment among Devlin's 'anti-partitionists'. In May 1923, a deputation of Devlinites allegedly told MacNeill and O'Shiel that 'the disfranchised state' of northern Catholics was 'all the fault of Sinn Féin', though they did not overtly advocate recognition of the northern state.[77] Hibernianism had already been reinvigorated by the formation earlier in the year of a provincial council for Ulster, and the return of a 'united Catholic party' of eight members to represent the interests of businessmen, publicans, and the clergy in the Belfast city council.

Devlin's formation of an active parliamentary opposition began haltingly in March 1925, with a nationalist convention in Belfast incorporating representatives of pro-treaty Sinn Féin and the southern government. The two nationalist factions resuscitated the pact of 1921, putting forward six Hibernians and five Sinn Féiners. All but one of these were elected, outscoring republican Sinn Féin by over four to one. In April 1925, Devlin entered the northern House of Commons along with one of his nine elected colleagues. The remainder dribbled into parliament over the following two years, despite the initial resolution in March that nationalists representing border constituencies would continue their boycott in the hope of eventual incorporation in the Free State. Following the confirmation of the unaltered boundary in December 1925, and then de Valera's progress in finding a political role for southern republicans, Devlin and the Catholic church began their opposition in earnest. In February 1926 Devlin's ally Patrick O'Donnell, during his brief tenure as cardinal archbishop of Armagh, pronounced almost with relief that 'the area of the Six Counties is now fixed as the area of Northern Ireland, and everyone within it has to take account of that fact'. Hinting that earlier Catholic representation might have helped 'to keep things right', O'Donnell declared that 'what matters now is that the case be made in such a way as to be thoroughly understood, and that it be pressed by every legitimate means, with nothing but good feeling for our neighbours'.[78] Though MacRory maintained his surly aloofness from northern institutions even after succeeding O'Donnell in Armagh, Devlin was able to recreate a makeshift replica of the pre-war alliance of constitutionalism and Catholicism.

Devlin was now actively encouraged in the strategy of parliamentary opposition by both major parties in the south, though de Valera's diehard republican opponents remained hostile. All ten nationalists were on parliamentary duty by 1927; and in May 1928, the party acquired a local organization grandly named the National League of the North. With Devlin as president, Cahir Healy as joint secretary, and an archdeacon as vice-president, the League soon secured letters of support from several bishops (including even MacRory).[79] The price for the clerical embrace was the abrupt termination of the informal alliance between nationalism and Labour, whose socialism and religious diversity filled the clergy with alarm. William McMullan, a Protestant trade union leader who had been elected on Devlin's surplus in 1925, was ruthlessly repudiated in Devlin's *Irish News*: 'The spectacle of a non-Catholic Socialist seeking the votes of Catholics, who, if they obey the Church, cannot be Socialists, against a Catholic candidate who is loyal to his Church, if it were not tragic, is truly ridiculous.'[80]

Despite the abolition of proportional representation, the parliamentary strength of nationalism was increased to eleven in 1929. Though far below the Catholic proportion of the province's population, the acquisition of nearly a fifth of the seats came close to the potential maximum, as a result of the clustering of Catholics in a few constituencies. The National

League, despite its titular link with Captain William Redmond's short-lived constitutionalist party in the Free State, developed far closer bonds with Fianna Fáil. It sought the unification of Ireland, but departed from republican Sinn Féin by recognizing the *fait accompli* of the northern state. The party further promised to defend Catholic interests and to pursue social reforms through the relief of unemployment by public works and other welfare measures. The effectiveness of Devlin's strategy depended partly on his success in uniting nationalism, but more crucially on the response of Ulster loyalism.

Drawing upon his proven brilliance as a demagogue and an organizer Devlin was temporarily successful in winning active participation from Catholic workers in Belfast and veterans of the Great War. Yet for all his managerial expertise, Devlin failed to maintain the National League as a populist organization after the electoral success of 1929, a fact which suggests popular scepticism about the probable benefits of loyal opposition. The still more daunting task of inducing the Unionist majority to allow nationalism an effective political role only briefly seemed capable of fulfilment. Once the spasm of reconciliatory rhetoric following the tripartite agreements had subsided, Craig's government reverted to treating northern nationalists as unwelcome guests rather than fellow citizens. By 1932, Protestant intransigence had been intensified by revived resentment against Catholic workers as unemployment mounted, and also by northern panic upon de Valera's accession to power in the Free State. Devlin's essay in democratic participation was curtailed by nationalist withdrawal over a seeming trifle in May 1932. The government ruled with increasing contempt for all opponents, causing the only remaining Labour member and an independent Unionist to follow the nationalist example four months later, when the speaker refused to allow debate on unemployment. Despite the return of nationalist members to their seats in October 1933, and the election of nine nationalists in November 1933 and eight in February 1938, the party subsided into terminal decline. After Devlin's death in 1934, no effective leader emerged, and no consistent policy towards abstention was practised. The attempt to cajole a dominant majority towards compromise had failed, leaving Northern Ireland in the seemingly perpetual custody of a still united and ever more implacable Ulster Unionist Party.

In the Irish Free State, the defenders of the treaty settlement were slow to develop a party appropriate to their novel situation as rulers rather than rebels. The lingering dream of restored unity, expressed in the creation of a 'National Sinn Féin panel' to maintain the status quo, had obviated the need for party organization for the general election of June 1922. During the civil war, the impotence of the Dáil and the primacy of military organization made the creation of a political party redundant. In March 1923, with the imminent prospect of an Irregular collapse followed by an electoral contest with the remaining republicans, Cosgrave established Cumann na nGaedheal (Fellowship of the Irish). Predictably, it claimed the sacred legacy of revolution: 'The new National Party would be but the successor of Sinn Fein. By direct political lineage the present Government are descended from the Sinn Fein organisation.' Cumann na nGaedheal hoped to retrieve the active support of those 'temporarily lost to us in the work of reconstructing and recreating the Gaelic State', especially those who had been seduced by the Anglo-centric Labour Party or the rent-obsessed Farmers' Party.[81] Cosgrave's organization received enthusiastic support from businessmen and commercial farmers, anxious to avert a republican or radical resurgence, and its membership was concentrated in the more prosperous midland and eastern regions. Even so, in August 1923 the party secured almost half of first-preference votes in Connaught, the poorest province, compared with a third in Munster and rural Leinster and a bare majority in Dublin.[82] The party had almost 800 branches by May 1926, having survived bruising collisions between its standing committee (purporting to represent 'the common people of Ireland') and the executive council.[83]

Somewhat unfairly, Cumann na nGaedheal was constantly derided by republicans as the party of the rich, ruled by an unseen hand. In the words of Seán Lemass in February 1925:

'Ireland today is ruled by a British garrison, organized by the Masonic lodges, speaking through the Free State parliament, and playing the cards of England all the time.'[84] It might seem ludicrous to suggest that the devout Cosgrave, soon to acquire his private chapel and papal knighthood of the Grand Cross of the Pian Order, was the tool of a masonic conspiracy. Yet, in an era when Catholic paranoia was divided almost equally between communism and freemasonry, it was all too easy to fantasize that the president (like business, the banks, and the professions) had been captured by a secretive, close-knit, and supposedly ruthless Protestant brotherhood. The fraternal experience of many leading republicans made them alert to rival conspiracies: Lemass himself became a leading member of the Knights of St Columbanus, having been fascinated as a young man by the *Mysteries of Freemasonry*.[85] The Knights, formed in 1917 to secure Catholic professional and business pre-eminence through the application of masonic methods, included ministers of both major parties, despite the disapproval of de Valera and a decreasing number of bishops. The principal evidence of a masonic plot, tirelessly paraded in J. J. O'Kelly's ever popular *Catholic Bulletin*, was Cosgrave's dependence (especially after 1927) on the support of Protestant deputies who were often freemasons, such as the grand inner guard, William Edward Thrift of Trinity College.[86]

Damaged by these insinuations of class bias and hidden hands, the party never embodied the full range of those accepting the Anglo-Irish settlement. Many supporters of the Free State continued to vote for sectional parties, and at no general election did Cumann na nGaedheal secure even two-fifths of the valid first-preference votes. Its percentage share was 39 in 1923, 27 in June 1927, 39 in September 1927, 35 in 1932, and 30 in 1933. Though never securing a majority of seats, Cosgrave managed to govern with the help of minor parties even after Fianna Fáil's entry to the Dáil in August 1927. Having been virtually free from parliamentary opposition for its first four years in power, the party proved dismally sluggish in responding to Fianna Fáil's methodical and zestful challenge. By 1932, when the onset of economic depression had rendered dubious the return of any incumbent government in Europe, Cosgrave was reduced to following British precedent by manufacturing a 'red scare', so returning Lemass's masonic compliment of 1925. Fianna Fáil was a mere front organization for the international communist conspiracy and its Irish associates, the IRA and Saor Éire (Free Ireland). This short-lived party, proscribed along with the IRA by the Catholic hierarchy as well as the government, had been founded by a splinter-group of faintly socialist republicans in September 1931. The hierarchy had admittedly been reluctant to support Cosgrave's previous attempts to besmirch his opponents as communists, and even in 1931 it was persuaded by de Valera to avoid explicitly extending that smear to Fianna Fáil.[87] The ascription of socialist precepts to de Valera was if anything more absurd than picturing Cosgrave in a masonic apron, though the slur was vigorously disseminated by many Catholic clergymen before the election of February 1932. Fianna Fáil's success, however, prompted the upholders of the Free State to seek alternative means of subduing republicanism.

A week before the election, veterans of the national army had regrouped to form the Army Comrades' Association, whose first president was Colonel Austin Brennan, elder brother of the chief of staff, with the Corkonian Commandant Ned Cronin as secretary. The association aimed 'to uphold the state', as well as to honour the freedom fighters by raising a national memorial. In August 1932, the presidency passed to Dr Thomas Francis O'Higgins, brother of the murdered minister for justice and formerly the army's director of medical services. O'Higgins declared that 'the time is ripe for the creation of a composite body, with the object of neutralizing the influence of those hidden forces of disorder which are operating in our country, and may grow into a ruthless tyranny if not checked in time'. Appalled by such outrages as the removal of an Australian flag from a house in Lansdowne Road, Dublin, the association was soon providing stewards, vigilantes, and guards of honour for meetings of Cumann na nGaedheal.[88] During the sometimes violent campaign before the election of January 1933, squads of

Comrades and IRA men confronted each other as 'protectors' of the rival candidates.

Six months later, immediately after his dismissal as commissioner of the Garda Síochána, Eoin O'Duffy took command of perhaps 30,000 Comrades, whom he evocatively renamed the National Guard. Its popular appeal was greatly enhanced by the government's prohibition of the customary commemorative parade for the founders of the state (abandoned in the previous year), which was expected to result in an attempt to seize control of military barracks and the Dáil. Despite the anticlimax when O'Duffy abandoned the parade scheduled for 13 August 1933, calling to mind Daniel O'Connell's 'surrender' at Clontarf ninety years before, the sustained severity of repression maintained the popularity of the National Guard and its successors. Indeed, membership allegedly rose to 120,000 over the following year, though more reliable returns of paid-up card-holders indicate that the true figure never exceeded 50,000.[89] The strongest support came from commercial farmers facing ruin as a result of de Valera's economic war. In September 1933, the militarization of Cumann na nGaedheal became starkly manifest upon its amalgamation with the National Guard and the Centre Party. The latter had been launched in January 1933 by James Dillon (son of John, and a future leader of the amalgamated party between 1959 and 1965); and Frank MacDermot (a former British army captain, barrister, and emigrant banker who had briefly headed a National Farmers' and Ratepayers' League). The new coalition was named Fine Gael (United Ireland Party), being led from outside the Dáil by O'Duffy. Cosgrave sank into a brooding vice-presidency, while many of his former executive council breathed fire and recovered morale. Partly through emulation of its rival Fianna Fáil, Fine Gael was organized more efficiently and systematically than its predecessor, claiming over a thousand branches at its ard fheis in February 1934.

The National Guard, with its core of middle-aged ex-servicemen, was improbably reconstituted as the party's youth section, now entitled the Young Ireland Association (subsequently the League of Youth). Ignoring these reiterated changes of identity, mainly designed to evade legal suppression, contemporaries universally identified O'Duffy's army as 'Blueshirts' (the uniform adopted by Cronin in April 1933). The emphasis on shirts deliberately evoked Mussolini's Fascisti or Blackshirts, whom O'Duffy had so much admired on his police pilgrimage to Rome in 1928. His debt to Fascism was more to its style, regalia, and methods of organization than to its political ideology, although O'Duffy was eventually to become an intellectual Fascist as his popular following shrank from a legion to a cult. The parade of August 1933, with its special excursion trains glinting with blue breasts, was to have been O'Duffy's march on Rome; the pugnacity of many of his followers also had Fascist parallels. More importantly, the Blueshirts' campaign of civil disruption drew upon O'Duffy's Volunteer heritage, enabling supporters as well as opponents of the Free State to experience an after-quiver of the anarchic thrills of revolution. Although faction-fighting resulted in only one death, that of a Blueshirt, the campaign involved numerous acts of violence against both property and the person. The grounds of conviction by one Special Powers tribunal confirm the nostalgic element of Blueshirtery: obstructing the highway by felling trees, cutting telegraph wires, and possessing rifle cartridges without a certificate, all 'with the object of impairing the administration of justice and impeding the machinery of government'.[90] Blueshirts, like Orangemen, had no compunction in defying laws and rulers in order to uphold the rule of law.

Eventually, the insidious effect of this inconsistency and the severity of coercion led to the marginalization of O'Duffy and his militia by his political associates. In September 1934, O'Duffy resigned as leader of Fine Gael and the League of Youth after only a year's tenure; in October 1935, his competitor and successor as Blueshirt leader (Ned Cronin) was expelled from Fine Gael; and in November 1936, after a brief experiment with Greenshirts (the overtly Fascist National Corporate Party), O'Duffy attempted to retrieve his prestige by leading an Irish brigade of about 700 members to fight for Franco against irreligion, anarchism, and communism in Spain. Here too he was thwarted, his brigade returning to the Free State without reaching the front line, where they might have confronted their former republican antagonists among the 200 natives of Ireland enrolled in the International brigade. Though ridiculous in retrospect, O'Duffy's crusades in Ireland, and even in Spain, had aroused impassioned support for the would-be Duce among army veterans, underemployed youths, bishops and priests, journalists, and poets such as W. B. Yeats (ever hopeful that O'Higgins, O'Duffy, or indeed de Valera, might have the heart to become Ireland's Mussolini). In a curious gesture of solidarity, de Valera allowed O'Duffy a state funeral in 1944. Meanwhile, Fine Gael had long since reverted to the more conventional techniques of parliamentary opposition. Having ousted O'Duffy in September 1934, Cosgrave resumed party leadership for another decade before retiring in favour of his former minister for defence, Richard Mulcahy. Fine Gael's percentage of first-preference votes steadily declined, from 35 in 1937 and 33 a year later to only 23 in 1943. Even in 1937, its support fell 5 per cent short of the combined vote for Cumann na nGaedheal and the Centre Party in 1933. The party's brief and ineffectual reversion to martial populism had seriously undermined its credentials as the democratic defender of law and order. Never again did Fine Gael dare to delve among the embers of militarism to be found in every Irish political enterprise.

The republican opponents of the Irish Free State had self-consciously emulated the devices of revolutionary propaganda and organization, in their campaign to subvert its institutions. In March 1922, the anti-treaty deputies constituted themselves as Cumann na Poblachta (Fellowship of the Republic), with de Valera as president. He was assisted by Cathal Brugha, Mary MacSwiney, and Austin Stack (the former tax-inspector from Kerry who had administered the revolutionary judiciary as minister for home affairs). Desultory attempts were made to maintain the unity of Sinn Féin, but the government's supporters closed its central office and allowed the organization to lapse. After the ceasefire of May 1923, de Valera reclaimed the contested legacy of Sinn Féin: 'We wish to organise not merely

Republican opinion, strictly so-called, but what might be termed "Nationalist" or "Independence" opinion in general.' All Irregular 'Volunteers' were ordered 'to immediately join and organise Sinn Féin clubs', particular attention being directed to the 'wonderful opportunity for political discussion and reorganization offered by the present concentration of some of our best men and women in jails and camps'.[91] As reorganized at a convention in Dublin's Mansion House in June 1923, Sinn Féin presented itself as a broad coalition of those rejecting the state's right to exist, so replicating the rhetoric of October 1917. Once again, Sinn Féiners were to seek election to an illegitimate parliament, only to 'abstain' from participation if successful. Once again, they were urged by arguments of expediency rather than principle to set aside violence, and to rely upon propaganda and collective protest to destabilize the régime. The republican hall of mirrors also contained de Valera's 'republican government' inaugurated in October 1922, the rump of the Second Dáil (revived in August 1924), and an even more bizarre medley of republicans who had won seats at any election since 1921, convened in December 1924 and grandly entitled Comhairle na dTeachtaí (Council of Deputies). All of these political and parliamentary bodies had the same policies and organizers, often meeting in rapid succession on the same occasion.[92]

The fundamental flaw in this elaborate historical re-enactment was the absence of massive popular support for Sinn Féin's protest. By June 1924 over a thousand branches had been formed; but almost a third of these failed to pay the affiliation fee, and over the following two years both income and the number of branches dropped drastically. By April 1926, only about 170 branches remained.[93] Although republicans secured 44 of the 153 seats in the Dáil (and 27 per cent of first-preference votes) at the general election of August 1923, they undeniably represented only a minority of those who had supported Sinn Féin's campaign for self-determination. The republican vote was strikingly low in Cork and much of Munster, the supposed heartland of Irregular resistance in the civil war. Sinn Féin's weakness was confirmed in June 1925, when it secured only one seat in nine at the triennial elections for local authorities. Without overwhelming support from nationalists, Sinn Féin could not expect to arouse substantial interest among its former benefactors in Britain, America, or Australia, who mostly dismissed it is as a divisive faction rather than the voice of the Irish people. Veteran revolutionary polemicists like Mary MacSwiney, sister of Terence the deceased hunger-striker, could not easily reconcile themselves to this 'betrayal' or accept its implications. Even de Valera, unable to deny his lack of a popular mandate as president of Sinn Féin, retreated into the comfortable role of a once and future king, confident that the 'real will' of the people would eventually be reasserted. In June 1923, his 'policy for the near future' was 'educating the people and winning them back to their true allegiance and the courage to express their *real will* as they did before'.[94] The corollary that the expressed preferences of the people were the product of delusion, and should therefore be disregarded, provided an obvious threat to the exercise of democracy.

De Valera's solution to Sinn Féin's evident obsolescence was characteristically ingenious. The electoral outcome in 1923 had suggested the possibility of a future republican majority in the Dáil, which if translated into government under de Valera's presidency would at last allow democracy to incorporate the 'real' popular will. Despite his initial assertion that the treaty was incapable of providing the basis for step-by-step self-determination, de Valera soon decided otherwise. His aim thereafter was not to secure the destruction of the state, but to win over the majority of his followers to the opportunist strategy. Even the collapse of the boundary commission did not deflect him, so bringing about a breach between political republicanism and the somnolent but still brooding IRA in November 1925. By May 1926, he was able to carry most of Sinn Féin into a new party fancifully entitled Fianna Fáil ('Soldiers of Destiny'), their immediate destiny being the Free State's Dáil. In resigning the presidency of Sinn Féin, he reaffirmed his faith that 'the people will change', but admitted 'that they are not prepared at the present moment to go back on the things that they have done in the past few years'. Reverting to his familiar theological rhetoric of opportunism, de Valera declared that entry to the Dáil was 'the only policy for us on which there was a chance of success'.[95]

The principled objection to swearing fidelity to the monarch and allegiance to the constitution, so powerful an element of de Valera's previous abstentionism, was overcome by applying the Catholic practice of mental reservation to those uttering the dreadful words. If by swearing an oath one could make possible the abolition of that oath, what harm could be done by the lesser evil of a merely formal perjury? The fateful utterance of the 'empty political formula' was finally accomplished in August 1927, by the Fianna Fáil deputies returned two months earlier in the first general election since 1923. This breakthrough was soon consolidated by the requirement (emulated in Northern Ireland seven years later) that electoral candidates undertake in advance to take their seats and therefore subscribe to the oath if elected. MacSwiney, Plunkett, Stack, the egregious Father O'Flanagan, and a diminishing band of republican idealists, continued to offer allegiance to the residue of the Second Dáil and so maintain the pretence of a legitimate alternative authority. The manifest benefits of de Valera's compromise in the pursuit of power could never eradicate the appeal of an immutable principle, which had provided the losers in the civil war with so much consolation since 1922.

Nevertheless, the history of abstentionist republicanism after the creation of Fianna Fáil was one of virtually linear decline in popularity, increase in intransigence, and intensification of petty factional or ideological squabbles. Between 1931 and 1934, at the depth of the depression and while Fianna Fáil's future course seemed uncertain, the IRA did indeed pose a formidable challenge to democratic government. That challenge was renewed after the reconciliation of the Second Dáil with the IRA's army council in December 1938, soon followed by a bloody bombing campaign in Britain and the spectacular removal in December 1939 of the national army's entire stock of ammunition from the magazine fort in Phoenix Park. Despites these bursts of morale-boosting violence, ever more arcane conflicts fractured

republicanism, the most enduring issue being that of co-operation with radical and even Marxist movements. Though Saor
Éire disintegrated soon after its launching in September 1931,
its strategy of republican socialism subsequently reappeared in
a succession of ill-documented organizations, each with its paramilitary counterpart. The Republican Congress, formed by
Peadar O'Donnell and other radicals in March 1934, represented a radical but ineffectual attempt to wean the IRA from
its tunnel vision. Meanwhile, the dominant factions in both Sinn
Féin and the IRA remained socially conservative, clinging to an
increasingly narrow and anachronistic vision of the receding
republic. The rationale for a common front against Britain was
no longer strong enough to sustain republican unity. Nor, for a
gathering stream of former purists, was the republican dream
sufficiently attractive to overcome the lure of practical rewards
within an admittedly imperfect Irish state.

Fianna Fáil quickly became an efficient, highly centralized yet
populist party. On its foundation, the new party secured support
from only about half of Sinn Féin's deputies and standing committees. As its popular appeal became evident, the leakage of
Sinn Féiners intensified. The number of cumainn grew from 460
in November 1926 to over 1,000 by summer 1927, matching Sinn
Féin at its peak three years earlier.[96] Fianna Fáil, like Sinn Féin,
drew heavily on the Redmondite model. Although developing a
single network of party branches rather than several interlocking bodies, Fianna Fáil's organizers were well schooled in the
techniques developed by Devlin and Dillon in the Ancient
Order of Hibernians and the United Irish League. The party's
deputies were expected to work hard for the sectional and personal interests of their constituents, gradually forming bonds of
clientage and patronage far more powerful than those of ideology or programme. They were more inclined than their nationalist precursors to be natives of their own constituencies, yet head
office played a key role in the selection of candidates. De Valera,
like Redmond and Parnell before him, was venerated within his
party as leader of the Irish race: even in his final political performance as an aged, blind, and eventually incapable president

(1959–73), his devotees would excuse the Chief's foibles with the sigh that 'ah, but he was a great mathematician'. Though many of his party managers were populists in the mould of Craigavon, de Valera's dominance was expressed through aloofness rather than bonhomie and back-slapping. No public expressions of dissent were tolerated, no detailed minutes of internal debates were compiled, and former ministers were forbidden to publish memoirs. No other southern leader was to achieve the same supremacy and loyalty within his own party, or the same detestation beyond it.

Affiliation to de Valera's Fianna Fáil was primarily determined by the legacy of the civil war rather than by the appeal of specific policies. For half a century after 1922, the consequent divisions between and within families and neighbourhoods provided the basis for most political, social, and perhaps even marital and amorous alignments. Though far less deep-rooted than the sectarian divide in Northern Ireland, the barriers of bitterness and recrimination erected in the civil war provided the firmest basis for partisan solidarity in the Free State. Adherence to any clear social or economic ideology was a luxury that neither major party could afford, since it would tend to alienate part of its natural constituency. Both Fianna Fáil and its opponents were thus constrained by the same populist imperatives which had prevented revolutionary Sinn Féin from espousing social radicalism. So long as traces of dominion status remained to be eradicated, Fianna Fáil concentrated its rhetoric and legislation on constitutional rather than social issues. At the suggestion of Seán Lemass, de Valera's successor as leader and taoiseach between 1959 and 1966, Fianna Fáil had incorporated the subtitle 'the republican party'—a claim perfectly consistent with his memorable *mot* in March 1928 that it was 'a slightly constitutional party'. The constraints of republican populism did not preclude rhetoric appealing to labourers and small farmers, partly because the great majority of employers, capitalists, and rich farmers were assumed to have supported the treaty and the Free State from the outset. In its first decade, Fianna Fáil drew considerable energy from the campaign to provide plots for agricultural labourers and other minor social reforms; but once in government, the manifest possibility and allure of winning support from the rich and powerful led to the progressive abandonment of practical radicalism. The election of 1938 was the last at which Fianna Fáil's support was concentrated in rural and poor constituencies.[97] Thereafter, Fianna Fáil presented itself as a forum for all classes of titular republicans.

Fianna Fáil's success in securing popular support from beyond its initial constituency is demonstrated by its sharp improvement in electoral performance between 1927 and 1938. In the six successive elections held during that period, Fianna Fáil's percentage of first-preference votes for the Dáil was 26 in June 1927, 35 in September 1927, 44 in 1932, almost 50 in 1933, 45 in 1937, and 52 in 1938 (its only popular majority before 1977). Between 1932 and 1944 the party failed to secure the majority of deputies in three of the six general elections (1932, 1937, and 1943), each of which was followed by a dissolution giving rise to a majority in the following year. Though many of Fianna Fáil's new supporters would previously have voted for minor parties, while others were new to the electoral register, it seems likely that the unpopularity of Cosgrave's later governments and his ineptitude in opposition caused some former supporters of the treaty to switch allegiance. Former Home Rulers and even Unionists were more easily converted, having been virtually excluded from the great debate in 1922. A startling example was de Valera's attorney-general from 1936 to 1940, Patrick Lynch (his constitutionalist opponent in East Clare and a former crown prosecutor in Kerry). The leadership of Fianna Fáil, however, was almost solely in the hands of former freedom-fighters who had supported the Irregulars, and (in due course) of their descendants. However doubtful of particular policies, the 'victims' of Free State persecution were reassured by the seemingly perpetual presence in de Valera's ministries of fabled revolutionaries such as Lemass, Aiken, Traynor, and Harry Boland's brother Gerald. The predominance in Irish politics of former revolutionary activists was not restricted to Fianna Fáil, and even in the election of 1944 (a quarter-century after the foundation of the Dáil) the majority of successful candidates were ex-revolutionaries. The leadership aged with the state. In 1922, over a third of deputies had yet to reach 35; by 1937, that proportion was one in twenty.[98] Yesterday's victims found their compensation as today's and tomorrow's rulers, claiming support for their past record rather than their promised future performance.

Not surprisingly, class and sectional affiliations failed to outweigh the loyalties sealed in blood during the civil war. Even without that conflict, it seems unlikely that the struggle between labour and capital would have dominated Irish party politics. The subtraction of the six counties left the Free State with a minute urban proletariat, so that the conventional programmes of European Labour and socialist parties could never have attracted even a substantial minority of the electorate. Though almost half of the occupied population remained in farming in 1936, the scarcity of labourers and the ubiquity of owner-occupancy limited the range of grievances capable of mobilizing the agricultural classes. Apart from the possible polarization of rural and urban interests, the initial presence of 100,000 marginalized veterans of the Great War created the potential for political collision with those who had condemned and subverted Ireland's participation. The tiny Protestant minority, though even less likely than war veterans to sustain a major political party, remained a potential focus for Catholic hostility and, conceivably, a unifying factor in nationalism. After all, the existence of an admittedly much larger religious minority in Northern Ireland had permitted Ulster Unionism to retain a surprisingly united front for the first half-century of partition. The political history of the Free State records traces of all of these potential conflicts and alignments.

The Labour Party succeeded from the first in securing substantial non-proletarian support. This was in part a by-product of Sinn Féin's electoral pact in 1922, which affirmed that 'every and any interest is free to go up and contest the election equally with the National Sinn Féin panel'.[99] The collapse of the pact on election eve had enabled Collins to urge voters to support minor parties rather than opponents of the treaty. Since the popular majority favouring the treaty manifestly exceeded the narrow margin among panel candidates, many voters would have adopted this strategy even if the pact had survived. All but one of Labour's eighteen candidates were returned, the party exceeding a fifth of all first-preference votes. In assigning their lower preferences, Labour voters strongly favoured supporters as against opponents of the treaty.[100] Thereafter, Labour's percentage of first-preference votes declined sharply. From 21 per cent in 1922, it fell to 11 in 1923, 13 in June 1927, 9 in September 1927, 8 in 1932, 6 in 1933, and 10 in both 1937 and 1938. Even so, the presence of a substantial block of Labour deputies (as many as twenty-two in the hung Dáil elected in June 1927) allowed the party a prominent voice. Indeed, its working alliance with Fianna Fáil in 1932 was crucial to de Valera's accession to power, heightening the illusion that his government would espouse radical social reform.

Labour's attempt to transcend its class basis entailed its effective repudiation of socialism, exaggerated affirmation of conservative Catholic morality, and eventual separation between the political and industrial movements. The replacement of Thomas Johnson by the Mayo schoolteacher, Thomas J. O'Connell (leader from 1927 to 1932), did nothing to radicalize the party. Connolly's slogan of 'the Workers' Republic', with its demand for nationalization of the means of production, was dropped in 1930, briefly resumed in 1936, and abjectly abandoned under pressure from the Catholic hierarchy in 1939. The special congress of February 1930 also agreed to separate the Labour Party from the Trades Union Congress (with its restricted constituency of 'wage-earners'), having heard that 'a democratic political party must have a wider appeal, embracing all the productive and creative elements in the community'. The divorce was also motivated by the fact that an increasing majority of Irish trades unionists belonged to British unions, so reducing the Irish congress to an unrepresentative rump. Despite protests from those who still dreamed of a unified Labour movement for the entire island, the party's loosening bond with the Northern Ireland Labour Party was symbolized by the alteration of its own title from the 'National' to the 'Irish' Labour Party. By the end of 1931, the reorganized party had formed 180 branches, about a quarter of the current number of Fianna Fáil cumainn.[101] The onset of depression further weakened all Labour organizations, as heavy unemployment eroded working-class solidarity and Labour's capacity to bargain with employers. Under William Norton, the post office clerk from Kildare who led the party from 1932 to 1960, Labour's electoral performance fluctuated dizzily. Though the most significant and enduring of the minor parties, Labour had little effect on the formation of social policy in the Free State.

Like most movements unconstrained by the likelihood of securing power, Labour was fractured by numerous doctrinal disputes. The intelligence services bombarded the executive council with scary accounts of sinister cabals plotting to overthrow the social order. The Communist Party of Ireland, formed in November 1921, had played a significant part in the soviet movement of 1922, but fell into neglect after its repudiation by the Communist International in 1923. The International preferred the equally ineffectual Irish Workers' League, formed by Connolly's former leader Jim Larkin after his return from America. Larkin's dissatisfaction with Labour's lack of militancy led to his expulsion from the ITGWU in March 1924, and his rival Workers' Union of Ireland was excluded from the Trades Union Congress until that organization fragmented in 1945. By November 1923, the vestigial Communist Party was busy expelling undisciplined members, debating the relationship of communism to anarchism, and anticipating an army attempt to 'set up a Military dictatorship throughout the Free State'. Various bodies attempted to mesh republican and socialist grievances, including Saor Éire and earlier organizations such as the Workers' Defence Corps, the Irish Labour Defence League, and Irish Class War Prisoners' Aid. By April 1930, the department of justice enumerated no less than fifteen 'revolutionary organisations', remarking that 'much the same people appear to be behind several organisations, Mrs. Maud Gonne McBride being as ubiquitous as it is possible to be'.[102] Larkin's son (also James) was instrumental in reconstituting the Communist Party in June 1933, and numerous British and foreign activists visited Ireland in the vain hope of stimulating working-class enthusiasm for the cause. The revived Communist Party sought an independent Irish republic led by workers and farmers (the counterpart to Lenin's 'peasants'), hoping for Irish unity following parallel struggle in Northern Ireland.[103] Despite the fine words and the intricate networks of sometimes clandestine societies with grandiloquent titles, Irish socialism was inconsequential and virtually devoid of popular support.

Though proletarians were vastly outnumbered by farmers in the Free State, the Farmers' Party formed by the Irish Farmers' Union in May 1922 had limited success in mobilizing its class. Its function was not to govern but to lobby governments: 'With a Farmers' Party growing in strength, there is little doubt that under the new regime in Ireland agriculture will not be neglected.'[104] In 1922 and 1923, the recurrent menace of strikes and intimidation by farm labourers, most notably in Waterford, revived the spirit of rural class antagonism which had briefly flared up in 1920. After 1923, the Farmers' Party concentrated on more prosaic issues such as rates, rents, tariffs, and the iniquity of measures against foot and mouth disease. Its percentage of first-preference votes rose from 8 in 1922 to 12 in 1923, thereafter declining to 9 (June 1927), 6 (September 1927), and 2 (1932), after which it was effectively absorbed by the Centre Party and then Fine Gael. The radical demand for non-payment of land purchase annuities, which some branches of the Irish Farmers' Union had espoused in 1921, was renewed under more radical leadership in 1928. The ostensible aim of the initial campaign, led by the Donegal teacher, novelist, and former Irregular Peadar O'Donnell and Colonel Maurice Moore (late commander of the National Volunteers), was to prevent transfer of the annuities to the British exchequer, an aim heartily endorsed by Fianna Fáil. O'Donnell declared that 'he had no objection to the payment of land annuities if the amount collected was kept in the Free State'.[105] Once in power, however, de Valera encountered as much resistance to restocking the Irish as the British exchequer, leading to energetic action against those withholding annuities (a cause now promulgated by the Blueshirts). Like many social causes, the campaign against annuities attracted opportunists from every political faction, without becoming the foundation for a unified farmers' movement. The creation in 1938 of Clann na Talmhan (Family of the Land) gave voice to the grievances of small farmers disappointed with Fianna Fáil's broken promises; but after securing a tenth of first-preference votes in 1943 and 1944, this party also rapidly lost its following. Neither class divisions nor the antagonism of country against town proved powerful enough to dominate party politics.

The principal southern losers in the fight for freedom had been Protestant Unionists and Redmondites, whose former political programmes were plainly anachronistic in the Free State. Unionists, fearful for their lives and property after the ravages of the revolution and especially the civil war, took care to avoid overt political reorganization. Several Protestants nevertheless entered the Oireachtas, often as 'Independents' emphasizing their commitment to the development of the Free State as a dominion. In addition to the many former Unionists nominated to the Seanad, as many as fourteen Protestants were elected to the Dáil under various labels in 1927 (twice the number elected in 1938). The Redmondite remnant was less afraid to speak its name: in September 1926, Captain William Archer Redmond launched a new National League seeking closer co-operation with both Northern Ireland and Britain. His party scored a momentary success with 8 seats and 7 per cent of first-preference votes in June 1927, immediately discrediting its principles by allying itself with Fianna Fáil and Labour in an unsuccessful attempt to supplant Cosgrave's government. Of all the minor parties, the National League probably had the greatest potential for cutting across the civil war polarity. It briefly provided a forum for the restive army of veterans of the Great War, who remained deeply disaffected from their neighbours and rulers despite the provision of excellent state-subsidized housing and British military pensions. Since 1920, these veterans had been peculiarly liable to unemployment, exacerbated by discrimination on the part of nationalist employers and hostility from organized Labour. Except for the substantial minority who had re-enlisted in the national army, they had no preferential access to employment in the civil service or local administration. The Irish section of the British Legion, which united the various ex-servicemen's associations from 1925, did not supply effective political advocacy. Although assiduous in cultivating amicable contact with Cosgrave's executive council, the Legion usually avoided public controversy except around the eleventh day of the eleventh month. The failure of parties such as the National League to exploit the sectional grievances of Ireland's most populous class of victims is one of the undiscussed puzzles of the Free State's early history.

Between 1922 and 1939, every major British and European political movement had sounded echoes in Ireland. Even the British Fascists had organized branches in both states, being however committed to self-denying ordinances unknown elsewhere: 'not to enter into politics under any circumstances'; 'not to have in their possession or carry firearms of any description'. The 'chief pastime' of the tiny Dublin branch was 'card playing', interrupted by two annual parades on Armistice Sunday and Armistice Day.[106] Every shade of Marxism, Stalinism, and Trotskyism attracted a few Irish adherents; and the short-lived Irish Christian Front (founded in 1935 by Patrick Belton) gave local expression to the European phenomenon of overtly Catholic and anti-communist political organizations. Neither these experiments, nor the more sustained attempts to unite workers or farmers, could fundamentally disturb the predominant antagonisms defined and forged in the bloody conflicts of 1922. Southern politics remained a product of the civil war, while sectarian divisions continued to determine party alignments in Northern Ireland. The post-revolutionary moulds were not easily shattered.

Power and Freedom

Revolution and civil conflict had left each Irish state with a dual political legacy. The institutions and forms of parliamentary government had survived the initial armed challenge, at the cost of relying on the instruments of terror to subdue terrorism. Thereafter, both states were governed in accordance with one fundamental tenet of parliamentary democracy, the granting of political power to the party securing greatest support in free elections. In Northern Ireland, the electoral predominance of Unionism was never seriously challenged, so that power reposed with a single party for half a century. In the Free State, the resilience of the Westminster system of representative government was demonstrated in 1932, with the relatively peaceful transfer of power to politicians who had, until quite recently, rejected the legitimacy of the state. It was in the treatment of minorities that the limitations of Irish democracy were exposed. Neither state hesitated to apply coercion and suspend civil rights when confronted by collective protest, whether violent or otherwise. The 'losers' (republicans under Cosgrave; Blueshirts and subsequently republicans under de Valera; nationalists of all descriptions under Craig) were treated all too readily as enemies of the state, and subjected to discrimination in public employment as well as harassment by the police. Reiterated coercion expressed the weakness rather than efficiency of social control, representing a further legacy of British government as it had been applied in Ireland under the Union. Britain's most notable political bequest to Ireland's new rulers was expertise in applying the tyranny of majorities. The exercise of that power repeatedly infringed the freedom of minorities, encouraging them to reject their rulers as illegitimate. In the Free State, the practicability of outvoting one's oppressors gradually induced all but the most disaffected republicans to participate in the democratic process. Likewise, most Blueshirts were soon effortlessly reabsorbed into constitutional politics through Fine Gael. But in Northern Ireland, where the exclusion of nationalists from power seemed irreversible, those without a stake in the state remained dangerously alienated.

In order to define the personal meaning of 'power' and 'freedom', it is necessary to stray beyond the issues of citizenship, constitutional rights, and representative government discussed in the previous chapter. Governments have only limited power to bestow well-being, and therefore limited power to withhold it. Furthermore, freedom of choice may be curtailed by many unofficial agents, such as clergymen, employers, trades unionists, parents, children, husbands, wives, indeed by any person capable of influencing the decisions of others. The broad analysis of Irish and Ulster life, with its intricate fabric of extra-political economic, social, or cultural conflicts and alliances, lies beyond the scope of this book. Yet, to the extent that the intervention of interest-groups influenced government, their morality and ideology become relevant to a study of Ireland's revolutionary legacy. The following sections examine the ideology underpinning post-revolutionary policies affecting welfare, education, and morality.

Welfare

Ireland's new rulers, even when revolutionaries, had been singularly conservative in their economic and social programmes. Northern loyalists saw themselves as defenders of a successful and efficient system of industrial capitalism, backed up by a productive and harmonious rural economy. Their task was to prevent the destruction of northern prosperity through dissolution of the economic Union, imposition of protective external tariffs, or internal subversion of the workforce. For most nationalists, the Union had equal but opposite economic significance. Southern poverty, unemployment, emigration, and industrial failure were all attributed to British misgovernment, economic exploitation, and free trade within the United Kingdom. It followed that the creation of a native government, willing to protect and develop Irish industries, would rapidly yield prosperity and remove the impulse for emigration. Despite the intermittent influence of socialists and syndicalists in the revolutionary leadership, their more searching demands for social transformation had been stifled even before the civil war. By 1923, protectionism was the only radical economic policy with widespread support among nationalists, whether defenders or calumniators of Cosgrave's government.

In both states, these expectations of home-grown prosperity were soon disappointed. In Northern Ireland, the economic optimism engendered by wartime demand for ships, munitions, and linen fabric for aeroplanes had already been extinguished by 1921. Demand for the province's staple manufacturing industries never fully recovered. Whereas the pre-war textiles trade had flourished while its competitors in Lancashire and lowland Scotland faltered, Northern Ireland gradually became among the poorest and most stagnant economic regions of the post-war United Kingdom. Gross Domestic Product increased by only £2 per capita between 1924 and 1938, when the northern figure of £55 was scarcely half that for the entire United Kingdom.[1] Despite attempts to attract industrial investment by guaranteeing private loans (even after their termination in Britain in 1927), and by offering small grants under the development acts of 1932 and 1937, only a few thousand new jobs were created.

The unprecedentedly high level of industrial unemployment intensified material inequality and created an ever more restive lumpenproletariat. At the inauguration of partition in June 1921, a quarter of the province's insured workforce was unemployed (compared with less than 18 per cent in Britain). By December the proportion was even higher, women being slightly more at risk than men. Although unemployment was slightly alleviated during 1922 and 1923, its subsequent cycles remained far above contemporary British levels. The rapid worsening of unemployment after 1929, peaking at 28 per cent of the insured workforce in 1931, soon exposed the fragility of the economy and also the inadequacy of welfare provision. During 1932, two-fifths of building and engineering workers were unemployed, and no less than three-quarters of those hitherto employed in shipbuilding. Even after the end of the depression and the economic war, the reported proportion in 1939 was 23 per cent of all insured workers, compared with a tenth in Britain.[2] The cherished freedom of access by northern manufacturers to the British market had manifestly failed to sustain the province's relative prosperity within the United Kingdom.

Among those registered at labour exchanges in 1932, almost a fifth did not qualify for insurance benefits. Though excluded from medical benefits until 1930, insured workers were entitled to unemployment benefits and transitional payments at British rates. However, except for spasmodic employment on public works, poor relief inside or outside the doors of the workhouse remained the only amenity for uninsured workers. The poor law restricted outdoor relief for able-bodied men to periods of dire distress, effectively leaving the definition of distress to the boards of guardians. The Belfast guardians proved particularly zealous in restricting expenditure, making no provision for outdoor relief in 1928 despite strong ministerial pressure. The government, anxious to avoid assuming the political responsibility and the full financial burden, desisted from dissolving the staunchly Unionist board. Though relief was again provided after the 'crash', the amounts offered were miserly. The number of Belfast recipients passing the means test rose from 1,800 in April 1931 to 9,100 almost a year later, the weekly allowance for a family being less than half that in Glasgow or Bradford. For able-bodied men, the allowances were only payable as wages for relief work. The refusal of the Belfast guardians to increase the allowances, and the government's continued insistence that poor relief was a local responsibility, led to organized protests, and eventually to serious rioting and looting. Though all strands of Labour and outdoor-relief workers of all religions became embroiled in the dispute, the protests were expertly manipulated by the minute Communist Party. After a fortnight's violence generating widespread predictions of socialist revolution and the collapse of capitalism, a moderate increase in payments terminated the strike by relief workers. The eventual outcome was the transfer of the formal obligation to maintain the able-bodied poor from local authorities to the state in 1934, and the extension of local powers for distributing outdoor relief in 1937.[3]

The political effect on northern loyalists of industrial and economic decline was not to discredit the British connection, but to intensify demand for British subventions, and also distrust of the Free State. Though reluctant publicly to admit the damaging effect of the Belfast boycotts and later the economic war, loyalists were confirmed in their suspicion of a southern and Catholic plot to destroy northern well-being. This supplied essential rationalization for the renewed expulsion of Catholic workers from Belfast firms in 1935 as in 1920, and for the unashamed demand that preference be given to Protestants in public employment, provision of housing, and other welfare measures. In the first years of partition, the northern government had grudgingly accepted British insistence that Catholics should receive at least a third of the payments allocated to unemployed ex-servicemen undertaking relief works. In June 1922, the minister of labour (John Andrews) vigorously defended the administration of these grants against Joseph Devlin's insinuations of sectarianism: 'Nine representatives of Catholics on Committee out of twenty-three and only one arrested. The others still actively co-operating in work of Committee which is proceeding harmoniously.' Despite objections from the minister of finance to subsidizing the employment of 1,300 married 'expelled workers', driven from their jobs in 1920, Andrews managed in October 1923 to secure cabinet support for the continuation of existing undertakings.[4]

Ten years later, a different spirit was exhibited by Sir Basil Brooke, the Fermanagh Orangeman who was eventually to supplant Andrews as prime minister (1943–63). Expressing shock at the suspected though fictitious employment of several Catholics in the parliamentary service at Stormont, Brooke demanded their replacement by loyal Protestants. Though embarrassing to less forthright colleagues, Brooke's proud if misleading boast that 'he had not a Roman Catholic about his own place', his advice to loyalists 'whenever possible, to employ good Protestant lads and lassies', and his assertion that 'ninety-nine per cent' of Catholics were 'disloyal', all aroused enthusiastic Orange echoes and cautious support even from Craigavon.[5] For Sir Joseph Davison, grand master of the Royal Arch Purple Chapter of Ireland as well as Belfast's Grand Orange Lodge, discrimination against Catholics was a moral imperative in 1933: 'When will the Protestant employers of Northern Ireland recognise their duty to their Protestant brothers and sisters and employ them to the exclusion of Roman Catholics?'[6] These shrill admonitions attest not only to prejudice on the part of some prominent politicians, but also to the persistent influence of more liberal practices in both public and private employment. The relative force of these conflicting attitudes depended in part on economic fluctuations, which help explain the timing of the sectarian campaign of 1933–4. The equation of Catholicism with subversion provided a convenient justification for firing Catholic workers, and thus reducing Protestant unemployment. Economic decline fuelled sectarian animosities, supplying the material motive for discrimination which might have been deemed needlessly divisive in a period of prosperity.

The welfare of northern Catholics was also to some extent imperilled by the discriminatory provision of housing. Yet the penalization of Catholic house-seekers, notorious in the era of public housing developments after 1944, was insignificant between the wars. Only 50,000 houses were built in Northern Ireland between 1919 and 1939, including 3,700 labourers' cottages, 3,800 other dwellings erected by local authorities, and 32,600 private houses subsidized by minor state grants under a dozen Westminster-inspired statutes. The number of houses built without any public assistance was scarcely 10,000. Since a planning committee considered in 1944 that the province required another 100,000 houses to supplement the current stock of 323,000, it is obvious that neither Catholic nor Protestant requirements had been adequately met.[7] Moreover, the predominance of private house-building reduced the feasibility of systematically excluding Catholic buyers. Even though the most extensive private housing scheme in inter-war Belfast was intended to become a '100 per cent Protestant colony' for respectable working-class tenants, the half-occupied estate was successfully invaded by evicted Catholic households after the riots of 1935. Half of the 'refugees' were eventually accepted as tenants in Glenard (renamed 'New Ardoyne' in 1938), many Protestants departed in fear or disgust, and chain colonization by Catholics proved sufficient to wrest the local constituency from Unionist control in 1945.[8] Even the allocation of public housing did not universally favour Protestants. Under an extensive scheme for building houses for ex-servicemen, administered by a trust funded by the British government, applicants were ranked according to a strict system of points without regard for religion. This provoked outrage from a legless and subliterate railway worker in Enniskillen who complained unavailingly to Craigavon that several fully limbed 'RCs' or 'Romans' had been housed while he had to limp a mile and a half from home to workplace: 'nice recompence for loyal orangemen who gave of their best in Englands hour of need. We were promised a country fit for hero's to live in. But it would take a *hero* to live in it.'[9]

In the Irish Free State, the expected achievement of prosperity through freedom proved as elusive as in Northern Ireland. Neither state matched the modest growth of income in inter-war Britain. Though Éire's Gross Domestic Product per capita was still slightly below the northern figure in 1938, the improvement since the mid-1920s had been somewhat less feeble than in Northern Ireland.[10] The southern economy remained depressingly dependent on the United Kingdom, which supplied over four-fifths of its imports and received almost all of its exports during the 1920s. Though formally distinct from 1927, the Irish currency remained at par with sterling until 1979. As in Northern Ireland, industrial unemployment appears to have exceeded the British proportion, and the continuing predominance of agriculture meant that many idle children of farmers and casual labourers were unrecorded in the official register. Cosgrave's governments followed British and northern practice by providing benefits for insured workers but no general 'dole', distress being alleviated by occasional relief works and outdoor payments labelled as 'home assistance'. Relief schemes for veterans of the Great War continued for some years after independence, and grants benefiting other groups (especially national ex-servicemen) were approved by the department of local government in 1924, 1925, 1927, and 1928. Such schemes affected a substantial minority of those without jobs.[11] In December 1923, 80,000 workers were officially estimated to be unemployed, the number being equally distributed between agricultural and other sectors. By April 1926, when 20,000 insured workers were receiving weekly benefits, it was estimated that five times that number had received some payment from the unemployment fund during the previous year.[12] Though minor by today's standard, post-revolutionary unemployment was sufficiently widespread and persistent to proclaim the failure of nationhood to deliver the promised well-being.

Cosgrave's ministers, sternly advised by conservative mandarins and preoccupied with the expensive enterprises of coercion and reconstruction, were half-hearted in their economic initiatives. Tariff protection was progressively applied to selected products after 1924, without generating any coherent policy of industrial development or attraction of capital investment. Particular tariffs, often affecting the welfare of only half a dozen workers, were introduced haphazardly in response to lobbying by individual firms or deputies. The most ambitious modernizing measure was the electricity supply scheme, inaugurated in August 1927 to provide a national network of generating stations, initially producing power for urban consumption (rural electrification followed two decades later). The first of these harnessed hydro-electric energy from the river Shannon at Ardnacrusha, Co. Clare, a project initiated in August 1925. The electricity supply board was the prototype for numerous 'semi-state bodies', financed by government loans but administered by autonomous boards including a minority of state nominees. With few exceptions, however, Cumann na nGaedheal allowed the economy to follow its accustomed sluggish course, with less official intervention than that practised by the 'constructive' Conservative administrations of the turn of the century.

The accession of Fianna Fáil coincided with a rapid increase in the mean number of applications at labour exchanges, which rose from about 25,000 in 1932 to 63,000, 72,000, 104,000 and 120,000 in the four succeeding years. Despite a slight subsequent respite, unemployment had climbed back to 93,000 by 1939. With consummate skill, de Valera exploited the constitutional struggle with Britain to mask the inability of republican economic policy to deliver prosperity in the context of worldwide depression. The 'economic war' of 1932–8 not only allowed British import restrictions to be blamed for Irish agricultural catastrophe, but also justified economic reprisals implementing Griffith's doctrine of industrial protection. Though tariff barriers were in any case being raised by most countries in the early 1930s, the punitive duties imposed on Irish cattle exports caused substantial additional unemployment and impoverishment. During the first seven weeks of 1934, the agricultural and non-agricultural workforces both recorded an increase of over a quarter in unemployment. The effects were far more serious in certain sectors of manufacturing, such as woollen goods and footwear, while the number of unemployed general labourers rose by almost half. Children suffered more than adults, and girls more than boys.[13] Fianna Fáil, like its predecessor, relied mainly on emergency relief works to mitigate the distress caused by loss of employment.

The government's attempt to protect home manufactures by imposing retributive tariffs on imports from Britain and Northern Ireland was ambitious and systematic. It undoubtedly created tens of thousands of new industrial jobs (neatly balancing the loss of demand in agriculture), curtailed the impact of urban depression, and accelerated rural–urban migration. Even so, the negative effect of the economic war was far greater for the Free State than for Britain, Northern Ireland being the major sufferer. The agricultural crisis was somewhat alleviated by the 'coal–cattle pact' of 1935, which allowed an increased quota of cattle exports in return for a British monopoly of coal imports to the Free State. The abandonment of punitive tariffs by both governments in April 1938, though undoubtedly beneficial to Irish exporters, soon led to the retrenchment of most of the additional industrial employment generated since 1932. De Valera's experiment in economic nationalism brought no obvious long-term benefit. In the short term, the policy of protection had further undermined the state's economic self-sufficiency by attracting massive investment from British and foreign capitalists, lured by low rates of interest and the assurance of a captive market of consumers. By 1939, the southern state was once again an economic dependency of the United Kingdom, virtually devoid of other export markets and no longer attractive to foreign investors. Admittedly, the foreign share of imports, which had risen to nearly half by 1938, was sustained near that level after the Anglo-Irish agreement (scarcely changing, indeed, up to the mid-1970s). But no appreciable increase in foreign exports had been achieved during the economic war, the proportion dropping from a tenth in 1935 to about 3 per cent a decade later (before gradually increasing to a quarter in 1960 and a third in 1970).[14] National freedom had brought no economic transformation or marked material betterment, fulfilling the chilling prophecy ascribed by Yeats to Parnell:[15]

> Parnell came down the road, he said to a cheering man:
> 'Ireland shall get her freedom, and you still break stone.'

The most poignant symbol of material failure was the renewal and persistence of extensive emigration. During 1920 and 1921 Collins and the Dáil ministry, perturbed by the leakage of Volunteers to America and convinced that patriots could be arm-twisted into staying at home, had issued ferocious decrees prohibiting emigration without a ministerial permit. These had little obvious effect, as the resumption of the passenger shipping trade prompted emigration at pre-war levels from spring 1921 onwards. The demand for passages reflected not only Ireland's endemic incapacity to provide jobs for more than half of each generation born in the country, but also the creation of a long queue of would-be emigrants whose intentions had been thwarted by wartime isolation. Discrimination against former 'Irregulars' encouraged an unmeasured additional movement in 1923, though many of these political exiles were to return as republicanism found a place in the political process. A second stream of exiles, more often directed towards Britain, Northern Ireland, or the dominions, was drawn from the casualties of revolution: former policemen; persecuted war veterans; isolated Protestants with looted or gutted houses, hostile neighbours, and often 'notices to quit'. The extent of Protestant emigration is unrecorded, but the Anglican population of the Free State area declined from a quarter of a million in 1911 to a sixth of a million in 1926. The decline was proportionately sharpest in the border counties and along the western seaboard, where the Protestant minority had long been vestigial.[16]

The most disturbing characteristic of post-war emigration was its direction. Despite shameless discrimination in favour of white Anglophones, the American quota system imposed stringent 'quality controls' upon immigrants which ensured that the Free State never quite exhausted its annual allocation. Furthermore, the reduced demand for domestic servants and unskilled labourers made the American option less alluring and more risky than in the nineteenth century. The renewal of subsidized movement from Britain to the dominions, with preference for ex-servicemen, was not extended to the Free State, whose government sniffed suspiciously at tentative proposals from Canada and Australia. The remaining option, always popular but hitherto secondary to the American movement, was to cross the water to Britain. Despite recurrent Conservative demands for the restriction of Irish access to British jobs and social services, no restrictions by passport or permit were imposed on inter-war travel across the Irish Sea, and citizens of the Free State retained a curious dual status as British subjects with the voting and residence rights of British citizens. Tens of thousands of young Irish people migrated annually to Britain, for terms varying between a season and a lifetime. Only at the depth of the depression, when the prospect of employment in Britain was no better than at home, was the drift towards Britain temporarily curtailed. The ultimate humiliation for the doctrine of national self-sufficiency was the decision of Parnell's 'cheering man' to break British rather than Irish stone.

In Northern Ireland, particularly in the border counties of mid-Ulster, emigration was likewise a universal career option and a frequent necessity. As in the Free State, the impulse to settle elsewhere was vigorously renewed from 1921 onwards. Far from deploring emigration within the British Isles and the empire, Craig's government applauded it as a sign of imperial integration and took full advantage of empire settlement and other schemes of assistance. Richhill Castle in Co. Armagh was acquired in 1926 as a training centre for up to seventy-five would-be empire settlers, hampered by inexperience of 'outdoor life, the effect on their physique of prolonged unemployment, etc.'[17] Even movement to the United States was quietly encouraged, since it was believed that Catholics were more likely to depart and thereby reduce disaffection at home. The calculation of the American quota was based on the pre-war intake from each country, Britain and Ireland being treated separately. Since British emigration had been far less intense than Irish, the inclusion of Northern Ireland within the British rather than the Irish quota imposed a severe and unfair restriction. Unable publicly to demand equitable treatment as a part of Ireland, Craig's government nevertheless struggled unavailingly in 1926 to secure preferential regional treatment within the British allocation.[18] Net outward movement from inter-war Northern Ireland peaked in 1926, and after 1931 inward movement seems actually to have exceeded emigration.

Loyalists, unworried by emigration, were constantly fearful of unwanted arrivals from the Free State. Convinced that southerners, perhaps with subversive designs, would otherwise take advantage of northern social services and urban employment, the northern government introduced 'certain deterrents to emigration of labour from the Irish Free State into Northern

Ireland'. By 1928, these included stringent residence qualifications for recipients of unemployment insurance benefits (which were not likewise restricted in Britain) and old-age pensions. In the absence of a law of settlement, northern boards of guardians were as yet unable to refuse relief to destitute southern immigrants, though 'private arrangements for returning the paupers' were commonplace.[19] For Ulster loyalists, the problem raised by migration was not how to keep patriots at home, but how to keep intruders out.

Education

The most bitterly resented object of official discrimination in Northern Ireland was elementary schooling, in which the Catholic church had a massive economic as well as spiritual investment. Though all teachers were paid by the state, the extent to which running and capital costs were reimbursed depended on how much of their autonomy managers were prepared to surrender. Londonderry's initial attempt in 1923 to give preferential funding to schools not offering doctrinal instruction in school hours had generated equal objection from all major churches, a rare moment of ecumenical unity. Ruthless campaigning by the United Education Committee of the Protestant Churches, eventually supported by the Orange Institution, had yielded amending legislation in 1925 and 1930 which allowed maximum grants to be given to schools teaching basic Bible studies (acceptable to virtually all Protestants but no Catholics). Since Catholics were scarcely represented on the regional education committees administering the allocation of grants, there was ample opportunity for inequitable distribution even of the inferior grants available to 'untransferred' schools. This was compounded by the initial refusal of most Catholic managers and nationalist councillors to collaborate in administering the iniquitous system.

Yet the increasing pragmatism of the Catholic church after 1925, and the government's positive response in raising capital grants and reducing the channels for local interference, meant that most Catholic boards eventually accepted a few representatives of the local authority in order to secure superior subsidies (second only to those for transferred schools). In 1930, even 'voluntary' schools were allowed to recoup half of their capital expenditure direct from the ministry, a settlement far more lucrative than that available to denominational schools in England or most parts of the empire. In the Free State, admittedly, two-thirds of capital costs were covered by the state. Craigavon was obliged to placate the outraged Grand Orange Lodge of Co. Down by affirming 'that an obligation rested on the government to go as far as possible—even beyond what might seem justifiable on strict grounds of equity—to settle the question on a basis satisfactory to every party in the State'.[20] The compromise was not unfavourable to the government, which at relatively low cost was exempted from the need to provide state schooling for over a third of the province's children. Yet Londonderry and Charlemont had proved even less successful than Whately and his nineteenth-century successors in restricting denominational control over state-subsidized schools. Education remained a formidable mechanism for inculcating and reinforcing Catholic alienation from the northern state.

The government's admittedly half-hearted attempt to incorporate Catholic schools in the state system partly explains its reticence in using the schools to disseminate the patriotic creed of Ulster Unionism. Despite state control of the elementary school curriculum, the ministry of education did not attempt to inculcate Ulsterness through the teaching of history or geography. Although several textbooks on regional history were prepared, the curriculum concentrated on Britain rather than any part of Ireland. Like the nineteenth-century commissioners of national education, the northern administrators chose to downplay the teaching of history for fear of inflaming sectarian emotions: the brief political chronicle in Chart's *A History of Northern Ireland* stopped short at the act of Union, more than a century before the foundation of the state named in its title.[21] Catholic secondary schools were permitted to teach the southern history curriculum, but the formal exposure of Protestant children to the perils of Irish and Ulster history was increasingly perfunctory at all levels. Even this seemed excessive to Sir Wilfrid Spender, who in 1937 privately deplored 'the pointless and ghoulish digging up of the results of British policy'. History teachers should concentrate on the inspiring examples of ancient Greece and the Bible, 'with only the broad outlines of English and Irish history'.[22] The inculcation of patriotism through symbolic gestures was focused on Britain rather than Ulster, being in any case minimal. In protesting against the cautious recommendations of Sir Robert Lynn's committee in June 1923, which provided the basis for most elements of educational policy under Londonderry, two Unionist MPs formulated an alternative approach. 'In our opinion not only should the flag be flown over every State-aided school but even the youngest children should be assembled at very frequent intervals and taught to salute the flag, thus inculcating loyalty in the children and preparing the soil in which the seeds of Civics, as they grow more advanced, could be planted.'[23] Prudently, however, the ministry of education avoided rigorous enforcement of symbolic demonstrations in Catholic schools.

Craig's cultural strategy was defensive, being designed to minimize official amenities for the exposure of his people to the insidious influence of Irish culture. To teach the recent history of Ulster would be to invite contrary nationalist interpretations, so distracting loyalists from the more abstract affirmation of fealty to the British monarch and empire. Official defensiveness was increasingly evident in policy concerning the Irish language, which had virtually disappeared from the province as a vernacular outside the Glens of Antrim, but quickly became a rallying point for nationalist dissidents whether or not Irish-speakers. The use of Irish was forbidden in addressing letters, naming streets, and other official transactions. Nevertheless, a small subsidy was initially available for teaching the language as an optional subject in elementary schools. Catholic objections to the anodyne history curriculum were ingeniously defused by directing schools to teach either Irish or history. As Charlemont observed, such concessions 'disarmed criticism on the part of anti-British elements in the population, while the actual results in spreading a knowledge of the language are insignificant'.[24] This ecumenical gesture came under increasing attack from the Orange Institution and many clergymen, leading to the withdrawal of the subsidy in 1933. Thereafter, while the government did not prohibit the teaching of the language or of Irish history, it offered no state support for these pursuits. Beyond the classroom, northern nationalists and loyalists alike were left to develop their ethnic identity informally, through the agencies of religion, the press, family fraternities, or simply conversation.

Informal though it was, the sense of belonging to Ulster, rather than merely to the United Kingdom or the empire, was essential to loyalist identity. The experience of revolutionary mobilization and the assumption of provincial power had heightened the loyalist sense of Ulsterness, albeit thinly disguised by the rhetoric of British patriotism. The efflorescence of Irish cultural nationalism in the later nineteenth century had been answered by a substantial if less distinguished literary celebration of Protestant Ulster's distinctive culture, expressed in dialect verses, whimsical tales of Ulster ways, compendia of Ulster idioms and proverbs, tracts on the superiority of the 'Ulster custom', and historical studies of the so-called 'Scotch-Irish' in America. The vision of a province peopled by hospitable philosophers of home and hearth, God-fearing yet canny, cosmopolitan if well-nigh incomprehensible in speech, was promulgated in newspapers and public lectures as well as in fraternal meetings of the 'loyal orders'. Incorporation of Ulsterness in the practice of government was an obvious option for Craig's administration, through the choice of official symbols as well as the control of schooling discussed above. Yet any overt affirmation of Ulster's cultural distinctiveness carried severe political risks, threatening to undermine British commitment to sheltering Northern Ireland within the United Kingdom. The equation of Northern Ireland with the province of Ulster was also bound to irritate not only Free Staters and Catholics, but the Protestants of Cavan, Donegal, and Monaghan. Craig's ministers therefore made no systematic effort to institutionalize

Ulster culture. The Union flag was normally preferred to the sinister Red Hand of Ulster at official ceremonies, although the provincial emblem was used in ministerial seals, in the gubernatorial flag, and sometimes in marketing campaigns.[25] The appropriation by de Valera of the term 'Ireland' provoked the northern government to consider, yet reject, the retaliatory renaming of Northern Ireland as 'Ulster', the designation customarily used in the loyalist press, in private correspondence between civil servants and politicians, and occasionally in public notices.[26] The feeling that Northern Ireland embodied Ulster culture remained a comfortable assumption rather than an official assertion.

By contrast, all factions of southern nationalists were unabashed in invoking Pearse's dream of a nation 'not free merely, but Gaelic as well; not Gaelic merely, but free as well'.[27] Perhaps more than the achievement of independence, the prospect of restoring Gaelic culture in Ireland had justified the horror and suffering of revolution and civil conflict. Even before the statutory date for transferring administrative powers to the provisional government, that body had peremptorily seized control of the office of national education upon learning that the commissioners had 'sanctioned the attendance of schoolchildren at a cinema performance entitled "With Lord Allenby in Palestine".'[28] Elementary education immediately became the chief official instrument for Gaelic cultural revival, through the compulsory teaching of Irish history and the language. Despite depressing evidence of the inefficacy of compelling children to learn a language usually unknown to their parents, and unspoken as a vernacular in most regions, the policy of mandatory instruction in Irish has never been abandoned. With great energy and greater optimism, the state imposed linguistic tests on all would-be teachers (as well as civil servants and even diplomats), aiming also to convert current teachers into purveyors of Gaelic culture through crash courses. In a heroic attempt to capture the mouths and ears of children at the most susceptible age, the provisional government had ordered on 1 April 1922 that all preschool classes should be conducted in Irish, despite the fact that over nine-tenths of national teachers were not yet competent in the language. The frenzied programme of retraining failed dismally, necessitating grudging exemption for teachers lacking the required fluency; yet the official aspiration was maintained until 1971.[29] The accession of Fianna Fáil merely intensified the concentration of educational policy on the language, a pass in which became mandatory for the various secondary certificate examinations after 1934. Despite the laxity with which compulsion was applied, the principle remained a source of grievance for Protestant managers, teachers, and pupils, who in other respects were treated with surprising generosity in the Free State's educational system.

It had long been a commonplace of Gaelic revivalists such as Douglas Hyde that Irish nationality required a knowledge of the nation's history and literature as well as its former language. History had been belatedly introduced as a distinct and compulsory element of the primary curriculum in 1908, schools being allowed the option of concentrating on Irish or British history according to taste. Under the initial direction of Eoin MacNeill as minister for education, the Free State's government gave priority to Irish history at all levels and specified a suitable range of permitted textbooks by orthodox nationalists such as Alice Stopford Green (and Professor MacNeill). Though rigorous control of the curriculum was not feasible in secondary education, which remained in private hands despite increasing state subsidies, history remained a core subject at lower levels with examinations concentrating on Ireland. The attempt to infuse Irishness through history lessons was reinvigorated in 1933, when Fianna Fáil's minister for education (Thomas Derrig, formerly headmaster of Ballina technical school, Co. Mayo) released the revised *Notes for Teachers*. Reissued without amendment to the text or bibliography until 1962, this unique ideological manifesto called upon teachers scrupulously to convey the facts of Irish history in order to counteract the lies promulgated by historians adopting 'the enemy's standpoint'. Youngsters would be saturated with 'sublime examples of patriotism' (and balancing tales of 'those who served Ireland in humbler ways'), progressing year by year to later centuries and deeper analysis of British oppression, with the creation of the Gaelic League providing a 'fitting close' to their primary studies. The awkward period of revolution, partition, civil war, and the establishment of the state was to be ignored, matching the silence of the history curriculum in Northern Ireland. Derrig's dream of history pupils entranced by stories of their ancestors' pugnacious exploits was soon shattered: despite the rapid generation of a battery of doctrinally acceptable textbooks (with less colourful Protestant options for the cherished minority), history remained the most dismally unpopular of school subjects. The obstinacy and irreverence of children wrecked the attempt to impose an intellectual tyranny more concerted than any such experiment under the Union.[30]

The resistance of children and their teachers to compulsory Gaelicization negated the cultural revolution that Hyde and Pearse had envisaged. The perpetuation of economic dependency on Britain, and extensive emigration to English-speaking countries, ensured that the English language and Anglophone culture would remain paramount in the Free State. The constitutional description of Irish as 'the national language' (upgraded to 'the first official language' in 1937) highlighted the gap between official aspirations and vernacular practice. In the revolutionary years, the acquisition of the language (in however rudimentary a form) had been an exhilarating expression of national defiance and fraternity, providing a code for identifying friends and confusing enemies. The daunting challenge of restoring a virtually defunct language prompted enthusiasts to establish and patronize Irish-speaking schools and pubs, to use the language within families or circles of friends, and even to ban the use of English by employees. Though never extinguished, these experiments lost their vigour during the civil war, which stripped nationalism of much of its romance. Compulsory indoctrination proved a miserable substitute for the missionary enthusiasm of the pre-revolutionary Gaelic League and kindred cultural organizations, which rapidly lost support after 1922. The private cultivation of Gaelicism became exceptional, providing solace for alienated republicans, intellectual stimulus for a few civil servants and scholars, and an alternative but unremunerative medium for a slowly expanding network of poets and authors writing mainly for each other. More conspicuously, the routine and stumbling utterance of a few ill-chosen phrases in Irish became *de rigueur* for politicians and public speakers. The increasingly lifeless Gaelic 'revival', once the most sacred of nationalist aspirations, became the very hallmark of political hypocrisy in all parties.

Morality

The Anglo-Irish settlement of 1921–2 had prohibited the establishment of any church in either state, protected the institutional interests of all churches, and proclaimed the equality before the law of citizens of all denominations. These safeguards did not interfere with the self-conscious creation of a Catholic Free State and a Protestant province in Northern Ireland. In a celebrated statement in 1934, Craigavon justifiably claimed 'that in the South they boasted of a Catholic State. They still boast of Southern Ireland being a Catholic state. All I boast of is that we are a Protestant Parliament and a Protestant State.'[31] For Craigavon and at least some of his fellow loyalists, this was perfectly consistent with according full civil rights and welfare benefits to Catholics: to be 'Protestant' was to be tolerant, just, and protective of freedom of conscience. A 'Catholic State', by contrast, would seek to impose its doctrinally regulated morality upon all citizens, so interfering with Protestant liberties.

In practice, the northern government seldom attempted to impose legislation morally repugnant to Catholics, partly because most Protestant churches were at least as rigorous in their moral conservatism as the Catholic church in Ireland. Apart from easier access to contraceptives, there was little difference between north and south in the range of legal restraints upon irregular liaisons and sexual intercourse. Indeed, the moral measure engendering greatest indignation among northern Catholics was a symptom of puritanism rather than licentious-

ness in the Protestant state. The Licensing act of June 1923 prohibited not only Sunday opening of pubs but also off-licence
sales by 'spirit grocers', many of whom were stalwart Catholics.
Though faintly applauded by the strong temperance lobbies in
all churches, the act outraged the publicans and grocers who
dominated Devlin's Hibernian and nationalist organizations.
The far more draconian threat of 'local option' was stoutly
rejected by Craigavon (a distiller's son) and most of his party.
The reformers sought to make 'Ulster dry' by restricting hours,
closing pubs, and allowing local prohibition by referendum as
in Scotland. Despite support from the extensive network of
Orange 'temperance lodges', the single attempt by local option-
ists to gain parliamentary representation, in 1929, was a dismal
failure.[32] Though the sabbatarian restrictions imposed by local
as well as central authorities were resented by Catholic cinema-
lovers, gamesplayers, punters, and topers, they constituted an
irritant rather than a moral despotism.

Northern loyalists, being drawn from many denominations,
did not identify Protestantism with any creed, beyond the repudiation of papal supremacy and affirmation of the supposed
principles of the Reformation. Loyalist laymen prided themselves on their independence from clerical authority, although
clergymen of all Protestant churches were entitled to become
deputy grand chaplains of the Orange Institution, and many
loyalist processions and demonstrations entailed attendance at
a church service. Loyalist repugnance for clerical dictation was
evident in the response of the Ulster Teachers' Union to demands from the United Education Committee of the Protestant Churches for 'special recognition of the Churches as such'
in the management of Stranmillis Training College, Belfast.
Delegates protested in March 1932 that 'it is incomprehensible
that such a demand should have the support of a democratic
body like the Orange Order'; and that 'we are more clerical-
ridden in the North than the people of the South, about whom
we have been talking for years as priest-ridden'.[33] In fact, as
Charlemont indicated in 1929, the Orange influence on education policy outweighed the clergy's. 'So long as I only had the

representatives of the Churches to deal with I thought a sympathetic attitude was all that was required, as I had no reason to think that they had any large body of public opinion behind them, but if the Grand Orange Lodge is also with them on this question it will make a certain amount of difference.'[34] Whereas Orangeism was recognized as an authentic expression of widespread popular opinion, there was no Protestant consensus concerning the proper bounds of clerical authority. Ranging from episcopalians to congregationalists and 'dippers', northern loyalists were never likely to tolerate political dictation from any particular church.

The same could not be claimed for Cosgrave's Free State. Cosgrave considered it proper that the Catholic hierarchy, as the moral authority for nine-tenths of the southern population, should be invited to pronounce upon the morality of proposed legislation. Even before the truce, he had proposed the creation for this purpose of an upper house of Catholic bishops. Once in power, it was his practice to seek informal guidance on potentially controversial proposals from the archbishop of Dublin, while maintaining close correspondence with influential well-wishers such as Michael Fogarty, the bishop of Killaloe. Cosgrave's unabashed deference to episcopal authority, though doubtless springing from personal conviction, was also politically astute. It enabled him at key moments to mobilize the bishops behind his government, re-enacting the alliance against conscription in 1918. Cosgrave's rewards included the remarkably wide-ranging excommunication of active Irregulars by the entire hierarchy in October 1922, and of their militant successors nine years later as Cumann na nGaedheal tottered towards defeat. Yet the governments of church and state were not always in accord over 'moral' issues, despite their frequent expressions of mutual admiration. Archbishop Byrne of Dublin protested privately to Cosgrave about the 'policy of reprisals' in December 1922 and the implacable treatment of republican hunger-strikers in October 1923: official sanction for the shooting of prisoners in reprisal was withdrawn, but the 8,000 hunger-strikers were left to starve until they prudently abandoned their futile protest.[35] Though supreme in matters not affecting the security of the state or the survival of the government, the bishops' moral authority could not in general outweigh political logic and the assertion of power.

In the Irish Free State as in Northern Ireland, Britain, the dominions, and the United States, the aftermath of the Great War created a widespread sense of moral collapse, followed by strong political pressure for restrictive legislation. Statutory censorship was applied to films (July 1923) and publications (July 1929), leading to an unusually severe and systematic attempt to suppress obscene and atheistic material (unless in the Irish language), a definition which eventually embraced almost the entire canon of contemporary literature. The second act had the effect of prohibiting advertisements for contraceptive devices, although their importation and sale remained legal until 1935. Whereas Fianna Fáil was eventually to surrender to episcopal pressure for a more comprehensive ban, Cosgrave's ministry had deflected the hierarchy's demand in 1929 by stressing the government's instability, and its need for Protestant as well as episcopal support in averting 'a grave upheaval in the country'.[36] Following the northern example of June 1923, some restriction of liquor licences and trading hours was enacted in May 1924, defying the persistent influence of publicans in the local organization of all major political parties. Yet Cosgrave's government was cautious in implementing the more radical demands for social regulation emanating from the burgeoning Catholic Action movement and increasingly from the clergy. In 1926, the executive council was shocked by a report on venereal disease, indicating that syphilis was widespread in every country town with an army barracks, while brothels continued to flourish above or behind Dublin's pubs and shebeens for all the sterling efforts of General Murphy's police and Frank Duff's Legion of Mary. Despite demands from a prominent Jesuit (Fr. R. S. Devane) that prostitutes be not merely fined but imprisoned, and despite the insistence of Kevin O'Higgins that the inquiry had revealed 'a very grave menace to public health, calling for definite legislation and administrative measures to cope with it', the executive council suppressed the report and left the law unchanged.[37] The risk involved in advertising immorality exceeded the probable benefit of trying to eliminate it.

As the depression deepened, Cosgrave's faltering government was bombarded with apocalyptic warnings and demands for stricter moral control. In March 1931, the county council of Tipperary North Riding solemnly condemned 'the "Daily Mail" for having published an article on Our Divine Redeemer which is blasphemous and detestable', and called 'on the Dáil to prevent the entry of foreign newspapers into Saorstát Éireann, except under special licence revocable at a moment's notice'.[38] The Lenten pastoral letters read in Catholic churches a few weeks earlier, carefully assembled and catalogued for the perusal of the executive council, provide vivid evidence of contemporary moral panic. Of the twenty-six episcopal pastorals, twelve reaffirmed the sanctity of marriage or inadmissibilty of divorce; eleven deplored the insidious effects of the press, wireless, or evil literature; eight inveighed against the cinema or theatre; six warned of the dangers of dancing; four alluded delicately to contraception, abortion, or infanticide; three condemned company-keeping; while irregular unions and immodesty in female dress each provoked two admonitions. No such pronouncements were forthcoming from the province of Dublin, the epicentre of Irish immorality; whereas the nine pastorals for the province of Armagh (embracing Northern Ireland) presented an almost united front against indecency in publications and dramatic performances. Cardinal Joseph MacRory of Armagh reflected that 'the country is still suffering from the effects of the excitement and moral laxity caused by the Great War, and intensified in the period of the "Black and Tans" and during the civil war'. William MacNeely of Raphoe (Co. Donegal) echoed the recent papal encyclical on Christian marriage, which presented 'a graphic picture of the diseases of post-war social life, that threaten to undermine family life'. The danger applied even in Ireland: 'No people can be entirely isolated nowadays; no atmosphere is morally germ-free.'[39] Independence had not resulted in the anticipated construction of a chaste and blameless Gaelic commonwealth.

The electoral triumph of Fianna Fáil in 1932 caused tremors of alarm in the hierarchy, which only a decade earlier had excommunicated almost the entire future leadership of the party in its pastoral condemnation of the Irregulars in October 1922. That astonishing display of episcopal unity fostered the illusion that the church was implacably hostile to republicanism and that republicans were antagonistic to the church. In fact, a small but dedicated army of sympathetic priests, mainly but not exclusively in regular orders outside direct diocesan control, had catered for the spiritual welfare of republican activists throughout the civil war. De Valera, Seán T. O'Kelly, and other well-connected republicans had developed remarkably strong links with key churchmen outside the hierarchy's jurisdiction, such as Archbishop Daniel Mannix of Melbourne and Msr. John Hagan, the former Roman correspondent of the *Catholic Bulletin* who exercised considerable influence in the Vatican as rector of the Irish College. In cajoling his followers towards participation in the Free State, de Valera re-enacted his strategy of 1917 by working tirelessly to reassure the clergy of republican respect for the church's spiritual authority, and desire to promote morality in both public and private life. By June 1924, the new bishop of Clonfert was already certain that the republicans would soon be returned to power, instructing his flock to 'prepare for that day and do your best for its quick approach, while in the meantime you obey the law of the Free State and subordinate your politics to the national interest'.[40] Though other bishops repudiated John Dignan's views, the practical necessity to prepare for government by de Valera gradually loosened the church's alliance with his opponents. As with Sinn Féin in 1917, the hierarchy avoided open embrace of Fianna Fáil until its popular following seemed overwhelming. After 1932, the hierarchy dropped its implicit imputation of communistic tendencies to de Valera's party; and in the following year's election campaign, numerous parochial clergy and a few bishops openly supported

Fianna Fáil. The party's acceptance as a Catholic instrument was symbolized during Dublin's Eucharistic Congress in June 1932 by the conspicuous participation of de Valera's ministry as well as Cosgrave's forlorn would-be hosts.

Once firmly in power, de Valera easily outscored Cumann na nGaedheal in moral zealotry, using legislation as an agent for moral reform. In February 1935, his government reinforced the clerical campaign against moral laxity by forbidding public dances without licence from district courts. In the same month, the Criminal Law Amendment Act answered the prayers of Fr. Devane by providing for the imprisonment of common prostitutes, as well as at last prohibiting the sale or importation of contraceptive devices. The second measure further infringed the freedom of Protestants, Jews, or disobedient Catholics to regulate their fertility: even in the two Irish states, as the records of the Marie Stopes foundation indicate, there was extensive demand for contraception among the urban middle classes.[41] The Dáil overrode the Seanad's attempts to penalize men importuning for immoral purposes, and to delete the ban on contraceptives.

De Valera's moral apotheosis coincided with the application in 1937 of his new constitution, much of which had been drafted by Jesuits and other clerical advisers. Though not specifically Catholic, its preamble invoked 'the Name of the Most Holy Trinity, from Whom is all authority and to Whom, as our final end, all actions both of men and States must be referred'. In a provision falling just short of church establishment, not removed by referendum until 1972, the constitution declared that 'the State recognises the special position of the Holy Catholic Apostolic and Roman Church as the guardian of the Faith professed by the great majority of its citizens' (art. 44.1.2°). Non-Catholics were faintly reassured by the parallel recognition of all 'religious denominations existing in Ireland', including 'the Jewish congregations' and by implication other non-Christian bodies. Though irritating to the proponents of Catholic Action, this ecumenical utterance had little practical force, since the recognition so accorded was presumably proportionate to the size of each minority. The new constitution retained the existing provision that 'freedom of conscience and the free profession and practice of religion are, subject to public order and morality, guaranteed to every citizen'. Yet the 'special position' of the Catholic church was incorporated in articles 41 and 42, concerning the family and education. The position of the family, unlike that of the church, was one of unqualified supremacy: 'The State recognises the Family as the natural primary and fundamental unit group of Society, and as a moral institution possessing inalienable and imprescriptible rights, antecedent and superior to all positive law.' This proposition was developed by several corollaries with notable consequences for individual liberty, including the statement that 'no law shall be enacted providing for the grant of a dissolution of marriage'.

The significance of this embodiment of Catholic doctrine in de Valera's constitution is all the more striking when contrasted with Cosgrave's hesitant and inconclusive handling of the divorce issue in the preceding decade. In early 1923, his government had been confronted with a handful of petitions for divorce from claimants who might hitherto have secured (at vast expense) a private act of parliament permitting their remarriage. Ireland had been exempted from the English act introducing cheaper and easier divorce in 1857, but the Irish Catholic church had never sought abolition of 'parliamentary divorces', which invariably affected wealthy Protestants. Upon the transfer of parliamentary powers from Westminster to Dublin, it was expected that standing orders would be introduced to permit the consideration of such divorce bills in the Oireachtas. Cosgrave took the precaution of seeking advice from Archbishop Byrne of Dublin. An intermediary reported 'that under no circumstances could the Church give any sanction to divorce. That the Church regards Matrimony as a Sacrament only, and claims sole jurisdiction in regard to it. That they could not even sanction divorce for non-catholics for the reason that all persons who had been baptised are members of the Church and under its jurisdiction.' Although 'persons desiring such facilities' might feel impelled to emigrate, the archbishop's view was 'that Ireland would not lose anything by this.'[42] The Irish Free State was indeed to be governed as a Catholic community, in which statutory sanction should never be conferred upon moral deviation.

The attorney-general's subsequent advice nonetheless to devise appropriate standing orders was again referred to Byrne and thence the hierarchy, which obligingly confirmed that 'it would be altogether unworthy of an Irish legislative body to sanction the concession of such divorce, no matter who the petitioners may be'.[43] After a furious outpouring of supportive theology in the Jesuit press, Cosgrave attempted in February 1925 to outlaw the introduction of any standing orders allowing for the introduction of divorce bills. He asserted 'that the whole fabric of our social organisation is based upon the sanctity of the marriage bond and that anything that tends to weaken the binding efficacy of that bond to that extent strikes at the root of our social life'.[44] Obstruction from the Seanad confounded Cosgrave's strategy, whereupon the Dáil rejected a placatory proposal from the Quaker banker, Senator James Douglas, to informally extinguish divorce by requiring that the first reading of each bill be passed in the Dáil. The outcome was a surly stalemate, the introduction of divorce bills being neither outlawed nor rendered practicable. Although Senator W. B. Yeats was disappointed in his excited prediction of a battle to the death between Protestant defenders of personal liberty and their Catholic oppressors, the divorce conflict had illuminated the political role of the Catholic church, its unconcealed desire to impose Catholic moral doctrine upon Irish Protestants, and its limited ability to implement this programme under Cosgrave's administration.

By contrast, De Valera's prohibition of divorce represented an undeniable triumph for Catholic morality over the inherited residue of secular and liberal precepts which Cosgrave had never quite managed to eliminate. Having fulfilled Cosgrave's unrealized dream, the Chief was rewarded appropriately by the Catholic hierarchy and press: 'Irish Catholics will rejoice in the fact that the fundamental provisions of the new Bunreacht [constitution] are in close accord with Catholic social teaching'.[45] Fine Gael could scarcely demur, restricting its criticism to de Valera's refusal to give constitutional force in civil law to the definitions of validity and nullity of marriages in Catholic canon law. John Aloysius Costello recalled that, when attorney-general, he had been advised to prosecute a case of bigamy in which an Irish Catholic girl exchanged vows with a non-Catholic 'Scotchman' in a registry office. After non-consummation followed by separation, which in Catholic but not civil law rendered the union void, she had been properly married in an Irish Catholic church. 'I need hardly say that I did not prosecute', chortled Costello.[46] The anomaly between the civil and canon law concerning nullity remained as a rare testament to Irish secularism. The outlawing of divorce was narrowly rescinded by referendum in 1995, having been emphatically upheld after a spirited clerical and lay campaign nine years earlier.

The manner in which divorce was prohibited reflected the general acceptance by the major political parties that the law of the southern state should incorporate Catholic morality even if this curtailed the liberty of religious minorities. Though civil marriage was a mere contract, whereas Catholic matrimony was a sacrament, all agreed that the availability of civil dissolution would imperil the always shaky adherence of Irish Catholics to their sacred duty. In abstract, the same applied to Northern Ireland, whose Protestants were likewise deemed to be schismatics who were nevertheless subject to papal authority and canon law. Yet, when Northern Ireland replicated British legislation extending the availability of civil divorce in 1939, the hierarchy made no concerted protest. The attorney-general declared that 'this measure is not a burden on the Roman Catholic community. If they care to stand apart well and good, but the majority of the community in Northern Ireland do not take that view.' After perfunctory protests from two nationalist members, the bill passed rapidly into law.[47] Far from being hypocritical, the hierarchy's acceptance of civil divorce in only one of the two states reflected a pragmatic admission of its relative capacity to mobilize the civil power in a moral crusade. In southern Ireland, perhaps more forcefully than in any contemporary society, the church succeeded in acting as the state's moral arbiter.

The secular influence of Catholic teaching was also increasingly evident in restrictions upon the civil rights of women. The post-war reaffirmation of the doctrine of 'separate spheres' was not restricted to Catholicism, and provided a powerful counterblast to feminism in Britain and Northern Ireland as well as in the Free State. Only there, however, did the glorification of housekeeping achieve constitutional and legislative embodiment. The basis of state policy was the view of women eloquently uttered in February 1931 by Bishop Morrisroe of Achonry: 'Upon the stouter shoulders devolves the task of winning by toil what is needed for the upkeep of the household, while to the weaker member belongs the duty of applying the resources to needs as they arise. In this way each partner has a separate sphere of activity. . . . The observance of neatness, tidiness, and orderliness in the house, coupled with a careful supervision of things destined for the table, will entitle the housewife to golden opinions, while a sympathetic word to the breadwinner after his day's toil will give the humblest meal a delicious flavour.'[48]

Encouraged by growing male unemployment, Fianna Fáil once in government acted resolutely to give legislative teeth to the bishop's normative aspiration. In 1933, female teachers were for the first time required to resign upon marriage. Under the subsequent Conditions of Employment act (1935), this provision was extended to the entire civil service (apart from subordinate workers such as cleaners), without discretionary exceptions as in Britain. Moreover, by contrast with Britain and Northern Ireland, female former civil servants had no claim for reemployment upon widowhood. According to a women's lobby struggling to secure an interview with de Valera in October 1936, this statute 'was one of the most reactionary pieces of legislation in recent times, and has placed the Irish Free State at the head of an international blacklist, prepared for the League of Nations at Geneva, of countries in which women in employment are penalised and restricted'.[49] The moral government of the Free

State had indeed been transformed since 1919, when the Sex Disqualification (Removal) act had ruled that neither sex nor marriage should disqualify a person from 'exercising any public function or for any civil office or post'. The government's advisers energetically repudiated the obnoxious principle of equal pay for equivalent work, pointing out that male salaries must be sufficient to 'attract and retain during the whole of their useful working lives the services of men who are married or will marry while in the Service'. Women received equal pay in only nine out of thirty-three categories of government work, otherwise averaging three-quarters of the amounts received by their male counterparts.[50] Likewise, the practice of excluding women from postal delivery (involving 'heavy loads'), veterinary inspection (for 'obvious reasons'), or forestry ('unsuitable for women'), was justified by enumerating female preserves such as typing ('particularly suitable for women', being work 'of a routine character' requiring 'dexterity').[51] Despite official unease at the egalitarian conventions emanating from the League of Nations, de Valera's government methodically translated the 'separate spheres' of men and women into law.

That process culminated in the state's constitutional undertaking from 1937 'to ensure that mothers shall not be obliged by economic necessity to engage in labour to the neglect of their duties in the home' (art. 41.2.2°). Though carrying the promise of family allowances, this provision also justified the exclusion of 'mothers' (though not childless wives) from the paid workforce. The constitutional embodiment of the family delighted Catholic theorists such as Alfred O'Rahilly, a Cork mathematician later to enter holy orders, but provoked numerous objections from women's organizations and from feminists. Even Dorothy Macardle, de Valera's favourite historian of *The Irish Republic* (London, 1937), protested that such clauses suggested 'that the State may interfere to a great extent in determining what opportunities shall be open or closed to women'. She did 'not see how anyone holding advanced views on the rights of women can support it, and that is a tragic dilemma for those who have been loyal and ardent workers in the national cause'.[52] As so often in Irish political history, the dilemma was resolved by reasserting the primacy of national over social issues. No powerful campaign was directed against the social clauses of the constitution, which secured a substantial majority of popular support by referendum.

In Northern Ireland, special treatment of women, whether in citizenship or employment, was conducted informally rather than through overt regulation. Whereas in the Free State women had been released from compulsory jury service in 1924, a similar proposal for Northern Ireland in 1925 was rejected after protest from Londonderry, who pronounced with his customary condescension that women 'should be educated up to their duties'.[53] When confronted in the same year by a motley array of women's organizations, ranging from the Girls' Friendly Society and the Belfast Women's Temperance Association to the Textile Operatives of Ireland, Craig was advised to dodge the issue of 'Equality of opportunity in the Civil Service, the Professions and in Industry'. Dawson Bates informed him that 'this is one of these vague generalities on which it is difficult to say anything definite. . . . I think our first duty is to the exservicemen and until their claims are satisfied it would not be fair to give women the same opportunities for employment as men'.[54] The principle was reaffirmed in 1926 by Spender's critique of a report on the northern civil service: 'There are certain recommendations which, though quite sound on strict business lines, the Government would be unwilling to enforce. For instance, the replacement of Ex-Service Clerks by cheaper female Writing Assistants.'[55] By making war service rather than sex the criterion for discrimination, overt collision with feminist principles was avoided. Such a collision would have alarmed the provincial journalist who snorted in 1931 that 'I got my first view of a Bowler hat on a female head in Bangor this week. Frankly, speaking editorially, we were not impressed. That hat was set firmly on the back of the lady's head and gave her an air of unswerving determination. It did not require a vivid imagination to picture her directing operations in her home with the bowler, set at a suitable angle, as a symbol of authority'.[56] In Northern

Ireland as in the south, men patronized women, and women's groups protested. Only in the southern state, however, was there a systematic attempt to incorporate the homeliness of women in the law of the land.

Conclusions

Through partition, Ireland's dual revolution had secured local power for the two dominant populist movements which had resisted British authority between 1912 and 1921. In Northern Ireland, this resulted in an unpredictably stable government dominated by the Orange Institution and its associates. In the Free State, the fracturing of republicanism made possible the alternation of power between the victors and losers in the civil war. Fianna Fáil, in particular, replicated the populist organization and appeal of revolutionary Sinn Féin, while rapidly adapting itself to the novel opportunities for selective dispensation of material benefits. The survival in both states of majoritarian democracy, despite recurrent armed challenges, demonstrated the enduring appeal of a system allowing ordinary nationalists or loyalists a voice in politics. The revolution had taught even the humblest Sinn Féiners and Orangemen that their political destiny was within their own grasp, so long as individual preference was subordinated to the collective interest. The populist outlook, fostered by revolutionary struggle, had profound negative effects for the forms of post-revolutionary democracy.

The triumph of populism had grim consequences for those excluded from the dominant community in each state. Catholics and nationalists had no effective voice at Stormont and very little influence even in local government. Though tolerated as citizens so long as they accepted decisions in which they played no part, Catholics had not been effectively integrated into the political process. In the southern state, the rise of Fianna Fáil had undermined the initial monopoly of political power by the supporters of the treaty. Initially no less alienated from the state than were Catholics in Northern Ireland, most republicans had progressively reconciled themselves to living and politicking in the Free State. By the late 1930s, Fianna Fáil's control over the organs of government was as comprehensive as that of Cumann na nGaedheal before 1932; yet few doubted that Fianna Fáil would peacefully cede power should it fail in a future general election. That confidence was to be vindicated in 1948 with the accession of the first inter-party government. Protestants and former Unionists, though a prime target for murder and outrage until 1923, did not constitute a permanently disaffected minority excluded from political participation. By contrast with northern Catholics, their wealth, skills, and connections proved essential to the state's welfare and protected them from systematic persecution. Nevertheless, both the rhetoric and ethos of the major southern parties were relentlessly Roman Catholic, matching the unapologetic Protestantism of those ruling Northern Ireland.

In both states, the consolidation of majority rule was secured through extensive coercion, abuse of the rights of minorities, and widespread infringement of religious, moral, and personal liberty. Northern discrimination against Catholics was no doubt endemic in private employment and the professions, where the fraternal networks of Orangeism and freemasonry provided initiated Protestants with preferential access to jobs and commissions. Protestant fraternalism also affected the allocation of civil appointments, official contracts, and welfare services, although the overt discrimination in favour of ex-servicemen obscured the independent force of sectarianism as a factor. When confronted in October 1932 by accusations in the Catholic *Tablet*, Craigavon composed a spirited defence of his government's impartiality towards Catholics. The abolition of proportional representation had benefited nationalists (typically 'poorer' than loyalists) by reducing the number of electoral contests and therefore the expense of political participation. In education, 'the treatment of the Roman Catholic community is infinitely more generous' than in Britain, matching capital grants being paid even to schools not transferred to the department of education. As for the RUC, Catholics had 'refused' to take up their assigned third of the force, so necessitating the recruitment of an extra 1,000

Protestants. Craigavon further asserted that 'the strictest impartiality is observed in all schemes for alleviating distress, unemployment insurance, old age and widows' and orphans' pensions, the building of workmen's dwellings, grants towards education or in any other field of social service'.[57] In short, any inequities resulted not from Protestant discrimination, but from Catholic alienation and voluntary abstention. Though perhaps tongue in cheek, Craigavon's apologia had an authentic element. The degree to which equity would have been observed, in the case of full Catholic participation in the state, was never put to the test.

The relative importance of official discrimination as against Catholic recalcitrance remains a prickly issue, not least for historians of Northern Ireland. Yet this debate neglects the force of social polarities long antedating partition, and also exaggerates the power of governments to transform societies. Pre-war Belfast and other Ulster towns were already sharply segregated between Catholics and Protestants, in terms of both residence and occupational status.[58] Northern Protestants under the Union were already practised in the sectarian arts of eviction, expulsion, exclusion from employment, fiddling electoral boundaries, and asserting communal dominance. Northern Catholics had developed parallel organizations and techniques for mutual protection and on occasion for sectarian aggression. Rival churches and fraternities had provided the foundation of autonomous and potentially antagonistic communities, in which 'mixed marriages' were rare and dangerous (though more common than either the Catholic hierarchy or the Orange Institution desired).[59] Under provocation, both Protestants and Catholics all too easily reverted to stereotyped assertions of each other's savagery and inferiority. For Sir Robert Lynn of the *Northern Whig* in November 1921, there were 'two peoples in Ireland, one industrious, law-abiding and God-fearing, and the other slothful, murderous and disloyal'.[60] Six months later, Bishop MacRory of Down and Connor was no more placatory when urging Pius XI to peruse an Orange songbook. This would 'give His Holiness an idea of the Orange spirit, . . . some idea, though faint, of the spirit of these savages'.[61] No government, even if well intentioned, lavishly funded, and armed with full powers, could easily have emptied those dank wells of mutual loathing and bitterness.

In the Irish Free State, sectarian animosity was more muted and far less forceful than in Northern Ireland. Southern Protestants were too useful to be tampered with, whatever government was in power. Furious clerical and republican denunciations of freemasonry and Protestant plutocracy failed to subvert the pre-eminence of Protestants in many sectors of business, banking, and the professions. Catholic fraternities such as the Knights of St Columbanus were slow to reproduce the social benefits of freemasonry for the Catholic bourgeoisie. Even before the foundation of the Free State, Protestant alarm at murders, land seizures, and other sectarian attacks had secured guarantees of minority rights from the provisional government (in May and September 1922). Cosgrave's nominees for the first Seanad included the masonic grand master, the 6th earl of Donoughmore, who courteously declined the offer since he was already chairman of committees in the House of Lords.[62] In the allocation of services such as education, all southern governments discriminated in favour of Protestants, subsidizing a plethora of undersized schools and permitting the use of alternative textbooks for controversial subjects. The resolutely 'Protestant bastion' of Trinity College was left undisturbed in its valuable central site. Although a land act of 1923 provided for the compulsory sale of the remaining tenanted estates to their occupiers, this measure relieved rather than alarmed the remaining landlords who might otherwise have lost their property without compensation. Faced with a small but wealthy and potentially useful Protestant minority, the state left its economic interests largely untouched. Occasional gestures of positive discrimination not only reassured Protestants of their security, but also disarmed insinuations of official sectarianism. In marked contrast with Northern Ireland, the rulers of the Free State provided some defence of the material security and interests of the religious minority against popular sectarianism.

In its moral jurisdiction, however, the southern state proved all too ready to give statutory or constitutional force to the precepts of the predominant church. Whereas Cosgrave had deferred to bishops while observing the forms of secularism, de Valera overcame the church's initial distrust by applying Catholic social doctrine to a widening range of social and economic regulation. Mainly because the various Protestant churches had no such coherent body of doctrine, de Valera's experiment had no significant counterpart in Northern Ireland. The severity of material discrimination against northern Catholics must therefore be balanced against the moral constraints officially imposed on southern Protestants (not to mention lapsing Catholics). Each state, after its own fashion, curtailed the liberty of religious minorities lacking access to effective political power.

The restriction of personal liberty through suspension of habeas corpus, the restriction of public assemblies, and other coercive measures, was common to both states. If the bloodiest and most ferocious coercion was accomplished under Mulcahy's supervision during the southern civil war, the most systematic and long-lasting apparatus of social control and repression was provided by the northern Special Powers legislation and the Special Constabulary. Craig's governments, unlike their southern counterparts, relied heavily upon popular mobilization of part-time vigilantes rather than the formal apparatus of full-time soldiers and police. In each state, however, coercion was conducted along lines developed by successive governments under the Union. The most significant contrast applied to the selection of targets rather than the techniques of repression. Whereas dissident nationalists were consistently targeted in Northern Ireland, the focus of repression in the Free State shifted from the Irregulars to the Blueshirts and then to the residue of the IRA. In both states, as in most countries in inter-war Europe, the assertion of authority typically outweighed respect for personal liberty. In this respect, the triumphant revolutionaries proved attentive pupils of their former adversaries.

The persistency of the demand for coercion reflected the

unextinguished strain of dissidence among alienated northern nationalists and intransigent republicans alike. Neither state proved fully capable of crushing armed dissent, although militant nationalism had been largely driven underground in Northern Ireland by the 1930s. The Free State, despite its ruthless legislation, failed to eliminate or disarm the IRA, and could not prevent the eruption of the 'border campaign' in 1938 or bombings in wartime Britain. This contrast in punitive efficiency masked a deeper cleavage in achievement. In Northern Ireland, coercion silenced but reinforced Catholic alienation, leaving no obvious path for reconciliation between communities. In the south, the state's inability to defeat private armies was balanced by its cumulative success in winning acceptance as a legitimate source of authority. Yet in both states the assertion of authority, formidable though it seemed by 1939, was partial and fragile. Six decades later, it seems depressingly clear that the terrorist's gun cannot be silenced either by *force majeure* or by adverse public opinion, however passionately felt and eloquently expressed. One armalite can still outvote a thousand ballot boxes.

The economic consequences of revolution and partition were no more satisfactory than its political outcomes. Nationalist republicans soon discovered that rural poverty and industrial sluggishness could not be eliminated merely through the accomplishment of 'native' rule. Memories of the wartime boom only sharpened the sense of frustration as successive governments half-heartedly applied Griffith's doctrine of protectionism to a stolidly backward economy. In Northern Ireland, the decline of the staple industries eroded the loyalists' conviction that their defence of the Union would also preserve the province's prosperity. Both ruling classes had pinned their economic hopes on securing political control, and remained predictably resistant to radical programmes after assuming power. In both states, the political appeal of socialist and corporativist alternatives was inhibited by the persistent popular absorption with the national issue. The collapse of Ulster loyalism into class-based factions was discouraged by the unrequited fear of nationalist subversion or imposed unification. Likewise, the animosities engendered in the civil war outweighed divisions of class and social ideology in determining southern alignments. The social and economic conservatism of both revolutionary movements was replicated in their practice of government.

Ireland's revolutionary legacy has been preserved, above all, by the widespread sense among nationalists that the revolution was incomplete. So long as partition endured, their expectation that Northern Ireland would eventually submit to Dublin's jurisdiction continued to foster loyalist fears and militant republican ambitions. Whereas most remaining southern loyalists were reconciled to Ireland's departure from the Union, if not entirely from the empire, northern nationalists did not generally accept the *fait accompli* of partition. That judgement continues to destabilize all attempts at governing Northern Ireland, and to fuel the lingering half-hope, voiced in moments of crisis by southern politicians of every party, that Ireland's revolution has yet to enter its final phase. Partition, designed to buy off both revolutionary parties with the prize of local territorial domination, almost worked. Its insidious and ultimately fatal flaw was the creation in Northern Ireland of a minority more disaffected than any Irish faction under the Union. And yet, after three-quarters of a century of struggle and reappraisal, no form of settlement demonstrably superior to partition has so far been propounded. The two Irelands, for all their cosmopolitan millennial glitter, have yet to escape the shadow of their revolutions.

Notes

Chapter 1 (pp. 9–23)

1. Lists of those expelled, initially giving details of offences, were published in each half-yearly *Report of the Proceedings of the Grand Orange Lodge of Ireland*. Annual returns of the number and often membership of lodges appeared in the printed reports of county Grand Lodges, many of which were consulted in the library at the House of Orange, Belfast.

2. After his eventual expulsion even from the Independent Orange Order, and emigration to Canada, Crawford was to reappear after 1922 at no. 1, Broadway, as the Irish Free State's first trade representative in the United States.

3. This analysis refers to 770 initiates into three divisions in the city of Cork, whose registers are preserved in the Cork Archives Institute, U389/7/1–3.

4. County statistics for the membership of national organizations are analysed in David Fitzpatrick, 'The Geography of Irish Nationalism, 1910–1921', in *Past and Present*, 78 (1978), 113–44.

5. T. W. Moody and Leon Ó Broin, 'The IRB Supreme Council, 1868–78', in *Irish Historical Studies*, 19, no. 75 (1975), 314.

6. Bulmer Hobson, *Ireland Yesterday and Tomorrow* (Tralee, 1968), 36. Police returns for the end of 1892 enumerated about 32,900 members, one-third of whom were 'in good standing'. Nine years later, two-fifths of the nominal strength of 20,300 had reportedly attended meetings and paid their subscriptions. See NA, S 26268 (Crime Special Branch, RIC).

7. Arthur Griffith (ed.), *Leabhar na hÉireann* (Dublin, 1908 edn.), 296.

8. Brian P. Murphy, *Patrick Pearse and the Lost Republican Ideal* (Dublin, 1991), 96.

9. Brian Ó Cuív, 'The Gaelic Cultural Movements and the New Nationalism', in Kevin B. Nowlan (ed.), *The Making of 1916: Studies in the History of the Rising* (Dublin, 1969), 12; Marcus de Búrca, *The GAA: A History* (Dublin, 1980), 94.

10. David Fitzpatrick, *Politics and Irish Life, 1913–1921: Provincial Experience of War and Revolution* (Dublin, 1977), 303.

11. David Fitzpatrick, 'The Disappearance of the Irish Agricultural Labourer, 1841–1912', *Irish Economic and Social History*, 7 (1980), 87, 89.

12. *Irish News* (Belfast), 5 Aug. 1907, quoted by Henry Patterson, *Class Conflict and Sectarianism: The Protestant Working Class and the Belfast Labour Movement, 1868–1920* (Belfast, 1980), 71.

Chapter 2 (pp. 24–43)

1. Facsimile in Patrick Buckland (ed.), *Irish Unionism, 1885–1923: A Documentary History* (Belfast, 1973), 224. Not all signatories were Protestants: according to the RIC, the covenant was signed by Catholics in every district of Antrim: Inspector General's Monthly Confidential Report, Oct. 1912, in PRO, CO 904/88.

2. T. M. Kettle, *The Open Secret of Ireland* (London, 1912), 64.

3. F. S. L. Lyons, *John Dillon* (London, 1968), 427.

4. Pádraic H. Pearse, 'Ghosts' (Christmas, 1915), in *Political Writings and Speeches* (Dublin, undated), 229.

5. Mabel FitzGerald to Shaw, 28 Nov. 1914 (concerning Garret's eldest brother), in Fergus FitzGerald (ed.), *Memoirs of Desmond FitzGerald, 1913–1916* (London, 1968), 184.

6. Eamon de Valera, *Ireland's Request* (Melbourne edn., 1921), 4.

7. Arthur Griffith, *The Resurrection of Hungary: A Parallel for Ireland* (Dublin, 2nd edn. 1904).

8. Typed transcript of speech, 26 Oct. 1917, in NLI, MS 21523, fo. 51.

9. Michael Collins, *The Path to Freedom* (Cork, 1968; 1st edn. 1922), 33. This formulation, though first published in February 1922, was Collins's paraphrase of his contribution to the Dáil's debate on approval of the treaty.

10. Dáil Éireann, *Minutes of Proceedings, 1919–1921* (Dublin, undated), 22.

11. James Connolly, *Labour in Irish History* (Dublin, 1971; 1st edn. 1910), esp. 2–3; Alasdair Mac Cába (ed.), *Leabhar na hÉireann* (Dublin, 1921 edn.), 39–40.

12. 'The Qualifications of an Orangeman' are reproduced annually in the *Diary* of the Loyal Orange Institution. Converts could be admitted only by resolution of the Grand Lodge of Ireland.

13. S. Rosenbaum (ed.), *Against Home Rule: The Case for the Union* (London, 1912), 13.

14. Memorandum of conversation, 13 Mar. 1915, originally enclosed in Graves to John Redmond, 2 Oct. 1915, in NLI, MSS 15261/2, 15261/8.

15. Hugh A. Law, *Why is Ireland at War?* (Dublin, 1916), 28–9.

16. De Valera, *Ireland's Request*, 60, 13.

17. Edith Wheeler to Bates and reply, 13 Sept. 1912, in PRONI, D 1098/2/3; facsimile of 'Women's Declaration' in Ulster Day Committee, *Ulster Day, 1912* (Belfast, 1912).

18. Minute book of executive committee, UWUC, 25 Jan. 1921, in PRONI, D 1098/1/2.

19. *County Down Spectator* (Bangor), 5 Feb. 1921.

20. Handwritten memorandum by Spender, in PRONI, D 1295/2/1A.

21. The county inspector's return for 31 July 1921 listed 4,297 men and 401 women (belonging to only 18 of the 60 Sinn Féin clubs): PRO, CO 904/116.

22. Margaret Ward, *Unmanageable Revolutionaries: Women and Irish Nationalism* (London, 1983), 93.

23. Beth McKillen, 'Irish Feminism and Nationalist Separatism, 1914–23', in *Éire-Ireland*, 17, no. 3 (1982), 57; 17, no. 4 (1982), 76; *The Times*, 7 and 10 June 1918.

24. P. T. Daly to Arthur Henderson, 10 Mar. 1917, in David Fitzpatrick, *Politics and Irish Life, 1913–1921: Provincial Experience of War and Revolution* (Dublin, 1977), 251.

25. Ibid. 246.

26. Thomas Johnson, *The Future of Labour in Ireland* (Dublin, 1916), 3.

27. *Irish Opinion* (new series), 1, no. 13 (23 Feb. 1918), 146.

28. Dáil Éireann, *Minutes*, 22–3, 78.

Chapter 3 (pp. 44–114)

1. A. T. Q. Stewart, *The Ulster Crisis* (London, 1979 edn.), 135.

2. County returns for the UVF in 1914, and also for the Irish and National Volunteers, appear in Breandán Mac Giolla Choille (ed.), *Intelligence Notes, 1913–16* (Dublin, 1966), 100, 109–12.

3. F. X. Martin (ed.), *The Irish Volunteers, 1913–1915* (Dublin, 1963), 57–61, 65.

4. David Fitzpatrick, *Politics and Irish Life, 1913–1921: Provincial Experience of War and Revolution* (Dublin, 1977), 106.

5. *County Down Spectator*, 17 July 1914.

6. Memorandum by the military members of the army council, 4 July 1914, in PRO, CAB 37/120, no. 81.

7. Leon Ó Broin, *The Chief Secretary: Augustine Birrell in Ireland* (London, 1969), 10; Augustine Birrell, *Things Past Redress* (London, 1937), 217.

8. *Parliamentary Debates* (5th series), lxvi, col. 911.

9. Parsons to war office, 29 Nov. 1914, in Parsons Papers, NLI, MS 21278.

10. Undated, handwritten return in Redmond Papers, NLI, MS 15259.

11. *Parliamentary Debates* (5th series), lxvi, col. 908.

12. This total included 21,000 pre-war regulars, perhaps 2,000 regular officers, 5,000 naval ratings, 18,000 reservists, and 12,500 members of the special reserve (mobilized in August 1914). Wartime enlistment included 134,000 army recruits, about 4,000 temporary commissions, and 10,500 recruits to the naval and air services. The returns by religion cover some 140,000 servicemen, of whom 58 per cent were Catholics. For sources and caveats, see David Fitzpatrick, 'The Logic of Collective Sacrifice: Ireland and the British Army, 1914–1918', *Historical Journal*, 38, no. 4 (1995), 1017–18.

13. 5 & 6 Geo. V, c. 8, s. 1 (1c); 5 & 6 Geo. V, c. 34, ss. 1 (1), 1 (7); regulations in NA, registered papers of chief secretary's office, 1920/25934.

14. Maj.-Gen. Friend to Kitchener, 16 Nov. 1914, in PRO, PRO 30/57/60, WK 12.

15. Fergus FitzGerald (ed.), *Memoirs of Desmond FitzGerald, 1913–1916* (London, 1968), 47.

16. Pádraic H. Pearse, *Political Writings and Speeches* (Dublin, undated), 216–17.

17. 'Notes on the Front', in *Workers' Republic*, 1, no. 27 (27 Nov. 1915).

18. Birrell, *Things Past Redress*, 212.

19. Arthur Mitchell and Pádraig Ó Snodaigh (eds.), *Irish Political Documents, 1916–1949* (Dublin, 1985), 17.

20. G. A. Hayes-McCoy, 'A Military History of the 1916 Rising', in Kevin B. Nowlan (ed.), *The Making of 1916: Studies in the History of the Rising* (Dublin, 1969), 299.

21. Diary of Miss Olive Armstrong, MA, 26 Apr. and 2 May 1916, in University of Leeds, Brotherton Library (Peter H. Liddle Collection).

22. David Fitzpatrick, 'Militarism in Ireland, 1900–1922', in Thomas Bartlett and Keith Jeffery (eds.), *A Military History of Ireland* (Cambridge, 1996), 392.

23. *Ireland* (New York), 6 May 1916.

24. Leon Ó Broin, *Revolutionary Underground* (Dublin, 1976), 178.

25. Fitzpatrick, *Politics and Irish Life*, 213.

26. Typed transcript of proceedings, 18 Oct. 1917, in NLI, MS 21523, fos. 50–1.

27. Mitchell and Ó Snodaigh, *Irish Political Documents*, 35.

28. NLI, MS 21523, fo. 10.

29. Ibid., fos. 5, 14.

30. Michael Laffan, 'The Unification of Sinn Féin in 1917', *Irish Historical Studies*, 17, no. 67 (1971), 368.

31. Mitchell and Ó Snodaigh, *Irish Political Documents*, 42–3.

32. Walter McDonald, *Some Ethical Questions of Peace and War, with Special Reference to Ireland* (London, 1919).

33. 'Ruthless Warfare', unattributed article in *An tÓglach*, 1, no. 4 (14 Oct. 1918); Piaras Béaslaí, *Michael Collins and the Making of a New Ireland* (Dublin, 1926), i. 211–12. The article was inserted at the request of Collins.

34. J. Anthony Gaughan, *Thomas Johnson, 1872–1963* (Dublin, 1980), 431–5.

35. Memorial to war cabinet, 8 Oct. 1918, in Imperial War Museum, French Papers, 75/46/12.

36. 8 & 9 Geo. V, c. 59. After its initial suspension by statute (4 & 5 Geo. V, c. 88), the Government of Ireland act was further suspended by a series of orders in council at six-monthly intervals: *Dublin Gazette* (1919), 1272–3.

37. W. A. Phillips, *The Revolution in Ireland, 1906–1923* (London, 2nd edn. 1926), 151.

38. 'A Soldier's View on Present Day Politics' (unsigned carbon copy), in PRONI, D 1295/6/20.

39. Inspector-general's monthly confidential report, July 1919, in PRO, CO 904/109.

40. Incomplete sets of printed annual reports for both orders in Belfast, stating the membership of each private lodge or preceptory, are held at the House of Orange, Belfast. Statistics for the Grand Black Chapter refer to the years 1917–18 and 1919–20.

41. William Corkey, *Gladly Did I Live* (Belfast, 1963 edn.), 196–243.

42. D. G. Boyce, *Englishmen and Irish Troubles* (London, 1972), 65–6,

83; David Fitzpatrick, 'A Curious Middle Place: The Irish in Britain, 1870–1921', in Roger Swift and Sheridan Gilley (eds.), *The Irish in Britain, 1815–1939* (London, 1989), 44.

43. Eamon de Valera, *Ireland's Request* (Melbourne edn., 1921), 4.

44. Robert Briscoe, *For the Life of Me* (Boston, 1958), 158.

45. Séamus Mac Ciarnáin (ed.), *The Last Post: The Details and Stories of Republican Dead, 1913–1975* (Dublin, 1976 edn.); cabinet sources cited in Fitzpatrick, *Politics and Irish Life*, 296 (n. 14). A republican tally enumerated 1,376 deaths between 1919 and 11 July 1921, involving 752 Volunteers and civilians and 624 members of the crown forces: Ministry of Defence Archive, A/0396: microfilm in NLI, P 915. The registrar-general's incomplete enumeration of 'homicides' (published in his official *Annual Reports*) rose from 32 in 1918 to 67 in 1919, 423 in 1920, and 1,199 in 1921. The annual rate per 100,000 of population (1919–21) ranged from 4 in Antrim to 77 in Clare, 90 in Tipperary, and 100 in Cork.

46. Fitzpatrick in Bartlett and Jeffery, *Military History*, 399.

47. Tom Barry, *Guerilla Days in Ireland* (Tralee, 1962 edn.), 8.

48. Richard Mulcahy, 'Chief of Staff, 1919', *Capuchin Annual*, 36 (1969), 351–2.

49. Correspondence in PRO, HO 351/63. This recently released file significantly amplifies Charles Townshend's account in *The British Campaign in Ireland, 1919–1921* (Oxford, 1975), 110.

50. Mark Sturgis, typed diary, in PRO, PRO 30/59/1, fo. 30.

51. Divisional Commissioner Smyth's orders to RIC in Listowel, Co. Kerry, 17 June 1920, in *Parliamentary Debates* (5th series), cxxxii, col. 1609; Prescott Decie's report to assistant under-secretary, 1 June 1920, in NA, Crime Special Branch Papers, carton 23.

52. Fitzpatrick, *Politics and Irish Life*, 20.

53. Maryann Gialanella Valiulis, *Portrait of a Revolutionary: General Richard Mulcahy and the Foundation of the Irish Free State* (Dublin, 1992), 257; Mulcahy Papers, in UCD Archives, P7/A/28.

54. Diary entry for 14 Dec. 1920 in Strickland Papers, Imperial War Museum, P 363.

55. Collins to de Valera, 27 June 1921, typed copy in NA, DE 2/296.

56. Austen Morgan, *Labour and Partition: The Belfast Working Class, 1905–23* (London, 1991), 269–71; Declan Hayes, 'Belfast Trade Unionism, from 1907 to 1922' (Ph.D. thesis, TCD, 1984), 188.

57. Dáil Éireann, *Minutes of Proceedings, 1919–1921* (Dublin, undated), 191–4; D. S. Johnson, 'The Belfast Boycott, 1920–1922',

in J. M. Goldstrom and L. A. Clarkson (eds.), *Irish Population, Economy, and Society* (Oxford, 1981), 294.

58. Townshend, *British Campaign*, 124.
59. Diary of Lady Spender, 1 June 1921, in PRONI, D 1633/2/24, fo. 91.
60. Bro. James Smyth at annual installation, Temple of Loyalty, LOL 481, in *County Down Spectator*, 22 Jan. 1921.
61. Message from Craig, 16 Apr. 1920, in Loyal Orange Institution of England, *Report of the Annual Meeting* (Birmingham, 1920), 13.
62. Bryan A. Follis, *A State under Siege: The Establishment of Northern Ireland, 1920–1925* (Oxford, 1995), 66–70.
63. Report by Lt.-Col. Charles Wickham, 12 Oct. 1921, in PRONI, CAB 9G/40. Wickham also commanded the Special Constabulary, and subsequently the RUC.
64. Undated typed return by divisions in Mulcahy Papers, UCD Archives, P7/A/32.
65. Maj.-Gen. Peter Strickland (OC, 6th division) to GHQ, 22 Aug. 1922, in Strickland Papers, Imperial War Museum, P 363.
66. Dáil, *Minutes*, 278.
67. For the text of the treaty and associated documents, see T. P. O'Neill (ed.), *Private Sessions of the Second Dáil* (Dublin, 1972), 285–324.
68. Dáil Éireann, *Official Report: Debate on the Treaty* (Dublin, undated), 330.
69. Ibid. 185; O'Neill, *Private Sessions*, 125.
70. Dáil Éireann, *Treaty Report*, 59, 221.
71. W. B. Yeats, 'Sixteen Dead Men' (Dec. 1917).
72. O'Neill, *Private Sessions*, 215–17.
73. Ibid. 317–24.
74. Ibid. 241–2; Maurice Moynihan (ed.), *Speeches and Statements by Eamon de Valera, 1917–73* (Dublin, 1980), 94.
75. Dáil Éireann, *Treaty Report*, 43; O'Neill, *Private Sessions*, 225–6.
76. O'Neill, *Private Sessions*, 216.
77. Cabinet conclusions in PRONI, CAB 4/35.
78. 12 & 13 Geo. V, c. 4, s. 2.

Chapter 4 (pp. 117–136)

1. James Woods (OC, 3rd Northern division) to Richard Mulcahy, 27 July 1922, in Eamon Phoenix, *Northern Nationalism: Nationalist Politics, Partition and the Catholic Minority in Northern Ireland, 1890–1940* (Belfast, 1994), 141.

2. 'Murders and Attempted Murders Committed in Northern Ireland', November 1921 to May 1923, in PRO, HO 348/53. These figures include 'non-political' crimes, which were not systematically distinguished but accounted for all four killings after October 1922. The various *Annual Reports* of registrars-general recorded 418 deaths attributable to homicide in 1922 (in the six counties), compared with 147 in 1921, 114 in 1920, and 8 in 1919. There were 13 homicides in 1923, only 6 in 1924, and a minor peak of 18 in 1935.

3. Typed returns relating to disturbances of public order, 1922–4, in PRONI, HA 5/316. The number of outrages reported in 1922 was 4,822, compared with the all-Ireland totals (perhaps using different criteria) of 4,471 from October 1920 to early July 1921, and 4,516 from January 1919 to September 1920: Charles Townshend, *The British Campaign in Ireland, 1919–1921* (Oxford, 1975), 214.

4. Collins to Louis J. Walsh (Draperstown), 1 Feb. 1922, in NA, Cabinet Papers, S 9241.

5. T. P. O'Neill (ed.), *Private Sessions of the Second Dáil* (Dublin, 1972), 29; Michael Farrell, *Northern Ireland: The Orange State* (London, 1980 edn.), 43; Dáil Éireann, *Official Report: Debate on the Treaty* (Dublin, undated), 225.

6. Bryan A. Follis, *A State under Siege: The Establishment of Northern Ireland, 1920–1925* (Oxford, 1995), 103–4.

7. Ronan Fanning, *Independent Ireland* (Dublin, 1983), 32.

8. Ulster Association, *Bulletin*, 1, no. 1 (Sept. 1922), 11.

9. Follis, *State under Siege*, 101, 108–9.

10. Eoin Neeson, *Civil War in Ireland, 1922–1923* (Cork, 1969 edn.), 11.

11. Maurice Moynihan (ed.), *Speeches and Statements by Eamon de Valera, 1917–73* (Dublin, 1980), 103.

12. David Fitzpatrick, *Politics and Irish Life, 1913–1921: Provincial Experience of War and Revolution* (Dublin, 1977), ch. 6.

13. O'Higgins, memorandum, *circa* 23–6 June 1922, in NA, Cabinet Papers, S 6695.

14. Wilson to TCD Dining Club, London, in *Irish Times*, 28 Apr. 1922.

15. Notice by Eoin O'Duffy, 2 Oct. 1922, in NA, Cabinet Papers, S 1810.

16. Capt. A. S. O'Muireadhaigh to Maj.-Gen. McGrath, TD, 12 Oct. 1923, in NA, Cabinet Papers, S 3331.

17. NA, Cabinet Papers, S 1322.
18. Paul Canning, *British Policy towards Ireland, 1921–1941* (Oxford, 1985), 46–7.
19. Collins, Report on Army Organization, 5 Aug. 1922, in Cabinet Papers, S 3361.
20. Churchill to Cosgrave, 26 Sept. 1922, in PRO, CO 739/2.
21. Macready, 'Personal Notes in Regard to the Present Position and Future of Troops in Southern Ireland', 4 Nov. 1922, in PRO, CO 739/11.
22. Collins, Report on Army Organization, loc. cit. n. 19 above.
23. De Valera to Joseph McGarrity, 10 Sept. 1922, in Seán Cronin (ed.), *The McGarrity Papers: Revelations of the Irish Republican Movement in Ireland and America, 1900–1940* (Tralee, 1972), 124.
24. O'Higgins, memorandum, loc. cit. n. 13 above.
25. Dáil Éireann, *Debates*, i, cols. 899–900.
26. Niall C. Harrington, *Kerry Landing, August 1922: An Episode of the Civil War* (Dublin, 1992), 148.
27. Executive council decision, 10 Jan. 1923, in NA, Cabinet Minutes, G 2/1 (C. 1/27). On 21 Feb. (C. 1/50) the government repudiated destruction as a form of counter-reprisal.
28. Cutting from *Irish Times*, 9 Dec. 1922, with messages of protest, in NA, Cabinet Papers, S 1884B.
29. Fanning, *Independent Ireland*, 39; Séamus Mac Ciarnáin (ed.), *The Last Post: The Details and Stories of Republican Dead, 1913–1975* (Dublin, 1976 edn.), 93–110. The 404 recorded republican deaths for 1922–3 include the 77 executions, as well as 39 deaths occurring before the civil war or outside the twenty-six counties. Several hundred fatalities were attributable to accidents with firearms rather than homicide. The returns for the twenty-six counties in the *Annual Reports* of the registrar-general enumerated 1,052 homicides in 1921, 470 in 1922, 328 in 1923, 79 in 1924, and only 24 in 1925.
30. Copy of circular from Dublin brigade headquarters to battalion commandants, 21 Aug. 1922, in NA, Cabinet Papers, S 1859.
31. Arthur Mitchell and Pádraig Ó Snodaigh (eds.), *Irish Political Documents, 1916–1949* (Dublin, 1985), 161–3.

Chapter 5 (pp. 137–204)

1. Churchill to Craig, 18 Sept. 1922, in Eamon Phoenix, *Northern Nationalism* (Belfast, 1994), 258. A parallel boycott by most

Catholic secondary schools, uncomplicated by the state payment of salaries, was more long-lasting.

2. NA, Cabinet Papers, S 1587A.

3. MacRory to Cosgrave, 2 Nov. 1922, and reply, 13 Nov., in NA, Cabinet Papers, S 8892.

4. Fisher to Stanley Baldwin, 21 Jan. 1926, in Cambridge University Library, Baldwin Papers, vol. 99, fos. 315–18.

5. Cleaver, the association's president and former director of a family linen business, proclaimed in *Who's Who* that he had 'organized and directed fitting out of Ulster division'.

6. PRONI, Cabinet Papers, CAB 9F/114/1.

7. Col. Wilfrid B. Spender to Capt. J. R. White, 31 Jan. 1923, in NA, Cabinet Papers, S 8042.

8. PRONI, Cabinet Conclusions, 10 Mar. 1924, CAB 4/105.

9. Bates to Craigavon, 2 July 1932, in PRONI, Cabinet Papers, CAB 9B/200.

10. Seán MacEntee to de Valera, 18 July 1935, in NA, Cabinet Papers, S 10549; Dennis Kennedy, *The Widening Gulf: Northern Attitudes to the Independent Irish State, 1919–49* (Dublin, 1988), 171, 199.

11. Ireland act, 1949: 12 & 13 Geo. VI, c. 41, s. 1 (2).

12. In 1932 a grandiose parliament building was opened in the grounds of Stormont Castle, already the site of the cabinet secretariat.

13. Patrick Buckland, *The Factory of Grievances: Devolved Government in Northern Ireland, 1921–39* (Dublin, 1979), 83.

14. Bryan A. Follis, *A State under Siege* (Oxford, 1995), 144. The intricacies of financing Home Rule are lucidly analysed in Nicholas Mansergh, *The Government of Northern Ireland: A Study in Devolution* (London, 1936), and R. J. Lawrence, *The Government of Northern Ireland: Public Finance and Public Services, 1921–1964* (Oxford, 1965).

15. Martin Wallace, *Northern Ireland: 50 Years of Self-Government* (Newton Abbot, 1971), 162.

16. Paul Bew, Peter Gibbon, and Henry Patterson, *Northern Ireland, 1921–1994: Political Forces and Social Classes* (London, 1995 edn.), 62.

17. Andrews to Craigavon, 29 Sept. 1927, and Cabinet Conclusion of 13 July, in PRONI, Cabinet Papers, CAB 9F/51/1.

18. The 'Balfour declaration' of Nov. 1926 asserted equality of 'status' but not 'function', Britain remaining paramount in

diplomacy and defence: David Harkness, *The Restless Dominion: The Irish Free State and the British Commonwealth of Nations, 1921–31* (London, 1969), 97.

19. John Andrew Oliver, *Working at Stormont* (Dublin, 1978), 17, 58.

20. Buckland, *Factory of Grievances*, 19–20.

21. Mansergh, *Government of Northern Ireland*, 263; 10 & 11 Geo. V, c. 67, s. 47 (1). Craigavon nevertheless claimed Henry as his own choice: letter to Lord Rankeillour, 20 Oct. 1932, in PRONI, Cabinet Papers, CAB 9B/205/1.

22. Michael Farrell, *Northern Ireland: The Orange State* (London, 1976), 82–5.

23. Ronan Fanning, *The Irish Department of Finance, 1922–58* (Dublin, 1978), 57; Lawrence W. McBride, *The Greening of Dublin Castle* (Washington, DC, 1991), 307–8.

24. J. J. Lee, *Ireland, 1912–1985* (Cambridge, 1989), 106–9.

25. Sir Nevil Macready, *Annals of an Active Life* (London, [1924]), ii. 551. Only about 400 civil servants were discharged for political activity between 1916 and 1921, of whom less than a quarter (including J. J. McElligott) subsequently secured employment in the Free State's service: McBride, *Dublin Castle*, 218.

26. Memorandum by J. J. Walsh, 13 Feb. 1925, and other files, in NA, Cabinet Papers, S 3406A.

27. Executive council decision, 26 Feb. 1935, in NA, Cabinet Minutes, G 2/11 (C. 7/169).

28. Mary Kotsonouris, *Retreat from Revolution: The Dáil Courts, 1920–24* (Dublin, 1994), 94, 112, 128.

29. Clark to Spender, 14 Sept. 1922, in PRONI, Spender Papers, D 1295/23A.

30. Mary Harris, *The Catholic Church and the Foundation of the Northern Irish State* (Cork, 1993), 112–13.

31. Returns for July 1925 and Dec. 1931, in PRONI, Cabinet Papers, CAB 9G/61A.

32. Farrell, *Northern Ireland*, 96; Buckland, *Factory of Grievances*, 31, 61–2; Phoenix, *Northern Nationalism*, 197–8.

33. *Belfast Weekly News*, 16 Aug. 1923, offprint in PRONI, Cabinet Papers, CAB 9G/45A.

34. Wallace Kennedy to Spender, 25 Nov. 1924, in PRONI, Cabinet Papers, CAB 9G/48A.

35. Cameron Report on C1 Division, 31 July 1923, in PRO, WO 32/5309; Sir Arthur Hezlet, *The 'B' Specials: A History of the Ulster*

Special Constabulary (London, 1972), 99, 108, 114–22; Follis, *State under Siege*, 168–9, 131.

36. PRONI, Cabinet Papers, CAB 9G/48A.

37. A. C. Hepburn, *A Past Apart: Studies in the History of Catholic Belfast, 1850–1950* (Belfast, 1996), ch. 10.

38. Maurice Manning, *The Blueshirts* (Dublin, 1970), 126–9.

39. Executive council statement for press, 19 June 1936, in NA, Cabinet Papers, S 8987.

40. *Garda Review*, 1, no. 7 (June 1926), 460.

41. Executive council decision, 24 June 1925, in NA, Cabinet Minutes, G 2/4 (C. 2/202); *Garda Review*, 1, no. 6 (May 1926), 437. See also Clare O'Halloran, *Partition and the Limits of Irish Nationalism: An Ideology under Stress* (Dublin, 1987), 116.

42. *Garda Review*, 3, no. 8 (July 1928), 764; 4, no. 1 (Dec. 1928), 24. The pope was to be supplied with a Latin translation of the poem, by Revd Professor Patrick Murray of St Patrick's College, Maynooth.

43. Conor Brady, *Guardians of the Peace* (Dublin, 1974), 93–4; Denis J. O'Kelly (ed.), *Salute to the Gardai, 1922–1958* (Dublin, 1959), 7, 22. Among nearly 8,000 recruits between 1922 and 1928, the counties with the highest rates of enlistment (per thousand of population in 1926) were Leitrim (5.0), Longford (4.8), and Clare (4.7). The lowest rates were in Waterford (1.1), Louth (1.0), and Dublin (0.9).

44. Executive council decision, 24 Jan. 1927, in NA, Cabinet Minutes, G 2/5 (C. 2/313).

45. Executive council memorandum, 25 May 1923, and decision, 16 Oct., in NA, Cabinet Minutes, G 2/2 (C. 1/111), G 2/3 (C. 2/12); report on CID, O'Muireadhaigh to McGrath, 12 Oct. 1923, in NA, Cabinet Papers, S 3331.

46. Eunan O'Halpin, 'Army, Politics and Society in Independent Ireland, 1923–1945', in T. G. Fraser and Keith Jeffery (eds.), *Men, Women and War* (Dublin, 1993), 160–6; Brady, *Guardians*, 31–3, 124.

47. Brady, *Guardians*, 137.

48. Executive council decisions, 4 Oct. and 10 Dec. 1923, in NA, Cabinet Minutes, G 2/3 (C. 2/7, C. 2/30).

49. Report by O'Duffy circulated to executive council, 29 June 1932, in NA, Cabinet Papers, S 2206; executive council decisions, 22 Feb. 1933 (dismissing O'Duffy from his post, with an offer of alternative employment or pension, and appointing Broy) and 17 Mar.

1933 (accepting Neligan's resignation from the force), in NA, Cabinet Minutes, G 2/10 (C. 7/4, 7/5, 7/11).

50. Dáil Éireann, *Debates*, vii, col. 3148.

51. Maryann Gialanella Valiulis, *Almost a Rebellion: The Army Mutiny of 1924* (Cork, 1985), esp. 48; memoranda and files in NA, Cabinet Papers, S 3678; executive council decisions, 7–8 Mar. 1924, in NA, Cabinet Minutes, G 2/3 (C. 2/60–1).

52. Report of the Army Inquiry Committee, 5 (7 June 1924), in NA, Cabinet Papers, S 3678C.

53. Seán MacMahon (the former chief of staff) informed the Army Inquiry Committee that 155 officers with previous service in other armies were retained after reorganization, of whom 80 had also served with the Volunteers before the truce. Of the remaining 75, 40 were in the technical services: Valiulis, *Almost a Rebellion*, 94–5.

54. John P. Duggan, *A History of the Irish Army* (Dublin, 1992 edn.), 155–6, 159.

55. Executive council decision, 29 Dec. 1924, in NA, Cabinet Minutes, G 2/4 (C. 2/156). This contradicts the assertion that 'disaffection never spread to the NCOs or enlisted men': Ronan Fanning, *Independent Ireland* (Dublin, 1983), 51.

56. Executive council decisions, 9 May 1929 and 17 Nov. 1930, in NA, Cabinet Minutes, G 2/7 (C. 4/100) and G 2/8 (C. 5/31); cutting from *Daily Mail*, 14 Nov. 1930, in NA, Cabinet Papers, S 6094.

57. Report by Lt.-Gen. Diarmuid O hEigeartaigh, *circa* 1 Apr. 1923, in NA, Cabinet Papers, S 3361.

58. O'Duffy, Army Reorganization Scheme, 2 May 1924, in NA, Cabinet Papers, S 3442B.

59. Return of 'serious crimes' reported to Garda and Dublin Metropolitan Police, in NA, Cabinet Papers, S 3527. A minority of these military suspects were demobilized rather than serving personnel.

60. David Fitzpatrick, 'Unofficial Emissaries: British Army Boxers in the Irish Free State, 1926', *Irish Historical Studies*, 30, no. 118 (1996), 206–32.

61. Typed minutes of subcommittee of Chiefs of Staff, Committee of Imperial Defence, 14 Oct. 1929, in PRO, WO 32/3074; Paul Canning, *British Policy towards Ireland, 1921–1941* (Oxford, 1985), 112–13, 180–1; Duggan, *Irish Army*, 150–1.

62. Typed translation from *An Realt* (The Star), 22 Mar. 1930, in NA, Cabinet Papers, S 6100.

63. Duggan, *Irish Army*, 159–62, 181.

64. Executive council decision, 2 Apr. 1935, in NA, Cabinet Minutes, G 2/11 (C. 7/178).

65. See O'Halpin in Fraser and Jeffery, *Men, Women and War*, 160–1.

66. John F. Harbinson, *The Ulster Unionist Party, 1882–1973* (Belfast, 1973), 118.

67. Frank Gallagher, *The Indivisible Island* (London, 1957), 262, 251–3.

68. Harbinson, *Ulster Unionist Party*, 91. These calculations incorporate Unionist members of both northern houses, and the British House of Commons, between 1921 and 1969. In 1968–9, three ministers left the Institution, while three new backbenchers did not belong to it.

69. Buckland, *Factory of Grievances*, 10–11.

70. Bew et al., *Northern Ireland*, 56.

71. Paul Bew, Kenneth Darwin, and Gordon Gillespie, *Passion and Prejudice: Nationalist–Unionist Conflict in the 1930s and the Origins of the Irish Association* (Belfast, 1993).

72. Buckland, *Factory of Grievances*, 16.

73. Ibid. 52, 63.

74. Ibid. 34.

75. Graham S. Walker, *The Politicis of Frustration: Harry Midgley and the Failure of Labour in Northern Ireland* (Manchester, 1985).

76. Capt. MacNaghten to provisional government, 7 Aug. 1922, in Harris, *Catholic Church*, 136; cf. 110–11.

77. Tallents to Anderson, 22 May 1923, in Phoenix, *Northern Nationalism*, 285.

78. Harris, *Catholic Church*, 173.

79. Phoenix, *Northern Nationalism*, 358–60; Harris, *Catholic Church*, 176–80.

80. Article by Revd T. McCotter, quoted in Harris, *Catholic Church*, 182.

81. 'Political Prospects of a National Party', in *United Irishman*, 8 Mar. 1923.

82. Basil Chubb, *The Government and Politics of Ireland* (London, 1970 edn.), 335.

83. Jeffery Prager, *Building Democracy in Ireland* (Cambridge, 1986), 210; Maryann G. Valiulis, 'After the Revolution: The Formative Years of Cumann na nGaedheal', in Audrey S. Eyler and Robert F. Garratt (eds.), *The Uses of the Past: Essays on Irish Culture* (Newark, 1988), 133.

84. *Irish Times*, 2 Feb. 1925, quoted by Richard Dunphy, *The Making of Fianna Fáil Power in Ireland, 1923–1948* (Oxford, 1995), 85.

85. My tattered copy of this work was inscribed by 'Sean Lemass Capel St. Dublin, 1917', and includes his entertaining annotations to diagrams of symbolic figures, each of which is identified with a prominent Sinn Féiner of similar physiognomy.

86. For a withering depiction of the future provost, see *Catholic Bulletin*, 15, no. 3 (Mar. 1925), 200.

87. Dermot Keogh, *The Vatican, the Bishops and Irish Politics, 1919–39* (Cambridge, 1986), 178.

88. Manning, *Blueshirts*, 23, 29–30.

89. Ibid. 135; Mike Cronin, 'The Socio-Economic Background and Membership of the Blueshirt Movement, 1932–5', *Irish Historical Studies*, 29, no. 114 (1994), 237.

90. Conviction papers for nine offenders from Cloyne, Co. Cork, 15 Nov. 1934, in NA, Cabinet Papers, S 7844.

91. De Valera to organizing committee, Sinn Féin, 31 May 1923; Adj.-Gen. to divisional and brigade officers, IRA, 22 May 1923; de Valera to TDs, undated: typed copies in NA, Cabinet Papers, S 1297, S 1859.

92. Brian P. Murphy, *Patrick Pearse and the Lost Republican Ideal* (Dublin, 1991), ch. 6.

93. Peter Pyne, 'The Politics of Parliamentary Abstentionism: Ireland's Four Sinn Féin Parties, 1905–1926', *Journal of Commonwealth and Comparative Politics*, 12, no. 2 (1975), 215–19; Dunphy, *Fianna Fáil Power*, 74.

94. Précis of speech, 13 June 1923, with annotations evidently in de Valera's hand, in NA, Sinn Féin Correspondence, 1094/9/2.

95. De Valera to ard fheis, 10 Mar. 1926, in Moynihan, *Statements by Eamon de Valera*, 129.

96. Dunphy, *Fianna Fáil Power*, 74, 82.

97. Tom Garvin, *The Evolution of Irish Nationalism* (Dublin, 1981), 166–7.

98. D. P. McCracken, *Representative Government in Ireland, 1919–48* (London, 1958), 89.

99. Dail Éireann, *Official Report* (for Aug. 1921 to June 1922), 479 (20 May 1922).

100. Michael Gallagher, 'The Pact General Election of 1922', in *Irish Historical Studies*, 21, no. 84 (1979), 414–20.

101. Irish Labour Party and Trades Union Congress, *Report of the Special Committee* (Dublin, 1930), 32; Enda McKay, 'Changing

with the Tide: The Irish Labour Party, 1927–1933', *Saothar*, 11 (1986), 32.

102. Report of Dublin meeting, 16 Nov. 1923; reports by department of justice, 19 June 1929 and 4 Apr. 1930, in NA, Cabinet Papers, S 5074.

103. *Irish Times*, 7 June 1933.

104. *Farmers' Gazette,* 4 Nov. 1922.

105. Garda report from Kinsale, Co. Cork, 17 May 1928, in NA, Cabinet Papers, S 8336.

106. Garda report, 12 Apr. 1933, listing additional rules for the Irish section, in NA, Cabinet Papers, S 11168. For the brief Irish involvement of Miss Rotha Lintorn-Orman's fragment of the British Fascists, see Richard Griffiths, *Fellow Travellers of the Right: British Enthusiasts for Nazi Germany, 1933–9* (London, 1980), 92–3.

Chapter 6 (pp. 205–243)

1. Estimates for GDP per capita (at current factor cost) indicate a decline in this ratio from 62 per cent in 1924 to 52 per cent in 1938: Kieran A. Kennedy, Thomas Giblin, and Deirdre McHugh, *The Economic Development of Ireland in the Twentieth Century* (London, 1988), 124.

2. D. S. Johnson, 'Northern Ireland as a Problem in the Economic War, 1932–38', *Irish Historical Studies*, 22, no. 86 (1980), 159.

3. Patrick Buckland, *The Factory of Grievances* (Dublin, 1979), 157–9; Angela Clifford, *Poor Law in Ireland, with an Account of the Belfast Outdoor Relief Dispute, 1932* (Belfast, 1983); Paul Bew and Christopher Norton, 'The Unionist State and the Outdoor Relief Riots of 1932', *Economic and Social Review*, 10, no. 3 (1979), 258–60; R. J. Lawrence, *The Government of Northern Ireland* (Oxford, 1965), 163–4.

4. Telegram from Andrews to Churchill, 15 June 1922; Andrews to Craig, 9 Oct. 1923; in PRONI, Cabinet Papers, CAB 9C/3.

5. These widely cited remarks are carefully analysed in *Brookeborough: The Making of a Prime Minister* (Belfast, 1988) by Brian Barton, who considers that a 'psychological' scar dating from 1922, rather than political opportunism, was responsible (p. 87).

6. John F. Harbinson, *The Ulster Unionist Party, 1882–1973* (Belfast, 1973), 116.

7. Martin Wallace, *Northern Ireland* (Newton Abbot, 1971), 144; Patrick Buckland, *The Factory of Grievances* (Dublin, 1979), 163–4.

8. A. C. Hepburn, *A Past Apart* (Belfast, 1996), 188–9.

9. Richard Murray to Craigavon, 4 Sept. 1928, in PRONI, Cabinet Papers, CAB 9B/6/3.

10. GDP per capita in 1938 (at current factor cost) was £51 in Éire, compared with £55 in Northern Ireland and £104 in the United Kingdom. The ratio of the figures for southern Ireland to those for the United Kingdom had declined from 56 per cent in 1926 to 49 per cent in 1938: Kennedy et al., *Economic Development*, 124.

11. Memorandum on unemployment measures by E. P. McCarron, 2 July 1929, in NA, Cabinet Papers, S 5893.

12. Report on unemployment statistics to minister for industry and commerce, 16 Apr. 1926, in NA, Cabinet Papers, S 4739.

13. Memorandum by department of industry and commerce, 29 Mar. 1934, in NA, Cabinet Papers, S 9571.

14. B. R. Mitchell, *European Historical Statistics, 1750–1975* (London, 1980 edn.), 515, 517, 557.

15. W. B. Yeats, 'Parnell' (28 Jan. 1937). A similar observation was ascribed to Daniel O'Connell by the mother of Maurice Hayes, as recorded in his *Black Puddings with Slim: A Downpatrick Boyhood* (Belfast, 1996), 81. On being advised by a road-mender in Kerry to use his legal prowess to 'pull down the landlords', O'Connell replied that 'I will be back this way tomorrow, and whether I win or lose, you will still be breaking stones'. I am grateful to Jane Leonard for this reference.

16. R. P. McDermott and D. A. Webb, *Irish Protestantism To-day and To-morrow: A Demographic Study* (Dublin, *circa* 1940).

17. Conacher (ministry of labour) to Blackmore (cabinet secretary), 29 Sept. 1926, in PRONI, Cabinet Papers, CAB 9C/20.

18. PRONI, Cabinet Papers, CAB 9C/17.

19. Dawson Bates to William Joynson Hicks (home secretary), 21 Sept. 1928, in PRONI, Cabinet Papers, CAB 9R/46/1.

20. Mary Harris, *The Catholic Church and the Foundation of the Northern Irish State* (Cork, 1993), 199, 239; Donald Harman Akenson, *Education and Enmity: The Control of Schooling in Northern Ireland, 1920–50* (Newton Abbot, 1973).

21. D. A. Chart, *A History of Northern Ireland* (Belfast, 1927), 24. This textbook, published by the Educational Company, was written by the deputy keeper of public records.

22. Paul Bew *et al.*, *Northern Ireland 1921–1994* (London, 1995 edn.), 245.

23. Ministry of Education, Northern Ireland, *Final Report of the Departmental Committee*, 19 June 1923, 83.

24. Harris, *Catholic Church*, 230.

25. The choice of the Red Hand, 'where the use of a national symbol is necessary to signify Northern Ireland', is documented in PRONI, Cabinet Papers, CAB 9E/105/1.

26. John Bowman, *De Valera and the Ulster Question* (Oxford, 1982), 158. Cosgrave's government had protested about official use of the provincial title for the six counties on 16 Jan. 1923: NA, Cabinet Minutes, G 2/1 (C. 1/30).

27. Graveside oration for Jeremiah O'Donovan Rossa, 1 Aug. 1915, in Pádraic H. Pearse, *Political Writings and Speeches* (Dublin, undated), 135.

28. Provisional government decision, 28 Jan. 1922, in NA, Cabinet Minutes, G 1/1.

29. The principle of exemption was belatedly introduced in 1926, and short daily periods of instruction in English were permitted from 1926 to 1934, and after 1948: John Coolahan, *A History of Irish Education* (Dublin, 1981), 39–43.

30. An Roinn Oideachais, *Notes for Teachers: History* (Dublin, 1956 edn.), 3, 28; David Fitzpatrick, 'The Futility of History', in Ciáran Brady (ed.), *Ideology and the Historians* (Dublin, 1991), 168–83, 254–62.

31. Northern Ireland, House of Commons, *Official Report of Debates*, xvi, col. 1095 (24 Apr. 1934), quoted in Buckland, *Factory of Grievances*, 72.

32. Harbinson, *Ulster Unionist Party*, 216–19.

33. Cutting from *Belfast Telegraph*, 31 Mar. 1932, in PRONI, D 3944/C/1.

34. Charlemont to Craigavon, 16 Jan. 1929, in Buckland, *Factory of Grievances*, 258.

35. Dermot Keogh, *The Vatican, the Bishops and Irish Politics, 1919–39* (Cambridge, 1986), 97–8, 124–5.

36. Ibid. 161, 205–6.

37. O'Higgins to executive council, 4 Jan. 1927, with copies of draft report and correspondence, in NA, Cabinet Papers, S 4183.

38. Copy of resolution of 26 Mar. 1931, with similar document from the South Riding, in NA, Cabinet Papers, S 2321A.

39. Copies of pastoral letters, 15 Feb. 1931, in NA, Cabinet Papers, S 6134.

40. Keogh, *The Vatican*, 129.
41. Cormac Ó Gráda, *Ireland before and after the Famine* (Manchester, 1993 edn.), 197–202.
42. Duggan to Cosgrave, 20 Mar. 1923, in NA, Cabinet Papers, S 4127. See also David Fitzpatrick, 'Divorce and Separation in Modern Irish History', in *Past and Present*, 114 (1987), 172–96.
43. Kennedy to Cosgrave, 5 Oct. 1923; Duggan [?] to Byrne, 7 Oct.; confidential, hand-written 'Resolution of the Archbishops and Bishops of Ireland', signed by Michael Cardinal Logue, 9 Oct.; in NA, Cabinet Papers, S 4127.
44. Dáil Éireann, *Debates*, x, cols. 158 *et seq.* (11 Feb. 1925).
45. Cutting from *Irish Catholic*, 6 May 1937, with a large file of other responses to the draft constitution, in NA, Cabinet Papers, S 9851A.
46. Dáil Éireann, *Debates*, xxxvii, col. 1882.
47. Northern Ireland, House of Commons, *Official Report of Debates*, xxii, cols 1267.
48. Cutting from *Western People*, 21 Feb. 1931, in NA, Cabinet Papers, S 6134.
49. Memorandum by Joint Committee of Women's Societies and Social Workers, 10 Oct. 1936, in NA, Cabinet Papers, S 9278. See also the accompanying memorandum for the president's use in interview, 29 Jan. 1937.
50. Based on memorandum by department of finance, 17 Nov. 1934, in NA, Cabinet Papers, S 6834A.
51. Memorandum by department of finance, 9 June 1937, in NA, Cabinet Papers, S 9278.
52. Macardle to de Valera, 21 May 1937, in NA, Cabinet Papers, S 9880; see also Mary C. McGinty, 'A Study of the Campaign for and against the Enactment of the 1937 Constitution' (MA thesis, UCD, 1987), 289.
53. Ibid. 15.
54. Notes for Prime Minister, 21 Mar. 1925, in PRONI, Cabinet Papers, CAB 9B/53/3.
55. Memorandum on Sir Russell Scott's report, 11 Oct. 1926, in PRONI, Cabinet Papers, CAB 9Q/7/1.
56. *County Down Spectator*, 22 Aug. 1931.
57. Craigavon to Lord Rankeillour, 20 Oct. 1932, in PRONI, Cabinet Papers, CAB 9B/205/1 (also cited in Eamon Phoenix, *Northern Nationalism* (Belfast, 1994), 376–7).

58. Hepburn, *A Past Apart*.
59. Harris, *Catholic Church*, 14, 38; Paul A. Compton and John Coward, *Fertility and Family Planning in Northern Ireland* (Aldershot, 1989).
60. Dennis Kennedy, *The Widening Gulf* (Dublin, 1988), 97.
61. Harris, *Catholic Church*, 134.
62. Donoughmore to Irish Office, 1 Dec. 1922, in PRO, CO 739/2.

Chronology

1912	11 April	Government of Ireland bill introduced in House of Commons
	28 June	Irish TUC renamed Irish TUC and Labour Party
	2 July	Catholics and nationalists expelled from Belfast shipyards
	28 September	Ulster's Solemn League and Covenant administered on 'Ulster Day'
1913	30 January	Government of Ireland bill defeated in House of Lords, a fortnight after passing through Commons for the first of three times
	31 January	Ulster Volunteer Force formed
	26 August	Tramways strike initiated by ITGWU, leading to lock-out and sympathetic stoppages throughout Dublin
	24 September	Ulster Unionist Council authorizes creation of an Ulster provisional government under Carson upon enactment of Home Rule
	19 November	Irish Citizen Army launched by Dublin Civic League
	25 November	Irish Volunteers launched at Rotunda Rink, Dublin
1914	18 January	ITGWU advises Dublin strikers to return to work
	20 March	Cavalry officers at Curragh camp, Co. Kildare, solicit dismissal in preference to enforcing Home Rule in Ulster
	2 April	Cumann na mBan inaugurated, Dublin
	24–5 April	Rifles for UVF landed illegally at Larne and elsewhere
	25 May	Government of Ireland bill passed for third time by House of Commons

	10 July	Ulster provisional government convened, Belfast
	26 July	Rifles for Irish Volunteers landed illegally at Howth, and four civilians killed by troops at Bachelor's Walk, Dublin
	3 August	Redmond pledges Irish support for Britain on the eve of declaration of war upon Germany, offering Irish Volunteers as coastal defence force
	8 August	Initial Defence of the Realm act facilitates censorship and emergency controls through executive order
	15 September	Government of Ireland bill (assented on 18 September) suspended, with promise of future amendment to cater for Ulster; Redmond urges Irish nationalists to enlist for overseas service
	24 September	MacNeill and executive members of the Irish Volunteers repudiate Redmond's leadership, causing split and formation of National Volunteers
1915	18 March	Defence of Realm legislation amended to restore entitlement of civilians to trial by jury
	25 May	Coalition ministry including Carson appointed by Asquith
	late May	Military committee formed by IRB to plan insurrection (expanded as military council in December)
	7 August	10th (Irish) division lands at Suvla Bay, Gallipoli
1916	27 January	Ireland excluded from first Military Service act, as from its successor (25 May)
	21 April	Casement disembarks from submarine in Kerry and is arrested; *Aud* intercepted and scuttled with her cargo of German arms
	22 April	MacNeill countermands order for field manœuvres by Irish Volunteers on following day (Easter Sunday)

	24 April	Proclamation of Irish Republic at GPO, Dublin, by Pearse and military council of IRB; seizure of Dublin buildings by Irish Volunteers, followed by proclamation of martial law in Dublin (25 April) and rest of Ireland (29 April)
	27–9 April	16th (Irish) division endures gas attack at Hulloch, in first major battle
	29 April	Surrender of rebel forces, followed by internment in Britain (from 1 May) and fifteen executions (3–12 May)
	23 June	Northern nationalist convention, Belfast, accepts Lloyd George's proposals for immediate Home Rule with perhaps temporary exclusion of six counties (accepted by Ulster Unionist Council, 12 June)
	1 July	Beginning of Somme offensive, decimating 36th (Ulster) division at Thiepval (offensive ended, 13 November)
	24 July	Redmond repudiates Home Rule scheme as revised by Asquith
	3 August	Casement hanged at Pentonville jail, London
	4 November	Maxwell replaced as army commander, and martial law terminated
	22–3 December	Release of remaining internees at Frongoch and Reading
1917	5 February	First of several by-election victories for candidates approved by Sinn Féin (Count Plunkett, North Roscommon)
	16 June	Convicted rebels released from jails in Britain
	10 July	De Valera returned for East Clare in by-election
	25 July	Irish Convention opened at TCD (reports published, 12 April 1918)
	25–6 October	De Valera elected president of Sinn Féin (likewise of Irish Volunteers, 27 October)
1918	6 February	Extension of suffrage to most women over 30

12 March	Dillon replaces Redmond (died 6 March) as chairman of Irish Parliamentary Party
23 March	16th and 36th divisions participate in retreat of 5th army in face of German offensive, leading to heavy losses and effective collapse of the divisions
9 April	Military Service bill introduced by Lloyd George, with provision for extension to Ireland by executive order (enacted 18 April)
18 April	Anti-conscription conference at Mansion House, Dublin, followed by meeting with Catholic bishops at Maynooth leading to co-ordinated declaration
21 April	Pledge to resist conscription administered in Catholic churches, with token but effective general strike on 23 April
17–18 May	Most republican leaders, including de Valera, arrested as parties to a 'German plot'
11 November	Armistice agreed between Germany and allies
14 December	General election, returning 73 Sinn Féin candidates
1919 18 January	Peace conference convened, Paris
21 January	Dáil Éireann convened at Mansion House, Dublin, approving declaration of independence and appeal for international recognition of Irish Republic
1 April	De Valera elected president of Dáil, after escape from Lincoln jail (3 February)
11 June	De Valera begins campaign of propaganda and fund-raising in north America (arriving back in Ireland on 23 December 1920)
28 June	Treaty signed at Versailles between Germany and the Allies, Dáil's delegates having been excluded from the peace conference
7 October	Cabinet appoints committee to discuss Irish constitutional settlement

	25 November	Membership of republican organizations proclaimed as illegal throughout Ireland, following proclamation of Dáil on 12 September
	19 December	Unsuccessful ambush near Dublin's Phoenix Park of the viceroy, Viscount French
1920	2 January	First enrolment in England of temporary constables to reinforce RIC ('Black and Tans')
	25 February	(Better) Government of Ireland bill introduced in House of Commons (enacted 23 December, with provision for partition into two states)
	4 April	Destruction by IRA of almost 300 unoccupied RIC barracks around Easter Sunday
	June	Sinn Féin dominate elections for county and rural authorities (following qualified success at urban elections, 15 January)
	19 June	Disturbances in Derry leading to eighteen deaths
	21–4 July	Catholic workers expelled from shipyards and engineering works, and fatal rioting in Belfast
	27 July	Formation belatedly sanctioned of force of ex-officers to assist RIC, later named Auxiliary division
	6 August	Boycott of Belfast firms inaugurated by Dáil Éireann
	9 August	Restoration of Order in Ireland act maintains and expands coercive powers under Defence of the Realm legislation
	25 October	Death on hunger-strike at Brixton jail of Terence MacSwiney, lord mayor of Cork
	1 November	First execution of rebel since 1916 (Kevin Barry); recruitment commenced for (Ulster) Special Constabulary
	21 November	Assassination of fourteen officers and others by IRA, followed by fatal reprisals at Gaelic football match in Croke Park, Dublin ('Bloody Sunday')

	28 November	Sixteen Auxiliaries killed by Tom Barry's West Cork flying column at Kilmichael
	10 December	Martial law imposed in four south-western counties (extended to four adjacent counties on 4 January 1921)
	11 December	Extensive burning and looting in Cork city by Auxiliaries and police, after ambush at Dillon's Cross
1921	1 January	First 'authorized' military reprisals against property, Co. Cork
	13 May	All Sinn Féin candidates for southern House of Commons returned unopposed
	24 May	Unionists win 40 of 52 seats in northern House of Commons
	25 May	Dublin's Custom House destroyed by IRA
	7 June	Sir James Craig elected as first prime minister of Northern Ireland (parliament opened by George V on 22 June)
	9–15 July	Belfast disturbances cause over twenty deaths
	11 July	Truce implemented between British army in Ireland and IRA
	16 August	Second Dáil convened by Sinn Féin MPs, Dublin
	26 August	De Valera elected president of Irish Republic by Dáil
	14 September	Dáil elect delegates to negotiate with Lloyd George and ministers, after prolonged preliminary exchanges
	11 October	Anglo-Irish conference opened in London
	22 November	Control of police in six counties transferred to northern government
	6 December	Articles of agreement for a treaty signed in London
1922	7 January	Dáil Éireann narrowly approves treaty, after acrimonious debate beginning on 14 December
	14 January	Provisional government appointed under Collins, in tandem with new Dáil ministry under Griffith (who replaced de Valera on 10 January)

21 January	Ineffectual pact between Collins and Craig to end Belfast boycott and protect northern Catholics
12–15 February	Belfast attacks cause 27 deaths, attributed to IRA, followed by four months of renewed sectarian rioting, sniping, and shooting
26–7 March	IRA convention establishes 'Irregular' executive council under Traynor, in defiance of Mulcahy's army staff
30 March	Second futile pact signed in London between Craig and Collins, along with Churchill; treaty given force of law in United Kingdom on the following day
7 April	Civil Authorities (Special Powers) act, NI, allowed internment and other emergency measures for one year, the act being periodically extended and made permanent on 9 May 1933
14 April	Rory O'Connor's faction of Irregulars establish headquarters in Four Courts, Dublin
20 May	Collins and de Valera sign electoral pact to maintain balance of parties in Second Dáil at forthcoming election
23 May	Northern government declares republican organizations illegal
31 May	Royal Ulster Constabulary established in place of RIC in Northern Ireland, the RIC in southern state being disbanded by 31 August
16 June	Pro-treaty candidates dominate election for provisional parliament to approve draft constitution for the Irish Free State, following collapse of electoral pact
22 June	Sir Henry Wilson (military adviser to northern government) killed by IRA in London
28 June	National army initiates open civil war by attacking O'Connor's garrison in Four Courts (surrendered 30 June)

	22 August	Collins killed in ambush at Béal na mBláth, west Cork, following Griffith's natural death on 12 August
	9 September	Third Dáil (provisional parliament) convened, and Cosgrave elected as president of provisional government
	11 September	Proportional representation abolished for local elections, Northern Ireland
	28 September	Dáil approves creation of military courts to try civilians
	10 October	Catholic bishops issue joint pastoral excommunicating active Irregulars
	25 October	Constitution approved by Dáil (ratified by British statute on 5 December); rival republican government constituted under de Valera, with support from IRA
	17 November	First of 77 Irregulars executed
	6 December	Cosgrave appointed president of executive council of new Irish Free State
	7 December	Northern parliament votes to opt out of Free State (implementing cabinet decision of 13 March)
1923	12 February	Cosgrave agrees secretly to payment of annuities, due from purchasers of Irish land, to British exchequer
	31 March	Customs control inaugurated between Free State and United Kingdom
	24 May	De Valera instructs republicans to abandon armed resistance, following suspension of Irregular offensive on 27 April
	11 June	Anti-treaty Sinn Féin reorganized at Mansion House, Dublin
	8 August	Garda Síochána given statutory force (inaugurated 21 February 1922)
	15 August	De Valera arrested in Ennis, Co. Clare, being interned until 16 July 1924
	27 August	Cumann na nGaedheal victorious in general election for Dáil
	10 September	Irish Free State admitted to League of Nations (treaty registered on 11 July 1924)

1924 6 March   'Army mutiny' following announcement of reorganization and reduction of national army on 18 February

10 March   Eoin O'Duffy (chief commissioner of Garda since September 1922) takes temporary command of defence forces until February 1925

12 April   Southern judiciary reconstituted by Courts of Justice act, followed on 21 April by Ministers and Secretaries act regulating civil service

10 May   Northern government declines to appoint delegate to boundary commission (MacNeill appointed by Free State on 20 July 1923)

6 November   Boundary commission convened in London, after legislation to allow appointment by British government of northern delegate

8 November   Amnesty for civil war offenders in Free State

24 December   Release of last remaining internees in Northern Ireland

1925 3 April   Unionists returned with reduced majority at general election, Northern Ireland; Devlin and nationalist colleague take seats on 28 April

15 November   IRA convention repudiates authority of de Valera's republican government

3 December   Under tripartite agreement in London, financial and constitutional settlement altered and boundary confirmed, after leaking of commission's report on 7 November and MacNeill's resignation on 20 November

10 December   Disbandment announced by Craig of A division, USC, leading to mutiny before settlement and discharge (followed by end of recruiting for CI division on 4 February 1926)

1926	11 March	De Valera resigns as president of Sinn Féin
	16 May	De Valera launches Fianna Fáil at La Scala theatre, Dublin
	14 November	Two gardaí killed in attacks on barracks by IRA
	19 November	Autonomy and equal status of dominions affirmed at Imperial Conference, London
1927	9 June	Cumann na nGaedheal narrowly retains power as minority government after general election, with Fianna Fáil taking oath and seats on 11 August
	10 July	O'Higgins, minister for justice, assassinated by IRA
	11 August	Further Public Safety act in Free State provides for special courts with military members and suppression of associations
	15 September	Cumann na nGaedheal again heads poll at general election, with reduced representation for minor parties
	9 November	Electoral candidates in Free State required to declare their intention of taking oath if elected
1928	12 July	Constitution amended to prevent popular initiation of bills and restrict referenda
	26 December	Further Public Safety act in Free State repeals draconian legislation of 11 August 1927
1929	16 April	Proportional representation abolished for House of Commons, Northern Ireland
	22 May	Failure of Labour and Local Option candidates in general election, Northern Ireland
1930	12 February	First censorship board appointed for Irish Free State
	1 April	Irish Labour Party separates from TUC
	17 June	Northern Education act gives greater state support for voluntary (often Catholic) primary schools
	17 September	Free State elected to League of Nations council

1931	26–7 September	First conference of Saor Éire (republican socialists) in Dublin
	17 October	Constitution amended to allow for military tribunal to suppress drilling and for proclamation of associations (effected, 20 October)
	18 October	Catholic bishops jointly condemn republican organizations
	11 December	Statute of Westminster releases dominions from legislative supremacy of the imperial parliament
1932	9 February	Army Comrades Association formed in Dublin
	16 February	General election in Free State allows formation of minority government by Fianna Fáil and election of de Valera as president (9 March)
	18 March	Suspension of act of 17 October 1931 sanctioning military tribunal
	11 May	Nationalists leave northern House of Commons over curtailment of debate
	10 June	De Valera declines international arbitration over proposed revision of treaty, following United Kingdom's objections to his proposal on 16 March to abolish the oath of fidelity and withhold land annuities payable to the British exchequer under the agreement of 12 February 1923
	30 June	Free State suspends payment of land annuities to British exchequer
	15 July	Punitive duties imposed by British treasury on goods imported from Free State, followed by retributive application of tariffs by Free State on 23 July
	26 September	De Valera addresses League of Nations assembly in Geneva as its chairman
	4–13 October	Strikes and riots over lack of unemployment relief, Belfast
	16 November	New parliament building opened at Stormont, Belfast

1933	4 January	Formation of Centre Party agreed, Dublin
	24 January	Fianna Fáil gains small majority at general election in Free State
	22 February	O'Duffy dismissed as chief commissioner of Garda
	24 March	Blue shirt adopted as uniform for Army Comrades Association
	3 May	Oath of fidelity removed from constitution
	9 May	Permanent force given to Special Powers legislation, Northern Ireland (repealed in 1972)
	20 July	O'Duffy elected as leader of Blueshirts (renamed National Guard)
	22 August	National Guard proclaimed as unlawful association, following prohibition and abandonment of procession proposed for 13 August
	2 September	United Ireland party (later Fine Gael) launched under O'Duffy, combining Cumann na nGaedheal with Centre Party and National Guard
	2 November	Powers of governor-general further restricted by constitutional amendment, appeal to the privy council being abolished on 16 November
	30 November	Northern general election returns Craigavon's Unionists to power as usual
1934	5 June	Electoral candidates in Northern Ireland required to declare their intention of taking seats if elected
	21 September	O'Duffy resigns as leader of Fine Gael
	21 December	Coal–cattle pact mitigates impact of 'economic war' on Irish farmers
1935	28 February	Sale and importation to the Free State of contraceptive devices prohibited under Criminal Law Amendment act
	12 July	Catholic families driven from their houses after renewed disturbances in Belfast
1936	29 May	Free State Senate abolished

	18 June	IRA proclaimed in Free State as illegal organization
	20 November	O'Duffy leads 'Irish Brigade' to support Franco's nationalists in Spanish civil war (arrives back in Ireland, 22 June 1937)
	11 December	Remaining references to the crown and governor-general removed from Free State constitution, but diplomatic functions of crown confirmed in Executive Authority (External Relations) bill enacted on following day
	16 December	Irish republicans under Frank Ryan join International Brigade opposing Franco in Spanish civil war
1937	1 May	Draft constitution for Éire published (approved by Dáil on 14 June)
	1 July	General election in Free State returns Fianna Fáil to power with reduced majority; new constitution approved by referendum
	28–9 July	George VI (having succeeded Edward VIII upon his abdication on 11 December 1936) visits Northern Ireland
	29 December	New constitution of Éire implemented
1938	9 February	Northern general election returns Unionists to power with increased majority
	25 April	Anglo-Irish agreement ends reciprocal tariffs and 'economic war', and provides for transfer of the 'treaty ports' to Éire's control
	26 April	British government agrees to maintain northern social services at British levels through subsidies from exchequer
	17 June	Fianna Fáil returned to power with slightly reduced majority at another general election in Éire
	25 June	Douglas Hyde inaugurated as first president of Éire
	12 September	De Valera again elected as president of League of Nations assembly

	22 December	Internment reintroduced in Northern Ireland under Special Powers act
1939	16 January	IRA initiates bombing campaign in Britain, abandoned in March 1940
	4 May	Chamberlain announces the exclusion of Northern Ireland from Military Service bill
	14 June	Offences against the State act facilitates coercion in Éire
	25 August	Five killed in Coventry bombing by IRA
	2 September	De Valera reaffirms intention to maintain neutrality in case of war (as previously announced on 19 February)
	3 September	Britain declares war on Germany; Emergency Powers act in Éire allows wide range of restrictive regulations
	23 December	Ammunition of national army stolen from Magazine Fort, Phoenix Park, in raid by IRA

Further Reading

Twentieth-century Ireland has been examined and interpreted in a multitude of surveys, textbooks, monographs, memoirs, and works of reference, of which a modest selection (restricted to the English language) is listed here. It is curious that few surveys of modern 'Ireland' give more than cursory attention to the six counties after 1921. This applies even to important works of synthesis such as R. F. Foster, *Modern Ireland, 1600–1972* (London, 1988), Oliver MacDonagh's searching *States of Mind: A Study of Anglo-Irish Conflict, 1780–1980* (London, 1983) and *Ireland: The Union and its Aftermath* (London 1977), Dermot Keogh's methodical *Twentieth-Century Ireland: Nation and State* (Dublin, 1994), and Ronan Fanning's refreshing *Independent Ireland* (Dublin, 1983). J. J. Lee, *Ireland, 1912–1985* (Cambridge, 1989) is a boisterous meditation on the political and economic performance of the southern state. F. S. L. Lyons, *Ireland since the Famine* (London, 1971) is almost unique in allowing extended, if separate, treatment to Northern Ireland. K. Theodore Hoppen gives compressed observations on both states in his *Ireland since 1800: Conflict and Conformity* (London, 1989), as does David Harkness in *Ireland in the Twentieth Century: Divided Island* (London, 1996). The pithiest analysis of partition is Michael Laffan, *The Partition of Ireland, 1911–1925* (Dundalk, 1983). Aspects of this topic are discussed by Clare O'Halloran, *Partition and the Limits of Irish Nationalism: An Ideology under Stress* (Dublin, 1987), Dennis Kennedy, *The Widening Gulf: Northern Attitudes to the Independent Irish State, 1919–49* (Dublin, 1988), and John Bowman's perceptive *De Valera and the Ulster Question* (Oxford, 1982). In *A History of Ulster* (Belfast, 1992), Jonathan Bardon draws from extensive sources for the entire province. The most useful brief accounts of the northern state are David Harkness, *Northern Ireland since 1920* (Dublin, 1983) and Patrick Buckland, *A History of Northern Ireland* (Dublin, 1981).

The Anglo-Irish relationship remains the province of Nicholas Mansergh, in works such as *The Unresolved Question: The Anglo-Irish Settlement and its Undoing, 1912–1972* (New Haven, 1991) and his still illuminating constitutional studies, *The Government of Northern Ireland: A Study in Devolution* (London, 1936) and *The Irish Free State:*

Its Government and Politics (London, 1934). Useful monographs include Sheila Lawlor, *Britain and Ireland, 1914–23* (Dublin, 1983), D. G. Boyce, *Englishmen and Irish Troubles: British Public Opinion and the Making of Irish Policy, 1918–22* (London, 1972), and Paul Canning, *British Policy towards Ireland, 1921–1941* (Oxford, 1985). For readable general accounts of the Anglo-Irish conflict, see George Dangerfield, *The Damnable Question: A Study in Anglo-Irish Relations* (London, 1979), and Joseph M. Curran, *The Birth of the Irish Free State, 1921–1923* (Alabama, 1980). For the constitutional sequel to partition, see David Harkness, *The Restless Dominion: The Irish Free State and the British Commonwealth of Nations, 1921–31* (London, 1969) and Deirdre McMahon's densely documented *Republicans and Imperialists: Anglo-Irish Relations in the 1930s* (New Haven, 1984). The evolution of the southern constitution is discussed by Basil Chubb, *The Government and Politics of Ireland* (London, 1970 edn.), Leo Kohn, *The Constitution of the Irish Free State* (London, 1932), Donal O'Sullivan, *The Irish Free State and its Senate: A Study in Contemporary Politics* (London, 1940), and Frank Litton (ed.), *The Constitution of Ireland, 1937–1987* (Dublin, 1988). The peculiar constitutional status of Northern Ireland has generated several analyses, including Martin Wallace, *Northern Ireland: 50 Years of Self-Government* (Newton Abbot, 1971) and Paul Arthur, *Government and Politics of Northern Ireland* (London, 1980). For broader analysis of the northern state and society, see Michael Farrell, *Northern Ireland: The Orange State* (London, 1976), and Paul Bew, Peter Gibbon, and Henry Patterson, *Northern Ireland, 1921–1994: Political Forces and Social Classes* (London, 1995 edn.).

Modern Irish nationalism and its 'political culture' have been usefully analysed by political scientists such as D. George Boyce, *Nationalism in Ireland* (London, 1982), John Hutchinson, *The Dynamics of Cultural Nationalism: The Gaelic Revival and the Creation of the Irish Nation State* (London, 1987), and Tom Garvin's iconoclastic studies, *Nationalist Revolutionaries in Ireland, 1858–1928* (Oxford, 1987) and *The Evolution of Irish Nationalist Politics* (Dublin, 1981). The question of the state's 'legitimacy' before and after 1922 is discussed in Gretchen M. MacMillan's schematic *State, Society and Authority in Ireland: The Foundations of the Modern State* (Dublin, 1993), Jeffrey Prager, *Building Democracy in Ireland: Political Order and Cultural Integration in a Newly Independent Nation* (Cambridge, 1986), and Tom Garvin, *1922: The Birth of Irish Democracy* (Dublin, 1996), in which the conflict over the treaty is tendentiously treated as a contest between preconceived democratic and élitist ideologies. There is still no extended study of the Home Rule movement after 1910, though Paul Bew examines its rhetoric in *Ideology and the Irish Question: Ulster Unionism and Irish Nationalism, 1912–1916* (Oxford, 1994). For Ulster, see Eamon Phoenix, *Northern Nationalism: Nationalist Politics, Partition and the Catholic Minority in Northern Ireland, 1890–1940* (Belfast, 1994).

Far more attention has been paid to the development of Sinn Féin and republicanism, in works such as Leon Ó Broin, *Revolutionary Underground: The Story of the Irish Republican Brotherhood* (Dublin, 1976), Dorothy Macardle, *The Irish Republic* (London, 1937), Sean Cronin, *Irish Nationalism: A History of its Roots and Ideology* (Dublin, 1980), Richard English, *Radicals and the Republic: Socialist Republicanism in the Irish Free State, 1925–1937* (Oxford, 1994), and Brian P. Murphy's quirky but subtle attempt to distil the essence of Irish republicanism, *Patrick Pearse and the Lost Republican Ideal* (Dublin, 1991). For the electoral history of the southern party system, see D. P. McCracken, *Representative Government in Ireland, 1919–48* (London, 1958), Michael Gallagher, *Irish Elections, 1922–44: Results and Analysis* (Limerick, 1993), and Cornelius O'Leary, *Irish Elections, 1918–1977: Parties, Voters and Proportional Representation* (Dublin, 1979). The major parties are surveyed in Richard Dunphy, *The Making of Fianna Fáil Power in Ireland, 1923–1948* (Oxford, 1995), Brian Girvin, *Between Two Worlds: Politics and Economy in Independent Ireland* (Dublin, 1989), and Maurice Manning, *The Blueshirts* (Dublin, 1970).

The political history of Ulster and southern Unionism before 1921 is chronicled by Patrick Buckland in *Irish Unionism* (2 vols., Dublin, 1972–3) and his edited collection *Irish Unionism, 1885–1923: A Documentary History* (Belfast, 1973). For the period after partition, John F. Harbinson's *The Ulster Unionist Party, 1882–1973* (Belfast, 1973) provides essential data on political organization. There is still no adequate documented analysis of modern Orangeism or the political culture of Ulster Unionism, although David W. Miller offers a probing long-span analysis of loyalist ideology in *Queen's Rebels: Ulster Loyalism in Historical Perspective* (Dublin, 1978). For innovative studies of the persecution of southern Protestants and the camaraderie of British ex-servicemen in Ireland, see the essays by Peter Hart and Jane Leonard in Richard English and Graham Walker (eds.), *Unionism in Modern Ireland* (Dublin, 1996).

Three essays on the twentieth century appear in Thomas Bartlett and Keith Jeffery (eds.), *A Military History of Ireland* (Cambridge, 1996).

The classic study of Ulster's preparation for rebellion after 1912 is A. T. Q. Stewart, *The Ulster Crisis* (London, 1979 edn.). Since publication of the Trinity History Workshop's volume of essays, *Ireland and the First World War* (Dublin, 1986 and 1988), that once forgotten theme has been usefully elaborated by Terence Denman, *Ireland's Unknown Soldiers: The 16th (Irish) Division in the Great War, 1914–1918* (Dublin, 1992), Philip Orr, *The Road to the Somme: Men of the Ulster Division tell their Story* (Belfast, 1987), Tom Johnstone, *Orange, Green and Khaki* (Dublin, 1992), and Myles Dungan, *Irish Voices from the Great War* (Dublin, 1995). Perhaps the most useful accounts of the Easter Rising appear in Kevin B. Nowlan (ed.), *The Making of 1916* (Dublin, 1969); while the military prelude is documented in F. X. Martin (ed.), *The Irish Volunteers, 1913–1915* (Dublin, 1963). There is still no thorough general account of the revolutionary conflict; but studies of local experience include my *Politics and Irish Life, 1913–1921: Provincial Experience of War and Revolution* (Dublin, 1977; new edn. Cork, 1997), Joost Augusteijn, *From Public Defiance to Guerrilla Warfare: The Experience of Ordinary Volunteers in the Irish War of Independence, 1916–1921* (Dublin, 1996), and Peter Hart's impressive analysis, *The Irish Republican Army and its Enemies: Violence and Community in County Cork, 1917–1923* (Oxford, forthcoming, 1998). Useful essays appear in D. G. Boyce (ed.), *The Revolution in Ireland, 1879–1923* (Dublin, 1988), and the Trinity History Workshop's volume *Revolution? Ireland, 1917–1923* (Dublin, 1990). Charles Townshend's *The British Campaign in Ireland, 1919–1921* (Oxford, 1975) and *Political Violence in Ireland: Government and Resistance since 1848* (Oxford, 1983) remain the most thorough studies of counter-insurgency.

Michael Hopkinson's *Green against Green: The Irish Civil War* (Dublin, 1988) is the most adequate survey of that military conflict, which nevertheless demands further documentation using recently released archives. The Free State's security forces are discussed in John P. Duggan, *A History of the Irish Army* (Dublin, 1992 edn.), Conor Brady, *Guardians of the Peace* (Dublin, 1974), and Liam McNiffe, *A History of the Garda Síochána* (Dublin, 1997). The shadowy history of military republicanism since the civil war is anecdoted in Tim Pat Coogan, *The IRA* (London, 1971) and J. Bowyer Bell, *The Secret Army: A History of the Irish Republican Army, 1916–1970* (London, 1970). There is still no published scholarly history of either the RIC or the RUC, though John D. Brewer, *The Royal Irish Constabulary: An Oral History* (Belfast, 1990) provides fascinating accounts of the conflict of

1919–21. Radically dissimilar depictions of the Ulster Special Constabulary appear in Sir Arthur Hezlet, *The 'B' Specials: A History of the Ulster Special Constabulary* (London, 1972) and Michael Farrell, *Arming the Protestants: The Formation of the Ulster Special Constabulary and the Royal Ulster Constabulary, 1920–7* (London, 1983).

For aspects of the Irish administration under Dublin Castle, see R. B. McDowell, *The Irish Administration, 1801–1914* (London, 1964), Lawrence W. McBride, *The Greening of Dublin Castle: The Transformation of Bureaucratic and Judicial Personnel in Ireland, 1892–1922* (Washington, DC, 1991), Eunan O'Halpin, *The Decline of the Union: British Government in Ireland, 1892–1920* (Dublin, 1987), and Leon Ó Broin, *Dublin Castle and the 1916 Rising* (London, 1966). The transfer of administrative powers after partition is examined in John McColgan, *British Policy and the Irish Administration, 1920–22* (London, 1983) and Bryan A. Follis, *A State under Siege: The Establishment of Northern Ireland, 1920–1925* (Oxford, 1995). The revolutionary counter-administration is most fully treated in Arthur Mitchell, *Revolutionary Government in Ireland: Dáil Éireann, 1919–22* (Dublin, 1995), supplemented by Mary Kotsonouris, *Retreat from Revolution: The Dáil Courts, 1920–24* (Dublin, 1994). The most exhaustive bureaucratic study of the southern state is Ronan Fanning, *The Irish Department of Finance, 1922–58* (Dublin, 1978); while diplomacy is examined in Dermot Keogh's *Ireland and Europe, 1919–1948* (Dublin, 1988). The administrative history of Northern Ireland is probed in Patrick Buckland, *The Factory of Grievances: Devolved Government in Northern Ireland, 1921–39* (Dublin, 1979) and R. J. Lawrence, *The Government of Northern Ireland: Public Finance and Public Services, 1921–1964* (Oxford, 1965).

The most innovative studies of the modern Irish economy are Cormac Ó Gráda's *Ireland before and after the Famine* (Manchester, 1993 edn.) and *Ireland: A New Economic History, 1780–1939* (Oxford, 1994). As in the case of Kieran A. Kennedy, Thomas Giblin, and Deirdre McHugh, *The Economic Development of Ireland in the Twentieth Century* (London, 1988), and Mary E. Daly, *Social and Economic History of Ireland since 1800* (Dublin, 1981), little attention is paid to the economy of Northern Ireland. Southern economic policy is dissected in Daly's *Industrial Development and Irish National Identity, 1922–1939* (Dublin, 1992). David Johnson, *The Inter-War Economy in Ireland* (Dundalk, 1985) offers a brief comparison of the two regional economies; and some aspects of the northern economy after partition are analysed in Líam Kennedy and Philip P. Ollerenshaw (eds.), *An Economic History of Ulster, 1820–1939* (Manchester, 1995). The political and industrial history of Irish Labour has received perhaps excessive attention by comparison with that of other class-based movements. Useful studies include Arthur Mitchell, *Labour in Irish Politics, 1890–1930: The Irish Labour Movement in an Age of Revolution* (Dublin, 1974), Emmet O'Connor's *A Labour History of Ireland, 1824–1960* (Dublin, 1992) and *Syndicalism in Ireland, 1917–1923* (Cork, 1988), C. Desmond Greaves, *The Irish Transport and General Workers' Union: The Formative Years, 1909–1923* (Dublin, 1982), and Mary Jones, *These Obstreperous Lassies: A History of the Irish Women Workers' Union* (Dublin, 1988). For Northern Ireland, see Austen Morgan, *Labour and Partition: The Belfast Working Class, 1905–23* (London, 1991) and Henry Patterson, *Class Conflict and Sectarianism: The Protestant Working Class and the Belfast Labour Movement, 1868–1920* (Belfast, 1980).

Social and cultural history remain fairly uncultivated fields in modern Irish studies, though recent changes in academic fashion promise future scholarship to supplement the outpouring of fine words which has already occurred. Terence Brown's thoughtful *Ireland: A Social and Cultural History, 1922–1979* (London, 1981) is unfortunately restricted to the southern state. F. S. L. Lyons's reflections on *Culture and Anarchy in Ireland, 1890–1939* (Oxford, 1979) are mainly concerned with the political cultures of nationalism and southern Unionism. Emigration has been studied less thoroughly for the twentieth century than for its predecessors, but some analysis is provided in Donald Harman Akenson's numerous studies such as *The Irish Diaspora, a Primer* (Toronto, 1993). For the Irish in America and their politics, see Kerby A. Miller, *Emigrants and Exiles: Ireland and the Irish Exodus to North America* (New York, 1985), Alan J. Ward, *Ireland and Anglo-American Relations, 1899–1921* (London, 1969), and Francis M. Carroll, *American Opinion and the Irish Question, 1910–23: A Study in Opinion and Policy* (Dublin, 1978).

John Coolahan's *A History of Irish Education* (Dublin, 1981) is a useful survey, which however excludes Northern Ireland. For the religious politics of education, see D. H. Akenson's *A Mirror to Kathleen's Face: Education in Independent Ireland, 1922–1960* (Montreal, 1975) and *Education and Enmity: The Control of Schooling in Northern Ireland, 1920–50* (Newton Abbot, 1973). Brian Farris, *The Politics of Irish Education, 1920–65* (Belfast, 1995) compares the experience of the two states. Among the many studies of sport and recreation are two valuable accounts of Gaelic athletics in political context: W. F. Mandle, *The Gaelic Athletic Association and Irish Nationalist Politics, 1884–1924* (London, 1987) and Marcus de Búrca, *The GAA: A History* (Dublin, 1980). No comparably wide-ranging studies of the Gaelic revival have yet appeared in English, although there is a massive body of writing on the Anglo-Irish literary revival and its cultural significance which cannot even be summarized here.

The study of women's history, though still mainly concerned with political activity, is belatedly generating significant research. This is evident in several volumes of essays, including Margaret MacCurtain and Donncha Ó Corráin (eds.), *Women in Irish Society: The Historical Dimension* (Dublin, 1978), Maria Luddy and Clíona Murphy (eds.), *Women Surviving: Studies in Irish Women's History in the 19th and 20th Centuries* (Swords, Co. Dublin, 1990), and Janice Holmes and Diane Urquhart (eds.), *Coming into the Light: The Work, Politics and Religion of Women in Ulster, 1840–1940* (Belfast, 1994). For women in politics, see Margaret Ward, *Unmanageable Revolutionaries: Women and Irish Nationalism* (London, 1983), Cliona Murphy, *The Women's Suffrage Movement and Irish Society in the Early Twentieth Century* (Hemel Hempstead, 1989), and Rosemary Cullen Owens, *Smashing Times: A History of the Irish Women's Suffrage Movement, 1889–1922* (Dublin, 1984).

For the political entanglements of the Catholic church, see David W. Miller, *Church, State and Nation in Ireland, 1898–1921* (Dublin, 1973), John H. Whyte, *Church and State in Modern Ireland, 1923–1979* (Dublin, 1980 edn.), and Mary Harris, *The Catholic Church and the Foundation of the Northern Irish State* (Cork, 1993). Unfamiliar archival sources are quarried in Dermot Keogh, *Ireland and the Vatican: The Politics and Diplomacy of Church–State Relations, 1922–1960* (Cork, 1995), amplifying his findings in *The Vatican, the Bishops and Irish Politics, 1919–39* (Cambridge, 1986). For brief and sometimes cursory accounts of the major churches, see Patrick J. Corish, *The Irish Catholic Experience: A Historical Survey* (Dublin, 1985), R. B. McDowell, *The Church of Ireland, 1869–1969* (London, 1975), Michael Hurley, SJ (ed.), *Irish Anglicanism, 1869–1969* (Dublin, 1970), and Peter Brooke, *Ulster Presbyterianism: The Historical Perspective, 1610–1970* (Dublin, 1987). Sociological studies of religion include Kurt Bowen, *Protestants in a Catholic State: Ireland's Privileged Minority* (Kingston and Montreal, 1983) and Tom Inglis, *Moral Monopoly: The Catholic Church in Modern*

Irish Society (Dublin, 1987). Among the few social histories of sectarian division, the most innovative is A. C. Hepburn, *A Past Apart: Studies in the History of Catholic Belfast, 1850–1950* (Belfast, 1996).

In addition to monographs and works of synthesis, there is a huge range of biographies and autobiographies illuminating twentieth-century Irish history. Important historical documentation abounds in the major political biographies, such as Tim Pat Coogan's vindictive but well-informed *De Valera: Long Fellow, Long Shadow* (London, 1993), his hagiographical *Michael Collins: A Biography* (London, 1990), and the equally reverential 'authorized' biography of *Eamon de Valera* (London, 1970) by the Earl of Longford and Thomas P. O'Neill. Other useful studies of nationalist leaders in context include F. S. L. Lyons, *John Dillon* (London, 1968), Richard Davis, *Arthur Griffith and Non-Violent Sinn Féin* (Dublin, 1974), Ruth Dudley Edwards, *Patrick Pearse: The Triumph of Failure* (London, 1977), Maryann Gialanella Valiulis, *Portrait of a Revolutionary: General Richard Mulcahy and the Foundation of the Irish Free State* (Dublin, 1992), and Terence de Vere White, *Kevin O'Higgins* (London, 1948). For northern Unionist leaders, see Edward Marjoribanks and Ian Colvin, *Life of Lord Carson* (3 vols., London, 1932–6), St John Ervine, *Craigavon, Ulsterman* (London, 1949), and Brian Barton, *Brookeborough: The Making of a Prime Minister* (Belfast, 1988). Labour leaders are predictably well represented in biography, with several valuable studies such as Graham S. Walker, *The Politics of Frustration: Harry Midgley and the Failure of Labour in Northern Ireland* (Manchester, 1985), Emmet Larkin, *James Larkin: Irish Labour Leader, 1876–1947* (London, 1965), C. Desmond Greaves, *The Life and Times of James Connolly* (London, 1961), and J. Anthony Gaughan, *Thomas Johnson, 1872–1963* (Dublin, 1980). Political women also figure large in Irish biography, including Leah Levenson and Jerry H. Natterstad, *Hanna Sheehy Skeffington, Irish Feminist* (Syracuse, 1986) and Jacqueline van Voris, *Constance de Markievicz: In the Cause of Ireland* (Amherst, 1967). It would be invidious in this brief reading guide to offer a selection from the vast corpus of biographies and memoirs of less prominent figures.

Twentieth-century Ireland is increasingly well supplied with reference works, despite the current absence of the Royal Irish Academy's long-promised *Dictionary of Irish Biography*. Notwithstanding strange omissions of topic, much valuable material for the period 1870–1921 is presented in W. E. Vaughan (ed.), *A New History of Ireland*, vol. vi (Oxford, 1996); the final volume is still unpublished. See also vol. viii,

A Chronology of Irish History to 1976 (Oxford, 1982), an essential source for this book and in particular for my chronology of major events. Three valuable ancillary collections of population and electoral data have been published separately by the Royal Irish Academy: W. E. Vaughan and A. J. Fitzpatrick (eds.), *Irish Historical Statistics: Population, 1821–1971* (Dublin, 1978), Brian M. Walker's *Parliamentary Election Results in Ireland* for 1801–1922 (Dublin, 1978), and for 1918–92 (Dublin, 1992). The most reliable of several available biographical dictionaries is Henry Boylan, *A Dictionary of Irish Biography* (Dublin, 1978), which may be supplemented by D. J. Hickey and J. E. Doherty, *A Dictionary of Irish History since 1800* (Dublin, 1980). *Who's Who* and the *Dictionary of National Biography* incorporate extensive information on Irish biography, even for those flourishing in the Free State and Éire. For useful collections of historical documents, consult Arthur Mitchell and Pádraig Ó Snodaigh (eds.), *Irish Political Documents, 1916–1949* (Dublin, 1985) and Maria Luddy, *Women in Ireland, 1800–1918: A Documentary History* (Cork, 1995). Readers wishing to graduate beyond this brief catalogue of useful studies should consult bibliographical guides such as Alan R. Eager, *A Guide to Irish Bibliographical Material: A Bibliography of Irish Bibliographies and Sources of Information* (London, 1980 edn.) and Michael Owen Shannon (ed.), *Modern Ireland: A Bibliography of Politics, Planning, Research, and Development* (London, 1981).

Index

36, 44, 47, 52, 54, 75; (1920) 100–1, 137, 144, 146; *see also* Council of Ireland
Grant, William (1877–1949) 181
Graves, Alfred Perceval (1846–1931) 33
Graves, Robert Ranke (1895–1985) 33
Great War (1914–18) 4, 27, 37, 38, 39, 44, 46, 51–62, 75, 79, 80, 95, 96, 114, 180, 227, 228, 242; German spring offensive (1918) 53, 70; Hulloch 53; Messines 66; Somme 27, 53, 61–2, 90; Suvla Bay 53, 71; Ypres 53
Greece 219
Green, Mrs John Richard (Alice Sophia Amelia Stopford; 1847–1929) 26, 222
Greenwood, Sir Hamar, 1st Bt. (1st Viscount Greenwood; 1870–1948) 89
Gregg, (Sir) Cornelius Joseph (1888–1959) 157
Griffith, Arthur (1872–1922) 16, 28, 29, 65, 66, 67–8, 73, 76, 82, 97, 106, 110–11, 113, 129, 132, 133, 159, 213, 242
gun-running: (1914) 47, 48, 49, 50 154; (1916) 58; (1920–1) 93
Gwynn, Stephen Lucius (1864–1950) 53

Hagan, Mgr. John (1873–1930) 229
Hales, Seán (d. 1922) 134
Hales, Tom 134
Harland & Wolff 21
Haslam, Mrs Thomas (Anna Maria Fisher; 1829–1922) 22
hats, bowler 181, 236
Healy, Cahir (1877–1970) 183, 185
Healy, Timothy Michael (1855–1931) 148
Henry, Sir Denis Stanislaus, 1st Bt. (1864–1925) 154
Heuston, Thomas 123
Hibernians, *see* Ancient Order of
Hickie, (Sir) William Bernard (1865–1950) 53

Hobson, Bulmer (1883–1969) 15
Home Rule, *see* Government of Ireland legislation, Irish Parliamentary Party
Hopkins, Sir Richard Valentine Nind (1880–1955) 146
Hughes, Peter (d. 1954) 171
Hungary 29
hunger-strikes 73, 88, 166, 194, 226–7
Hyde, Douglas (1860–1949) 16, 42, 147, 222, 223

imperial parliament: House of Commons 5, 9, 12, 13, 38, 40, 52, 75, 80, 100, 177; House of Lords 9, 12, 13, 240
Independent Labour Party 40, 181, 182
Independent Orange Order 11, 12, 40
India 5, 7, 29, 50, 148; *see also* Bengal
International brigade, Spain 192
international propaganda: republican 29, 67, 78–81, 84, 91–2; Ulster Unionist 77–8; *see also* diplomacy
Internationals: Communist 81, 201; Socialist 78, 81
IRA *see* Irish Republican Army
IRA Organization (1923–4) 172
IRB, *see* Irish Republican Brotherhood
Irish Association 180
Irish brigades: Germany 59; Spain 191–2; *see also* International brigade
Irish Christian Front 204
Irish Citizen Army 40, 57, 60
Irish Class War Prisoners' Aid 201
Irish College, Rome 229
Irish Convention 71, 101
Irish Dominion League 101
Irish Farmers' Union 43, 202
Irish history, study of 26, 31, 35, 94, 139, 218–19, 220, 221, 222–3, 235
Irish Labour Defence League 201
Irish Labour Party 21, 40, 41–2, 73–4, 133, 135, 181, 187, 199–201; *see also* National Labour Party